GENDER RECONSTRUCTIONS

Gender Reconstructions

Pornography and perversions in
literature and culture

Edited by
Cindy L. Carlson
Robert L. Mazzola
Susan M. Bernardo

Ashgate
Aldershot • Burlington USA • Singapore • Sydney

© The editors and contributors, 2002

All rights reserved. No part of this publication may be reproduced, stored in a retrieval system, or transmitted in any form or by any means, electronic, mechanical, photocopying, recording or otherwise without the prior permission of the publisher.

The editors have asserted their right under the Copyright, Designs and Patents Act, 1988, to be identified as the editors of this work.

Published by
Ashgate Publishing Limited
Wey Court East
Union Road
Farnham
Surrey, GU9 7PT
England

Ashgate Publishing Company
110 Cherry Street
Suite 3-1
Burlington
VT 05401-3818
USA

Ashgate website: http://www.ashgate.com

British Library Cataloguing-in-Publication data

Gender reconstructions: pornography and perversions in literature and culture
  1.Pornography 2.Pornography – Social aspects 3.Sexual deviation in literature 4.Women in literature
  I.Carlson, Cindy L. II.Mazzola, Robert M. III.Bernardo, Susan M.
  809.9'33538

Library of Congress Cataloging-in-Publication data

Gender reconstructions: pornography and perversions in literature and culture / edited by Cindy L. Carlson, Robert L. Mazzola, Susan M. Bernardo.
    p. cm
  Includes bibliographical references and index.
  1.Sex in literature. 2.Literature, Modern – History and criticism. 3.Erotic literature – History and criticism. I.Carlson, Cindy L. II.Mazzola, Robert L. III.Bernardo, Susan M.

PN56.S5 G46 2001
809'.933538
                                                                                2001022169

Transferred to Digital Printing in 2011

ISBN 978-0-7546-0286-6

 Printed and bound in Great Britain by Printondemand-worldwide.com

Contents

Preface vii
Notes on Contributors xii

1 'When female weakness triumphs': Torture and Perversion in Four Plays by Hrotsvit of Gandersheim 1
   Martine van Elk

2 Clothing Naked Desire in Marlowe's *Hero and Leander* 25
   Cindy L. Carlson

3 Seductive Confession in Mary Shelley's *Mathilda* 42
   Susan M. Bernardo

4 *Villette* and the Perversions of Feminine Identity 53
   Eleanor Salotto

5 Abjecting Freud: Masculinity, Maternity, and Perversion 76
   Deborah Caslav Covino

6 The Gaze and its Specular Perversions: Marcel Duchamp's *Étant donnés* 92
   Ernestine Daubner

7 Sade's Woman: Essential Pornogony and Virtual Embodiment 108
   Robert L. Mazzola

8 'On the Beach of Elsewhere': Angela Carter's Moral Pornography and the Critique of Gender Archetypes 125
   Gregory J. Rubinson

9 Perverse Writing – Maternity and Monarchy: Fictocriticism and Exorbitant, Plural Bodies 148
   Heather B. Kerr

10 White Trash Lesbianism: Dorothy Allison's Queer Politics 167
   Kelly L. Thomas

11 The Efficacy of Shock for Feminist Politics: Kathy Acker's *Blood and Guts in High School* and Donald Barthelme's *Snow White*   189
    Ann Bomberger

Index   205

Preface

Gender Reconstructions: Pornography and Perversions in Literature and Culture addresses the perverse as it relates to women in various cultural and literary contexts. The importance of the debate (that of Dworkin and others) surrounding the pornographic is underscored by current critical theories that address language, image and text as either gendered or neutral, author-based or the products of the history and contextualizing powers of language itself. Each contributor to this volume approaches the subject perversion and the subjects *of* perversion (those *subjected to* perversion and the initiators of perversion) from varying points of view, thus creating in the collection as a whole, not so much a consensus on what constitutes perversion for women, but a polemic that aims at redefining aspects of the perverse while also keeping open the debate to which this redefining process contributes. The collection ranges from manifestations of the erotic (Carlson's and van Elk's essays) to the question of pornography as perversion (the perverse family, perversion of narrative use, perversion of audience expectations of a text) and debates the equally vexing question of where might lie the line dividing the erotic from twentieth-century definitions of pornography (Thomas's, Kerr's, and Bomberger's work).

These issues, whether they address the pictorial or the verbal, are of ongoing interest to scholars and non-scholars alike, as they touch on the question of what constitutes the perverse and the pornographic. As an integral text *Gender Reconstructions* engages these related topics of interest to a broad spectrum of both academic and non-academic readers who wish to explore the modernist and postmodernist implications of the perverse for women's and cultural studies. In turn, this question may be seen as pivotal to a redefining of gender, its reconstruction through the cultural imperatives of literature and art. While we have in mind the university scholar and his or her students, both undergraduate and graduate, we recognize that this work will be of interest also to those for whom the questions raised here go beyond the researcher's desk and the classroom to embrace a truly universal concern about the ways 'gender' and 'pornography' in our time have elicited often heated attention from politicians (Mayor Rudolph Giuliani's debacle in 1999 over the Brooklyn Museum of Art's right to mount an avant-garde exhibition some saw as pornographic and irreligious, for example), the media, and those others who either applaud or decry the various uses to which the term gender, especially as it relates to pornography, is put.

My own interests in the pornographic and its place as a manifestation of perversion date from my first work on Sade in two papers for the *Conference on*

Early Modern Literature Studies. In a real sense Sade's novella, *Eugénie de de Franval*, and my response to it were the beginning of an effort to redefine what is productive of pornography in his work and what implications that productivity could have for a wider view of the ways in which literature and the other arts earn the title 'perverse.' While Cindy Carlson and Susan Bernardo, working in the English Renaissance and the Victorian period respectively, have not in previous writings addressed the pornographic, both delve into issues confronting women and gender, and both therefore were interested in this project from its inception.

The eleven essays that comprise this volume look at the notion of perversion as it impacts women through traditional and less than traditional modes of questioning. Eleanor Salotto, for example, is concerned to demonstrate that the perverse in writing can serve women as a 'narrative tool,' while I view the Sadian perverse enterprise as one that might empower women as a sexual and political tool of equality. Deborah Caslav Covino explores abjection in a Kristevian usage that calls into question (while relying on many of his precepts) Freud's views on women, maternity and the constitution of masculinity as a cultural construct. Susan Bernardo adds to the argument on the 'uses of the perverse' vis-à-vis women with her concept of 'seductive confession,' an element of Sade's as well as Mary Shelley's narrative arsenal. The tools of discourse thus take their place in these essays as weapons of the so-called culture wars, which in many if not all instances divide along modernist and postmodernist lines. Perhaps what emerges in these writings as most controversial is the possibility, investigated extensively by Gregory Rubinson, of pornography as just such a perverse tool or weapon wielded by woman in order to create a new viability of discourse at various levels, cultural, sexual, political. In his investigation of this tantalizing possibility, he relies upon and thereby elucidates what was in 1978 at the time of its first publication, and remains today, the 'shocking' feminist re-evaluation of Sade in Angela Carter's *The Sadeian Woman and the Ideology of Pornography*. Rubinson's penetrating critique of the gender archetypes Carter exposed in that seminal text furthers our understanding of what might be called the ability to *read differently*, to comprehend the reading *of* pornography as a process of pornographying reading and thus of reinventing the pornographic image and imagination as a tool with which to reach beyond the initial, pruriently layered reading of the pornographic text. In fact, both Rubinson's essay and mine serve to illustrate a postmodern view of the productivity of pornography, what I have called 'pornogony.'

The debate over the pornographic, as this is seen to affect and be affected by women, is not synonymous with perversion but is thought of as inextricably *linked* to cultural and woman-centered manifestations of the perverse. Conversely, the perverse is often considered the salient feature of pornography. Writers and artists represented in these essays have been responsible for many present-day definitions of this pornography/perversion dyad (Duchamp, Kristeva, Irigaray, Carter, Baudrillard, Sade, Acker). In the realm of the plastic arts Marcel Duchamp's horizontal urinal reversed the usual perverse formulation by turning a scatological artifact into an object of artistic contemplation. Ernestine Daubner brings her views of the perverse to bear on Duchamp's controversial installation *Étant donnés*. As she remarks, 'in no way is this a representation of the female nude aesthetically contained by the controlling device of a frame. Rather, enclosed in this cage, and so exposing herself only to 'his' eyes, . . . the female nude becomes a disruptive force, acting upon the viewer, suddenly aware of his role as a voyeur.' In emphasizing the 'disruptive force' of the enclosed and perverted female nude, Daubner comes close to paraphrasing Susan Sontag's now classic observation that '[p]ornography is one of the branches of literature – science fiction is the other – aiming at *disorientation*, at psychic *dislocation*' ('The Pornographic Imagination,' emphasis added). Disruption of the viewer's or reader's expectations disorients the viewing/reading experience and dislocates the psychic perceptions he or she brings to the painting, the photograph, the written text. In the Duchamp piece, that disruption revolves around the woman and the bizarre setting (the installation itself) into which the artist placed her and in which the viewer/voyeur glimpses her as through a keyhole.

Striking a note similar to Daubner's, Ann Bomberger, in her discussion of the efficacy of shock for feminine politics, describes the perverting sexuality of myth and fairy tale revisited in Donald Barthelme's *Snow White*:

> When sexuality has been mined as a topic so thoroughly that it has lost even the most remote ability to incite or excite, the novel adds a flash or two of sudden violence. In one scene the dwarves have a dream of violent, sexual group fantasy. Snow White is slowly cooked on a rotating spit over an open flame. The rotating motion of the spit parallels the ceaseless repetition of the characters' lives. While some passion and excitement are hinted at (we are told Snow White is screaming and 'making a lot of noise'), the language is still dull and uninviting. The narrator nonchalantly relays the events that occur while they are cooking Snow White in the most detached language possible: 'We regarded Snow White rotating there, in her pain and beauty, in the dream.' The verb 'to regard' appears repeatedly in the novel as an awkward substitute for 'to see' or another more common term. It gives a certain sense of distance, even intellectual curiosity to a scene which might otherwise shock. Sexualized murder would normally be considered an extreme expression of the perverse since it crosses the boundaries of most sexual activity, yet in *Snow White* it is just another unsuccessful attempt to break the monotony of late twentieth-century life.

Both Daubner and Bomberger stress the scoptophilic power of the perversion of images that leads to disorientation of vision and language (the hypertrophy of the verb 'to see'), a psychic dislocation (through the dwarves' dream and Duchamp's viewer's 'enforced' voyeurism), and ultimately a disruption, or perversion, of the faculty of sight itself. In each instance, a woman (Rrose Sélavy) identified by

Daubner as Duchamp's 'alter ego', and the iconic Snow White are the centerpieces of this disruption.

Disruption of the family circle as a theme is taken up by Deborah Caslav Covino's essay which imports Kristeva's abjection into a view of Arshile Gorky's *The Artist and His Mother* 'as a rebuke of Freudian Oedipal constructions of the mother.'

I take the scoptophilia of the Marquis de Sade as the instancing of a reduction of hot romantic seduction to a cold, theatrical and hyperreal seduction which the French culture theorist Jean Baudrillard equates with production. This is a pseudo-seduction lacking the reversibility Baudrillard deems necessary for true seduction. Once again, a naked woman, Eugénie de Franval in the Marquis's 1788 novella, is placed at the center of a scene in which two men, one her own father who has *produced* this play of cold seduction, enact the voyeur's *tableau vivant*.

Incest, the disruption of the family scene, is the theme that unites my concerns vis-à-vis Sade's theater to Susan Bernardo's consideration of father-daughter transgressions in Charles Perrault's 'Peau d'âne' (seventeenth-century French) and Mary Shelley's Mathilda (nineteenth-century British). Bernardo sees narcissism and monogamy as transforming factors in incest, and her appraisal of this perversion also calls into question the supposed sanctity of the family circle.

Eleanor Salotto focuses on another nineteenth-century text, Charlotte Brontë's novel *Villette*, as an example of the use of 'word perversion in a positive sense to suggest that Brontë uses perversion as a narrative tool to move outside the limiting enclosures of feminine autobiography.' Just as Ernestine Daubner's essay sees the enclosing, perverse effect of Duchamp's visual art, so Salotto's evokes that effect as a female author's own tool for working against the effect itself.

Heather Kerr and Gregory Rubinson tackle the notion of 'word perversion' in the writing of Kristeva and Angela Carter respectively. Kerr relates the perversion to maternity and the anorexic body in Kristeva, while Rubinson explores Carter's uses of moral pornography (the seeming oxymoron appearing as an exemplar of the perverse word) in *The Passion of New Eve*. Aspects of the perverse as a reversal of reader expectations in which the concerns of torture, homoeroticism, and lesbianism play their parts, inform readings by Martine van Elk, Cindy Carlson and Kelly Thomas respectively, on subjects as diverse as the tenth-century plays of Hrotsvit of Gandersheim, Christopher Marlowe's *Hero and Leander*, and Dorothy Allison's *Bastard Out of Carolina*.

For van Elk this perverting of Hrotsvit's discourse on torture has a narrative function. 'If we allow for the possibility of sexual dissidence by virtue of a teleology defined in opposition to dominant discourse,' she writes, 'the perverse dynamic can be seen to open up a space for a medieval representation of female empowerment.'

Carlson takes the reversal of expectation in a direction similar to the one in which van Elk sees the torture theme reversed in order to foil the expectation of female resignation and weakness. Just as the torture victim may turn the tables on the torturer, so may our prejudgment of what constitutes the perverse love object be turned on its head. As Carlson says, '[i]n the 'battle' of love between men and women, deceit is allowable, the threat of rape is omnipresent, and men are overcome with suicidal desire. In this world, women, not men, have become the perverse object of men's desire.'

From thwarted or perverted expectations of the workings of desire in tenth- and sixteenth-century texts, the focus in Thomas' essay shifts to the present century and the subject of lesbianism as a derailment of readers' expectations. Thomas succinctly states her interest in this process as:

> examining how [Dorothy] Allison negotiates and constructs a politically efficacious identity founded upon two radically different (and often contentious) cultures that are united in their disdain for different aspects of her 'perverse' sexual practices. By theorizing and historicizing marginal white identity and analyzing essays from Allison's essay collection *Skin: Talking about Sex, Class, and Literature* as well as her novel *Bastard Out of Carolina*, I will explore the problems the white-trash body poses for hegemonic as well as alternative notions of sexuality and social hierarchy. In this way, I will demonstrate how the white-trash body cuts across and confuses often different political and cultural lines . . . In asserting that her sexuality is shaped by class, Allison doesn't posit a causal relationship between poverty and sexual abuse and her homosexuality; rather, she seems more invested in exposing the ways in which the politics of taste in lesbian culture can become an expression of class prejudice.

Kelly Thomas' examination of the ways a 'perverted' reading of sexuality and politics carries within it the seeds of its strategic reversal as both a social and a narrative ploy is echoed in the other essays that comprise this collection. Each contributor conducts more than a simple survey of the ways perversions are enacted in the case of the representations of women found in the texts or artworks that form the basis of his or her investigation; instead, each writer truly conducts an *examination* of the implications of the cultural manifestation of the perverse contained within and exemplified by the chosen subject of her or his discourse here.

Robert L. Mazzola
Denver, August 2001

Notes on Contributors

Susan M. Bernardo is associate professor of English at Wagner College where she teaches courses in Victorian and Romantic literature as well as in Science Fiction and Fairy Tale. Her recent scholarly work includes an essay on George Eliot's *Romola*, a book review in *In-between: Essays & Studies in Literary Criticism*, and a piece on Oscar Wilde's fairy tales.

Ann Bomberger is an assistant professor and the Director of Expository Writing at Allegheny College. She has published essays on the politics of cross-racial characterization in the work of Joyce Carol Oates and Ellen Douglas. Currently, she is researching and writing on the use of technology in the writing classroom.

Cindy L. Carlson is associate professor of English at Metropolitan State College of Denver. She and co-editor Angel Jane Weisl have published *Constructions of Widowhood and Virginity in the Middle Ages* (1999). She is currently at work on a monograph on fashion commentary.

Deborah Caslav Covino is an assistant professor of English and Women's Studies at Florida Atlantic University. She teaches courses in feminist theory and aesthetics, literary theory, literature and medicine, and visual and literary representations of the body. Her current book project, *Aesthetic Surgeries: Grotesque Protest and the Sculpted Body*, deploys feminist theory and disability studies to examine the influence of the current aesthetic surgery boom on the contemporary bodily imaginary.

Ernestine Daubner received a PhD in the Humanities from Concordia University, Montréal, Canada, with a dissertation entitled, *Allegories of Nature, Culture, Gender: Dialogues with Marcel Duchamp's 'Étant donnés'*. Concerned with representational and discursive practices pertaining to gender construction, she is also interested in the histories and discourses of modernity and Enlightenment culture, particularly as these are reflected in contemporary art and new technologies. Her research has been presented in academic publications and in scholarly papers at national and international conferences and congresses. She currently teaches in the Art History Department of Concordia University.

NOTES ON CONTRIBUTORS

Martine van Elk is an assistant professor in Renaissance Studies and Shakespeare at California State University, Long Beach. She has forthcoming publications on different subjects, including an essay on *The Comedy of Errors* in *SEL* and an entry on Edna O'Brien in the *Dictionary of Literary Biography*. She recently completed her doctoral dissertation on scenes of recognition and identification in Shakespeare and is currently engaged in further research on this topic and on early modern women writers.

Heather B. Kerr teaches in the English Department at the University of Adelaide. She is co-editor of *The Space Between: Australian Women Writing Fictocriticism* (University of Western Australia Press, 1998) and two collections of Shakespeare criticism. She is working on a jointly authored critical study of fictocritical effects in the humanities and in social science qualitative research. She publishes in the areas of early modern and contemporary cultural studies, postcolonialism and electronic writing practice.

Robert L. Mazzola is a former professor of French literature and an independent scholar whose work includes a translation into English of Luce Irigaray's 'Égales à qui?,' and several essays on the novels of Marguerite Duras, including, most recently, 'Le schéma de la disparition: *Les petits chevaux* [imaginaires] *de Tarquinia*' in *Lectures de Duras: corps, voix et écriture* edited by Brian Stimpson in 2000 for *Dalhousie French Studies*. His essay on Kathy Acker and *pornogony* titled 'Kathy Acker and Literary Madness: Erecting the Pornographic Shell' will appear shortly in a commemorative volume edited by Michael Hardin and María González.

Gregory J. Rubinson is a lecturer in the UCLA Writing Programs. He received his PhD from the University of Rochester where he wrote his dissertation, 'Pointing at Frauds: Genre and Desacralization in Contemporary British Fiction' under the direction of David Bleich. He has recently published a related essay – 'Body Languages: Scientific and Aesthetic Discourses in Jeanette Winterson's *Written on the Body*' – in *Critique: Studies in Contemporary Fiction*.

Eleanor Salotto, assistant professor of English at Sweet Briar College, specializes in nineteenth-century British literature and culture. Her most recent publications include essays on identity and shopping in Emile Zola's *The Ladies' Paradise* and on secrets and the gothic plot in Wilkie Collins's *The Woman in White*. She is currently working on a book length project involving a feminist reading of the 'secret' in Victorian literature. Chapters include 'Bleak House', 'The Woman in White', 'Our Mutual Friend', and 'The Haunted Hotel'.

Kelly L. Thomas received her PhD in English from the University of Michigan in 1998. Her work has appeared in *The Road Movie Book* (Routledge, 1997) and *Classic Whiteness* (University of Minnesota Press, forthcoming).

Chapter 1

'When female weakness triumphs': Torture and Perversion in Four Plays by Hrotsvit of Gandersheim

Martine van Elk

Twentieth-century critics disagree about the depiction of women in the plays of the Saxon canoness Hrotsvit of Gandersheim (c. 935–1000). Her Christian imitations of Terence have been praised for their positive portrayal of women who 'appear to be strong, courageous, and resourceful people' and denounced for the extent to which the plays 'remain within, draw on, and reinforce oppressive structures of patriarchy.'[1] The position of the critic tends to depend on whether Hrotsvit is perceived as a product of her religious background or as an individual writer capable of reflecting on, rather than merely reflecting, her intellectual milieu. Reading her six plays together, it is not difficult to see where the disagreement comes from. While some of her female characters seem extraordinarily powerful, even in the face of brutal torture, others passively give in to male guidance and relinquish the self for the purpose of salvation. The conflicted nature of Hrotsvit's representation of women and female sexuality is paralleled by a contradictory depiction of torture and gender relations.

The type of ambiguity that marks her plays is perhaps unavoidable in, and certainly characteristic of, the work of medieval women writers. Jane Burns, among others, has pointed out that the complexity of medieval texts by women inheres in the lack of precedent for their role as the speaking subject of discourse: 'As the female author moves from the position of the object of discourse to become its speaking subject, she makes the shift only partially and incompletely' (10). In other words, the medieval woman writer ends up reinforcing and undermining dominant modes of discourse at the same time. If the female author's double voice seems to suggest an inability to free herself from patriarchal constraints, Hrotsvit has turned the complications that pertain to this position into a dramatic and rhetorical strength. Numerous critics of Hrotsvit insist on reading her oeuvre as unified.[2] A crucial feature of her work, however, is the extent to which it confirms and subverts patriarchal binary oppositions, particularly when it comes to the representation of illicit sexuality, violence, and gender.

Actual or potential violent behavior towards women is a part of all of Hrotsvit's plays, but four of her six plays are primarily concerned with torture of women. As might be expected, torture is endorsed when it is employed in a religious setting and ineffective when it is used in a pagan environment. In each of these four plays, female suffering is glorified because it leads to salvation and martyrdom. As male sexuality threatens to pervert the young women in the plays, violent redemption is presented as a defense against perversion because it enables a reconfiguration and desexualization of the female body. While torture erases a sense of self for two prostitutes, however, it becomes a means of female empowerment for young virgin martyrs, who humiliate their Roman persecutors. And even though perversion is imagined as uncontrolled sexual desire, the accusations of Roman emperors show that chastity can also be perceived as sexual deviance. There is a double standard with respect to the pagan and religious conceptions of the perverse, but it is nevertheless important that, in the case of the Roman authorities at least, the interpretation of sexually deviant behavior is shown to be contingent upon political power structures.

By virtue of these central contradictions, Hrotsvit's work deserves to be read as a major female text in the history of the representation of perversion and torture. Defying easy categorization, the plays offer valuable challenges to modern theories on these subjects because they foreground and deconstruct the very binaries on which these theories are based.[3] This discussion of Hrotsvit's plays reflects on two important theoretical accounts of torture and perversion. Hrotsvit's work confirms and complicates the theories of Elaine Scarry and Jonathan Dollimore by introducing the question of gender difference, which is undertheorized by both. Elaine Scarry's theory of torture resembles Hrotsvit's plays in that it too offers an idealized account of torture. In *The Body in Pain*, Scarry describes torture as a language, but what she gives us is a grammar of torture in which no allowance is made for ambiguity in the relation between torturer and tortured.[4] Hrotsvit's plays are similarly absolute in their representation of this relationship. Besides, both the theory and the artistic representation are based on binary oppositions. Scarry describes with great clarity the structure of torture as one of many contrasts between torturer and tortured. She writes that religious suffering does not reflect this particular structure, but the relation between women and their spiritual fathers in Hrotsvit's plays follows it closely. For that reason, the medieval texts suggest a wider context for the structure of torture than Scarry allows. Furthermore, Scarry fails to consider the question of martyrdom; Hrotsvit's plays offer the theoretical insight that martyrdom leads to a reversal of the relationship between torturer and tortured. This allows us to consider the importance of interpretation to torture and the extent to which torture can become subject to subversion.

Hrotsvit's plays permit this recognition because, unlike *The Body in Pain*, they do not represent power as monolithic and always capable of containing subversion. Jonathan Dollimore distances himself from containment theory in *Sexual Dissidence*. He stresses the political significance of perversion, both in its pre-sexual and in its modern, sexual form. Part of the radical potential of perversion, he claims, is its tendency to undermine dominant structures based on violently oppressive binary oppositions, a phenomenon for which he coins the phrase 'perverse dynamic.' Hrotsvit's plays depend on the oppressive structures of patriarchy, but its binary oppositions are reversed in the case of the virgin martyrs. The struggle between the virgins and their Roman torturers is really an interpretive one – the two parties define sexual deviance in radically different ways. By depicting the virgins' noncompliance with the sexual demands of the Roman authorities, the plays uncover the violence that is at the heart of political, male power. The resulting inversions of the power structure show that power is itself an unstable category and that a radical transformation can be achieved by means of a refusal to accept the binary oppositions imposed by power.

It is surprising that the confrontations between the martyrs and the pagan rulers can be read as examples of the perverse dynamic. After all, Dollimore insists that perversion is always anti-teleological. Following Dollimore, chastity should not be regarded as sexual dissidence. Hrotsvit's plays make clear that this binary (perversion vs. patriarchy, anti-teleology vs. teleology) can in turn be deconstructed. The connections between the terms of binary oppositions can be seen at work in these plays, which emerge from a dominant mode of discourse, but go back to the days of Christianity's own marginality and struggle for expression. Dollimore writes that 'the paradoxical dynamics of perversion in its pre-sexological senses enable an account of dissidence within sexuality which is not – hopefully can never again be – confined *to* sexuality' (33). An early representation of sinful perversion and sexual deviance, Hrotsvit's work extends the relevance of the perverse dynamic even further within the realm of sexuality than Dollimore has accounted for. If we allow for the possibility of sexual dissidence by virtue of a teleology defined in opposition to dominant discourse, the perverse dynamic can be seen to open up a space for a medieval representation of female empowerment.

The four plays analyzed here are *The Fall and Repentance of Mary, The Conversion of the Harlot Thais, The Martyrdom of the Holy Virgins Fides, Spes, and Karitas,* and *The Martyrdom of the Holy Virgins Agape, Chionia, and Hirena.*[5] The plays can be divided into two pairs since the first two, which I will call the hermit plays, and the last two, the Roman plays, tell very similar stories. All four plays are set in the third or fourth centuries, the days of the desert fathers and the Roman persecutions of the early Christians. These highly stylized constructions based on Christian legend begin and end in similar ways: male figures of authority try to gain control over the sexual behavior of women whose life style is considered a danger to society; ultimately physical suffering leads to spiritual salvation for the female victims.[6] The Roman plays, *The Martyrdom of the Holy Virgins Agape, Chionia, and Hirena* and *The Martyrdom of the Holy Virgins Fides, Spes, and Karitas*, stage repeated confrontations between pagan emperors or commanders and Christian virgins, who refuse to give up their faith. The virgins' proclamation of chastity is seen as a dangerous example to the female population; hence the use of increasingly cruel forms of torture, which eventually results in a glorious death for the young martyrs. *The Conversion of the Harlot Thais* and *The Fall and Repentance of Mary* are narratives of female transgression followed by penance under the guidance of a hermit father figure. Both tell the story of a young prostitute whose enclosure finally leads to a (re)incorporation into the Church. The plays resemble each other closely, although Thais is a more experienced prostitute while Mary has been raised by Abraham from childhood and is seduced by a man disguised as a monk. Mary's case involves a fall into sin and a return to the innocence of childhood through penance, both brought about by men. Thais's motivation for being a prostitute is unclear, but she too turns out to be a Christian in spite of her profession. This difference, the fact that Mary has been perverted while Thais herself perverts her lovers, explains the more cruel suffering that Thais has to undergo to be converted.

Elaine Scarry's definition of torture excludes religious suffering on the basis of three differences: its limited duration, the fact that the believer has control over the pain inflicted, and its benign purpose in the sense that 'the path of worldly objects is swept clean . . . to make room for the approach of some divinely intuited force' (34). Neither of the prostitutes knows how long their enclosure will last, and it is crucial to their redemption that they give up any sense of control over their destiny. Furthermore, while the benign purpose of salvation is certainly essential to the suffering of Mary and Thais, it should not blind us to the fact that the women are undergoing torture, especially because they do not formulate this benign purpose independently of their torturers. As Scarry points out, torture always masks itself by posing as something else, in the case of political regimes most importantly as information gathering. While redemption may be the ultimate goal of the women's enclosure, the actual body in pain may still be seen to undergo torture, particularly if the relationship between the spiritual guide and penitent believer accords with the structure of the relationship between the torturer and his victim.

The Body in Pain argues that the inexpressibility of pain makes it possible for the torturer to inflict pain, objectify pain's attributes, and ultimately deny it in order to turn it into a sign of his own and the regime's power without at any point being led to identify with the prisoner. The relationship with the victim is one of perfect oppositions in which 'for the prisoner, the body and its pain are overwhelmingly present and voice, world, and self are absent; for the torturer, voice, world, and self are overwhelmingly present and the body and pain are absent' (46). At times, the relationship between torturer and tortured is described in terms of contrasts that become mathematical in their precision: 'The direct equation, "the larger the prisoner's pain, the larger the torturer's world" is mediated by the middle term, "the prisoner's absence of world" '(37). Hrotsvit's plays are equally concerned with structure rather than character and the universal or ideal rather than the particular. They show a similar polarity between torturers and victims, as they introduce gender difference to enhance the contrast between the two parties.

The physical suffering of the young prostitutes in these two plays begins in an initial confrontation that resembles interrogation, an important first stage of torture in Scarry's analysis. Even though the questions are not supposedly asked to gain information, they do serve the dual purpose of 'deconstructing' the world, self, and voice of the victim and securing the world, self, and voice of the torturer by constructing a fictional justification for his actions. (Scarry uses the term deconstruction to show that it is the opposite of construction, not instantaneous destruction.) The process is mutually reinforcing: Abraham's sense of self as religious guide is established through asking questions that undo Mary's identity as a prostitute.

> ABRAHAM. Where is that angelic life that already here on earth you led?
> MARY. Destroyed, it fled.
> ABRAHAM. Where is the modesty of your virginity? Where your admirable countenance?
> MARY. Lost and gone from hence.
> ABRAHAM. What reward for the efforts of your fasting, prayers, and vigils can you hope for unless you return to your senses, you who fell from the height of Heaven and have sunk into the depths of Hell?
> MARY. Woe is me, alas! (Wilson 1989 85–6)

Pafnutius's interrogation of Thais closely corresponds to this dialogue. Although the hermits do not employ physical violence in the course of the exchange, the women experience the accusations as the infliction of physical pain. Mary falls down to 'stay immobile lying on the ground' (86), an act that is also questioned by Abraham. Thais says to Pafnutius, 'Your severe reproach's dart / pierces the inmost recesses of my heart,' to which he replies, 'O, how I wish you were pierced through all your flesh with pain / so that you wouldn't dare to give yourself to perilous lust again!' (107).

The location of these scenes is the most private room of the prostitute, into which the hermits intrude in their disguise as lovers. Mary is questioned in her bedroom, but Thais, the seasoned prostitute whose bedroom has become a public space, is confronted in an even more secret room, the hidden space that she has reserved for her prayers. Scarry notes that torture takes place in the setting of a room to destroy the victim's sense of safety and privacy. In these plays, the room stands for the former self of the prostitute, a place that has to be left behind for the cell in which the women will be enclosed. In abandoning their most private spaces and following their interrogators, Thais and Mary enact the renunciation of their sinful life. Thais has to go even further: in a final public performance she burns her colorful clothes and the gifts of her lovers, the material signifiers of her former identity, in front of her house in full view of a group of former lovers. Thus, the destruction or renunciation of self precedes actual penance.

The second stage of torture involves the loss of world, self, and voice for the victim. Confinement of the body in the monastic cell not only symbolizes but also literally enacts the loss of world, which becomes not much larger than the body itself. In *The Conversion of the Harlot Thais*, the space of the room functions throughout as a metaphor for the body. Thais's cell is dark and very small, it has no entry or exit, and, most importantly, there is no sanitary comfort. Scarry cites many examples of the transformation of the room from a place which 'keeps warm and safe the individual it houses in the same way the body encloses and protects the individual within' (38) into 'an agent of pain' (40). The cell turns the protective room into a cause of physical suffering as Thais is forced to sit in her own excrement.

This is how enclosure accomplishes Thais's perception of the body as a cause of pain. In torture, says Scarry, this view of the body causes a sense of the body's self-betrayal that contributes to the deconstruction of the self. This aspect of torture is particularly important in a religious setting since the notion of the body as traitor to the soul is essential to the rejection of secular life. Thais comes to associate her body with hell and repugnance. She tells Pafnutius after her final release, 'if you wish to know how I spent my time, I will tell you: in my conscience I enumerated my manifold sins and wickedness and gathered them as in a bundle of crime. Then I continuously went over them in my mind, so that just as the nauseating smell here never left my nostrils, so the fear of Hell never departed from my heart's eyes' (120). Fear has now been displaced from her physical to her metaphysical 'heart's eyes.' Having so thoroughly come to see her own body as a source of filth, pain, and degradation, her disgust with the body usurps her sense of self: 'Venerable Father, do not take me, stained and foul wretch, from this filth; let me remain in this place / appropriate for my sinful ways' (121).

Voice is obliterated in enclosure as in torture. According to Scarry, the voice of the victim is appropriated by the torturer, whose own voice grows as the victim is reduced to a body. After enclosure, the women in the hermit plays lose their stage presence. Saved from prostitution, Mary's own voice is no longer heard. Her penitential practices are reported with approval as the image of the silently suffering young woman remains with us. While in enclosure there is no communication beyond the cell, Thais is even forbidden to utter words in prayer. Pafnutius rebukes her for asking permission to pray: 'how can you have such great confidence that you would presume to utter the name of the unpolluted Divinity with your polluted lips?' He then takes over her voice (and 'enlarges' his own) by prescribing the formula, 'Thou who created me, / have mercy on me' (115). It is a preliminary to the final stage of torture, in which the torturer ends up denying the prisoner's pain and displacing it onto the power of the state, the ultimate objective of torture in *The Body in Pain*.

The deconstruction of world, self, and voice, Scarry argues, finally leads to the appropriation of the reality of pain for the state's power, a process for which she coins the phrase 'analogical substantiation' or 'analogical verification.' It requires the denial of pain and an interpretive move away from the body to the abstraction of power. Clearly, religious suffering more generally entails the denial of the body that has been at the center of attention all along. In the hermit plays, Abraham and Pafnutius displace the significance of the pain of the prostitutes from their bodies to their spiritual salvation in order to glorify the Christian faith. The loss of self, world, and voice on the part of the women has made this outcome possible. Mary's suffering body is off-stage in enclosure so that it is left to Abraham to report to his advisor and friend Effrem that she fulfills her penance '[e]ntirely to [his] governance' and that her body is weakened by wearing a hair-shirt, fasting, and keeping vigils (91). The men conclude that everything is as it should be, interpreting her suffering as evidence for the glory of Christ. Thais finally echoes Pafnutius's earlier lessons: 'praise Him all the company of Heaven . . . because He not only suffers men to live in sinful ways / but rewards the penitent with the gift of grace' (121). As she dies, Pafnutius literally takes over her voice and prays that 'the dissolving, diverse parts of this human being / may happily return to the source of their original being' (122). His words show that Thais has ceased to matter as an individual (even her name is no longer mentioned), and her 'dissolving' body has come to signify the glory of the faith.

In *Technologies of the Self*, Michel Foucault describes penance in words that are pertinent to the fate of Mary and Thais:

> Penance is the affect of change, of rupture with self, past, and world. It's a way to show that you are able to renounce life and self, to show that you can face and accept death. Penitence of sin doesn't have as its target the establishing of an identity but serves instead to mark the refusal of the self, the breaking away from self: *Ego non sum, ego*. . . . Self-revelation is at the same time self-destruction. (43)

Following Foucault, we can conclude that Christian self-definition in penance in its most extreme form entails the destruction of self.[7] For Hrotsvit's women, this is even more so because there is no agency involved in the initiation of the penitential process. Consent to undergo penance is constructed for them in interrogation. Foucault's formulation of penance as 'rupture with self, past, and world' comes significantly close to Elaine Scarry's description of the initial stage of torture as a deconstruction of 'self, voice, and world' even though 'rupture' fails to assign agency to the believer or the religious guide. If consent to undergo penance can be foregone or if penance can be imposed on the believer, the category of the benign purpose of religious suffering, such an important motive for Scarry's exclusion of this type of pain from her account of torture, is no longer unambiguous. Female penance depicted by Hrotsvit follows the structure of torture and is similarly used as a sign of the power of the institution that 'inflicts' it.

In spite of Jonathan Dollimore's suggestion that perversion did not become sexualized until the 19th century, Hrotsvit's plays indicate that in a religious context sinful perversion was defined, at least in the case of women, as primarily sexual.[8] In the hermit plays, Hrotsvit depicts women as prone to perversion by nature and only kept on the right path by proper male guidance. But her depiction of transgressive sexuality is based on a contradiction that parallels the ambiguities Dollimore discovers in the work of Augustine and as a result in the Western tradition at large: 'we find evil conceptualized simultaneously as, on the one hand, a foreign force or agency, at once alien, antithetic, and hostile; on the other as an inner deviation... evil becomes at once utterly alien and insidiously inherent' (143). In *The Fall and Repentance of Mary*, these contradictions become quickly apparent. Mary is led astray by a mysterious man (presumably the devil) disguised as a monk, who is never given a presence or voice in the play.[9] Evil is displaced to the margins of the text and personified as an incomprehensible other, whose actions are not examined, perhaps because religious women are not allowed to hear 'evil flattery,' as Hrotsvit writes in her 'Preface to the Dramas' (3). Yet, this mysterious character is capable of perverting a young virgin who was raised by a hermit in circumstances entirely conducive to a religious life. If a momentary lapse in attention on the part of her religious father can cause a paragon of female virtue to be led astray, evil comes dangerously close to innocence, and the possibility of perversion has to be always potentially present in female purity. Thus, the play stages what Dollimore calls the 'utterly alien and insidiously inherent' quality of evil and specifically of perversion in the case of women.

But these are not simply narratives of individual female redemption. The hermit plays represent female sexuality as having consequences far beyond the individual female sinner. For the male leaders of the religious community, control over female sexuality is indispensable to social harmony because it is bound up with the fate of the souls and bodies of men. Abraham and Effrem repeatedly refer to the effect of Mary's perversion on their own bodies. For example, when Abraham recounts his discovery of Mary's disappearance to his friend, he claims, 'my innermost parts trembled with fear, and my limbs quaked with terror' (78). Mary's behavior causes eternal damnation to the souls of her clients, but Thais, the worse sinner of the two, even affects male physical health as her lovers fight among each other for her favors. Depicting the influence of female sexuality on male bodies, Hrotsvit complicates the binary opposition between embodied female and disembodied male, showing the male body to derive its religious status mainly from its relation to the female body.[10]

In spite of the general tendency of these two plays to confirm patriarchal binaries, Hrotsvit also undermines the opposition between sin and salvation. Prior to the enclosure of the prostitutes, the bodies of both lovers and hermits are in a comparable state of distress due to female transgression. The hermit plays establish an unexpected parallel between sexual seduction and religious conversion. Like the devil who seduces Mary, Abraham and Pafnutius disguise themselves as lovers. Persuasion of females takes the same form whether it is used for perversion or for salvation so that purpose, determined by the male father figures for the women, becomes the only means of differentiation between leading someone astray and showing her the right path. Not surprisingly, before the hermits embark on their journeys to the brothels, anxiety is expressed about the effect of their acts on their bodies. Effrem wonders if Abraham will have to drink wine and eat meat; Pafnutius asks his disciples to pray that he 'won't be overcome by the vicious serpent's guile' (103). The bodies of the hermits take on the dangerous appearance of secular male bodies.

Abraham's body is saved from these anxieties when it turns out to be itself a source of evidence of faith. In this Christianized version of the narratives of mistaken identity and recognition so familiar in ancient comedy, Mary instantly receives a hint of Abraham's true identity. She recognizes his smell as 'the fragrance of chastity I once practiced' (84). The body is not only evidence of an essential self beyond the disguise but also a reflection of the state of the soul which transcends the boundaries of gender–Mary is reminded of her own smell.[11] This view of the body as a mirror of the spiritual state justifies the extreme physical suffering to be undergone by Mary at a later stage. In *The Conversion of the Harlot Thais*, the initial connection between male physical violence and female perversion undergoes a 'benign' transformation into institutionally controlled violence directed against the female body. While the religious men start out in physical pain, they end up without any expressed physicality while the women, defined by their attitude towards their bodies as a source of pleasure and income, are increasingly reduced to silently suffering bodies.

In the two hermit plays, Hrotsvit legitimates physical suffering inflicted on female bodies as a means to salvation for the women but also as a strategy for preventing social disorder. The Church, personified by the hermits, establishes its power by emphasizing the threat of female sexuality and then controlling it. Critics like Marina Warner and Elizabeth Robertson have pointed out that medieval texts on female sanctity often emphasize physical suffering and torture because women were seen as inescapably linked to their bodies and incapable of transcending the flesh.[12] Compared with the treatment of Mary, the enclosure of Thais is a much more graphic representation of torture as a method of desexualization of the female body, which becomes pure matter marked by decay in the eyes of the penitent. While her redemption differs from Mary's in its severity, it is also more clearly a reconfiguration of the body as a source of sin rather than pleasure.

Mary's suffering is intended to achieve a return to the innocence of her youth. As a child, she is told that she has to live up to the destiny indicated by her name; she is meant to be a virgin as well as a 'stella maris' or guiding star to sailors at sea, as Abraham tells her, 'through the unimpaired wholeness of your body and the pure holiness of your mind' (73). But once she has been led astray due to her female weakness, the narrative of redemption highlights the enforced, constructed character of her destiny. Dollimore perceives the potential for subversive readings of this type of conflict between perversion and dominance: 'At those moments when coercion reveals destiny as subjection, authoritarianism produces the conditions for its own delegitimation . . . and erring may become a kind of knowledge' (107). Transgressive knowledge is not achieved by the women in the hermit plays, however, precisely because coercion works by means of torture and therefore by a reduction of the perverted female to a suffering body without a self.

Unlike the prostitutes, the virgin martyrs in *The Martyrdom of the Holy Virgins Agape, Chionia, and Hirena* and *The Martyrdom of the Holy Virgins Fides, Spes, and Karitas* do achieve transgressive knowledge in their refusal to conform to the sexual demands of the Roman emperors. Analogical substantiation is behind the torture of the martyrs. Diocletian, the emperor in the former play, fears the advocacy of chastity and Christianity by the three virgins especially in light of their exceptional beauty, which places them in a position to influence others. The emperor Hadrian, in the latter play, feels threatened by the chaos that has already been caused by the arrival of three young virgins and their mother Sapientia from abroad. Antiochus warns him, 'Our wives despise us so that they refuse to eat with us, / or even more to sleep with us' (126). The Romans in both plays use torture to neutralize the disruptive force that originates in the presence, beauty, and behavior of these women with the purpose of maintaining control over the female segment of their society by confirming the power of the state. Fears of the social disruption that has occurred or may occur on a larger scale are therefore projected onto the virgins, who embody the threat of a lack of state control over marginalized subjects in general. As Peter Schroeder has remarked, 'The largely impersonal institution of the state, Hroswitha implies, rests on the largely relational institution of marriage; women, by exercising their power over the latter, can help bring down the former. Christianity is presented as a feminine attack on the male power structure' (54). This is precisely the mechanism designated by Scarry's analogical substantiation, which is particularly important, she writes, to societies that suffer from 'a crisis of belief–that is, when some central idea or ideology or cultural construct has ceased to elicit a population's belief either because it is manifestly fictitious or because it has for some reason been divested of ordinary forms of substantiation.' In such a situation, 'the sheer material factualness of the human body will be borrowed to lend that cultural construct the aura of 'realness' and 'certainty.''[13] The Roman rulers want to turn the physical suffering of the virgins into a sign of their own power and control over their subjects much as the hermits interpret the pain of the prostitutes as a sign of the power of Christianity.

The attempts to reduce the virgins to bodies in pain by destroying their sense of self, world, and voice, fail in each instance because the girls tell their torturers that by inflicting pain they are merely fulfilling the girls' wishes. In *The Martyrdom of the Holy Virgins Fides, Spes, and Karitas*, Fides declares under threat of torture: 'our souls exult in the reward so grand' (133) and 'To die in Christ is just what I desire' (136). Hirena, one of the virgins in *The Martyrdom of the Holy Virgins Agape, Chionia, and Hirena*, reacts to the execution of her sisters with the expression of a wish to undergo the same fate: 'I hope to follow their example and expire, /so with them in heaven eternal joy I may acquire'(45). When officer Sissinus threatens her by saying, 'What you abhor, I shall ordain' (46), it becomes clear that the problem is that there is no violence Hirena abhors. This premise, the martyrdom of the virgins, raises the question of what happens when the infliction of pain does not bring about the expected effect because the martyr embraces it. Pain is not experienced as a form of self-betrayal by the body and, rather than obliterating consciousness, it strengthens the martyr's sense of self.[14] The Roman plays suggest that desire transferred from the torturer to the tortured reverses the relationship described by Scarry.

As their names suggest, the virgins are personifications of religious concepts and therefore of course difficult to hurt physically. While they are emblems of stability and faith, our attention moves to the Romans, whose sense of self, world, and voice disintegrates. For the state and its representatives, these aspects of subjectivity depend on recognition by its subjects and the ability to command inferiors. The plays depict the Romans' loss of self, world, and voice as a loss of control over their words, bodies, and subjects, to emphasize that torture incapacitates the torturers. In the initial interrogation scenes, the Romans try to persuade the virgins to give up their former identities in ways that resemble the strategies of Abraham and Pafnutius. Emperor Hadrian flatters the young women and asks their mother what ages they are. When he ends up having to listen to Sapientia's elaborate display of mathematical virtuosity (for which he has no response), he is positioned as a pupil rather than a spiritual guide. His attempt at gentle persuasion fails to have the expected impact.

Diocletian tries more forcefully to destroy the confidence of the virgins by accusing them of madness and telling them that within Roman society, their chastity cannot be tolerated in light of their nobility and beauty. But Agape responds to Diocletian's accusation with a rational challenge: 'What signs of our madness do you see?' Finding his answer unconvincing, she persists in the denial of her own madness. Her sister Chionia turns the accusation back on Diocletian: 'My sister is not mad; she rightly reprehended your folly' (38). Madness becomes a matter of interpretation, and the virgins deny the emperor's right to attach the label to his subjects by virtue of his position. Moreover, failing to conform to the expectations that the torturers have of their victims, the virgins become such an interpretive problem to the Romans that the officers and soldiers end up accusing each other of madness.

This interpretive reversal is achieved in a narrative of destruction and torture of female and male bodies. The loss of the secure voice of the pagan authorities is followed by their physical incapacitation, in an exact reversal of the stages of torture described by Elaine Scarry. Contrasting responses to physical suffering allow for the inversion of binary oppositions between male and female, torturer and tortured, state and subject. While the virgins suffer no real pain, the torturers fall victim to the very violence that is intended to sway the virgins. In *The Martyrdom of the Holy Virgins Fides, Spes, and Karitas*, the boiling water into which Spes is thrown causes a flood that downs the emperor's servants, but the little girl swims around without a care. The fire that is meant to burn Karitas leaves her unharmed but leads to an explosion that kills five thousand soldiers. With the breakdown of the social order, the unforeseen effects of torture result not only in physical weakness on the part of the Romans, but also in mental degradation. Hadrian, for one, becomes more and more dependent on Antiochus, and his words show a progressive crumbling of certainties, of his identity as emperor, and therefore of his ultimate authority.

He repeatedly asks Antiochus for advice on how to behave towards the virgins and their impertinent mother (e.g. 135, 137, 141). Once the bodies of his soldiers begin to be affected, he says, 'What is happening to us? I am alarmed,' and finally, 'I admit defeat' (141). When the attempt to burn Karitas has had its disastrous outcome, the emperor admits, 'I blush to see her again; / my efforts to harm her are all in vain' (145).

Similarly, Dulcitius and Sissinus find that their commands are no longer followed up, which brings Sissinus to conclude that his soldiers must have gone insane. Ultimately, the loss of control felt by his men as a consequence of divine intervention and female empowerment leads to their admission of weakness and delusion. The soldiers fail to take Hirena, the youngest and only virgin left alive at this point, to a brothel as Sissinus has ordered, giving her up to the care of two God-like strangers instead. Sissinus, who has already cursed his own soldiers, realizes that he can no longer exercise his authority. His soldiers explain, 'We are all deluded by some intrigue; / we are afflicted with a great fatigue; / if you allow this insane person to stay alive, / then neither you nor we shall survive' (49). Although the accusation of madness is still directed at the martyr, their own delusion is perceived in terms of the body, and her death becomes a precondition for their physical survival. In other words, the suffering of the male body is accompanied by a loss of voice and the destruction of a secure sense of self. At the same time, the self, voice, and world of the virgins are strengthened as a result of their suffering.

As is the case with the traditional medieval depiction of the body of the female martyr, Hrotsvit's dramatic representation of the virgins' bodies is marked by duality. Warner explains that the ideal of wholeness and purity was characteristic of the virginal state (72). On the one hand, therefore, the bodies of the young girls are unharmed by male assault. In *The Martyrdom of the Holy Virgins Agape, Chionia, and Hirena*, for instance, the soldiers remark on the fact that Chionia and Agape are not disfigured by the fire that kills them and 'no traces of injury can be found' (45). On the other hand, the plays also follow tradition in showing the fragmentation of the body of the female martyr. Fides's nipples are torn off, but Spes's torture is even crueler. Hadrian orders her to be 'suspended in mid-air and torn to pieces with claws so that when her bowels have been severed / and her bones have been bared, / cracking, limb by limb, she dies' (140). For both Karitas and Spes, beheading is finally the only effective form of punishment – the process of torture has no effect on the body and only achieves a silencing of the martyr when it terminates her life and suffering.

At the conclusion of *The Martyrdom of the Holy Virgins Agape, Chionia, and Hirena*, Hirena tells Sissinus to 'blush for shame and proclaim your miserable defeat because without the help of weapons, you cannot overcome a tender little virgin as your foe' (49). Her emphasis on the disparity between the virgin and the officer indicates the extent of the reversals that have taken place.

The virgins are essentially untouchable because they conceive of the body only as a vehicle for suffering that will bring them closer to God. This upsets the structure of torture to the point of complete turnaround. Torture confirms the self and voice of the virgins because of the transferal of desire. In longing for the pain that will bring them closer to God, every instance of torture serves only to confirm the Christian identity that differentiates them from their surroundings. The basic problem of the Romans is that they are at a loss as to how to interpret the world now that the virgins provide such a crushing example of the tenuous nature of their assumptions with respect to femininity and control over the subject through violence. The men's loss of control is contrasted with the confidence of the martyrs, whose predictions come true, whose prayers have the desired effect, and whose identities are confirmed.

Clearly, these plays have many suggestions to offer to theories of torture. Their medieval, skillful rhetorical structure and symbolically meaningful juxtaposition of different attitudes to life result in a representation not altogether different from Elaine Scarry's equally rhetorically clever grammar of torture. Even though Hrotsvit's Roman plays offer a dramatic fantasy of ineffective torture, they point to the importance of interpretation and desire to the relationship between torturer and tortured. Once desire is moved from the torturer to the martyr, the plays suggest, the relationship between torturer and tortured undergoes an exact reversal as a consequence of the fact that the victim's interpretation of physical pain is radically different from what it should be to make torture have the crushing effect on self, world, and voice. The confrontation is no longer between a powerful representative of the state and a silenced prisoner, but between two different ways of interpreting pain and two different processes of analogical substantiation. In this interpretive battle, the virgins turn torture into a sign of the power of their faith and the strength of their own identities. Analogical substantiation fails to work for the Romans because the body in pain becomes a sign of the strength of the weak. Thus, it confirms the cultural construct advocated by the virgins.[15]

In transforming the spectacle of imperial power into an opportunity for weak females to triumph, Hrotsvit capitalizes on what Foucault has famously described as the ambiguity inherent in the spectacular style of punishment:

> There is ... an ambiguity in this suffering that may signify equally well the truth of the crime or the error of the judges, the goodness or the evil of the criminal, the coincidence or the divergence between the judgement of men and that of God. Hence the insatiable curiosity that drove the spectators to the scaffold to witness the spectacle of suffering truly endured. (1975 46)

Hrotsvit seems to have been a savvy playwright, who was well aware of the workings of this type of punishment, as she staged for her Christian audience the very reversal of signification that was potentially present in public torture and caused the 'insatiable curiosity' of the spectators. Even regardless of the signs of divine protection, the resistance of the virgins itself undermines the authority of the torturers to such an extent that the spectacle can only be deciphered as proof of the ineffectualness of power in the face of religious conviction. The asymmetry between the individual martyr and the powerful emperor and his soldiers makes the spectacle a sign of its own opposite.[16]

While public punishment can undergo a reversal of meaning, perversion may also undermine dominant modes of signification. Dollimore writes that the inversion of binary oppositions is a consequence of the perverse dynamic, or in other words, the presence of perversion itself undoes the binary oppositions by which it is produced in the first place. He explains the concept as follows:

> [it] denotes certain instabilities and contradictions within dominant structures which exist by virtue of exactly what those structures simultaneously contain and exclude. The displacements which constitute certain repressive discriminations are partly enabled via a proximity which, though disavowed, remains to enable a perverse return, an undoing, a transformation. The perverse dynamic signifies that fearful interconnectedness whereby the antithetical inheres within, and is partly produced by, what it opposes. (33)

The confrontations at the heart of the two Roman plays converge on the issue of female sexuality and gender difference. The oppositions set up by the dominant state between male and female, powerful and weak, torturer and tortured, are revealed to be not a consequence of the inherent attributes of gender, but of power over processes of attribution and signification. Thus, gender turns out to be one more construct that is employed by the state to acquire control over its subjects. In refusing to accept the ways in which the state constructs gender, the virgins cause a reversal of power relations that denaturalizes gender and exposes its attributes to contestation. As they do so, some of the conventional signs of femininity are transposed onto the male aggressors, showing that the binary oppositions that mark gender difference can be undone, a clear sign of the perverse dynamic at work.

The sexualization of the female body is one of the many signs of contrast between the Romans and the virgins that is reversed in the course of the plays. The attempt of the state to sexualize the chaste female body fails as the bodies of the officers and authorities themselves become the source of uncontrolled desire. The state employs explicitly sexual methods to reduce the girls to helpless female bodies, but their efforts to strip them or take them to a brothel are all thwarted and made to look ridiculous by divine intervention. Marina Warner contends of medieval narratives of female martyrs that

> the particular focus on women's torn and broken flesh reveals the psychological obsession of the religion with sexual sin, and the tortures that pile up one upon the other with pornographic repetitiousness underline the identification of the female with the perils of sexual contact. For as they defend their virtue, the female martyrs of the Christian calendar are assaulted in any number of ingenious and often sexual ways. (71)

Yet the sexual assaults on the virgin body in Hrotsvit constitute less a sexualization of that body than an interpretive reconfiguration by which sexuality becomes a male characteristic, as the men, not the women, lose control over their bodies and their actions.

This reversal is most clearly foregrounded in the case of Dulcitius, who is himself subject to his community's demonization as a consequence of his attempts to deflower the virgins. In the famous kitchen scene, male desire goes rampant. Dulcitius not only loses his capacity to interpret the world (as he kisses pots and pans thinking they are the virgins), but he also makes it impossible for others to identify and recognize him as a representative of the state because he is smeared with soot. His loss of identity in sexuality becomes externalized when, in the words of Agape, he 'appear[s] in body the way he is in mind: possessed by the Devil' (42). As Marla Carlson has remarked, there is an 'ironic contrast' between the virgins, who are above sexual desire, and the pagans, who are '*subject to* their bodies' (479). Dulcitius's soldiers, not realizing who he is, run away in fear, and his wife tells him he has gone mad. This results in his loss of position to another officer when Diocletian realizes that Dulcitius has been 'so greatly deluded, / so greatly insulted, / so utterly humiliated' that he has to assign someone else to the task of torturing the virgins (43). Male perversion is figured as uncontrolled desire causing a loss of authority.

Similarly, the male gaze is sexual while the female gaze is rational and defiant. The women return the gaze of male authority without fear, just as they return its accusations. Before confronting Hadrian, Sapientia declares, 'I do not fear to enter the palace in the noble company of my daughters, nor do I fear looking upon the Emperor's threatening face' (126). Her control over her emotions is contrasted with Hadrian's own lack of restraint, as he admits that, 'The beauty of every one of them stuns my senses; / I cannot stop admiring the nobility of their bearing, their many excellences' (127). The outcome of the attempted torture of the young girls is written on the male body: Dulcitius's sexuality covers his face in the form of soot, and the Emperor Hadrian and his men admit to blushing in embarrassment, the conventional sign of female modesty and weakness. By sexualizing the male gaze and the male body, Hrotsvit represents male authority as prone to the very weaknesses that supposedly characterize women, showing that in some ways male power over women is based on the repression of certain 'female' qualities within men themselves.

The martyrdom of the virgins has been read as evidence of their transcendence of the female gender. Charles Nelson, for one, writes that Hrotsvit gives in to the patriarchal tradition when she depicts Hirena's power as gendered male: 'The suggestion is that her 'masculine' will, courage, and faithfulness is separate from her female body which is vulnerable to pollution and lust' (54). This type of reading finds its source in the writings of St. Jerome, who was certainly an inspiration for Hrotsvit. His advocacy of chastity for women because it allows them to become like men, however, is not relevant to the Roman plays. On the contrary, Hrotsvit continues to stress the femininity of her martyrs throughout in order to strengthen the contrast between the dominant and the marginalized, who come out on top. It is precisely by depicting the inversion of binary oppositions that her plays acquire their radical potential as examples of the perverse dynamic.

The female refusal to conform to the sexual and gendered imperatives of the pagan authorities leads to an exposure of the violence and random sexuality at the heart of male domination. As a result, the behavior of the virgins permits the audience to achieve the kind of knowledge described by Dollimore as transgressive, a type of recognition based on political and sexual dissidence. The reversals of binary oppositions obtained by the martyrs reveal not only the coercive nature of gender politics but also the extent to which gender characteristics themselves are an effect of power. In presenting young, marginalized women as more capable of physical endurance, self-control, heroism, and insight than their rulers, Hrotsvit aims to glorify her religion, but she also makes clear that gender binaries are constructed for the purposes of maintaining social control. The virgins create a world upside down and cause the exposure of the powerful interests served by society's gendered binary oppositions, simply by refusing to conform to social stereotypes of female behavior.

Jonathan Dollimore insistently describes perversion as anti-teleological in nature. But what is represented in Hrotsvit's Roman plays turns out to match the subject of *Sexual Dissidence*:

> This is the transgression that this study explores: the kind which seizes upon and exploits contradictions and which, as a political act, inspires recognition first, that the injustices of the existing social order are not inevitable–that they are, in other words, contingent and not eternal; second, that injustice is only overcome by a radical transformation of the conditions that produce and sustain it; third, that all such transformations are at the cost of destructive struggle. (89)

The 'destructive struggle' of the Christian martyrs reveals not only that the oppression by the Romans is really an attempt to contain the female segment of the population, but also that the Roman assumptions about women are deeply flawed. Dramatizing the inversion of binary oppositions, the Roman plays offer a representation of the empowerment of marginalized figures by virtue of their subversive resignification of the body, gender, and the effects of pain. Dollimore's own opposition between teleology and anti-teleology does not allow for the inclusion of this particular representation of empowering chastity under the heading of sexual dissidence. The insights enabled by the perverse dynamic are in these plays coupled with an alternative teleology rather than an anti-teleological attitude towards sexuality because the non-compliance with the reproductive teleology of the Romans on the basis of Christian doctrine leads to female empowerment. For these reasons, Hrotsvit's work suggests that sexual dissidence needs to include the possibility of a teleology that is radically different from accepted beliefs and incomprehensible to the dominant forces in society. In writing the history of perversion, it is necessary to consider the different configurations of perversion in specific texts and historical periods. Moreover, it should be recognized that in particular circumstances even the binary opposition between teleology and anti-teleology needs to be deconstructed so that all kinds of sexually subversive behavior, even chastity, can be termed perversion if the political ramifications require it.

Hrotsvit's dramatic representation of female martyrdom in all four of these plays involves the confrontation between different systems of signification, under the aegis of the pagan state and religion. The confrontation converges, specifically, on female sexuality. Aberrant sexual behavior, whether sexual abstinence or prostitution, is a marker of uncontrollability for male authority figures. Surprisingly, if one accepts the premise that sexuality was not considered essential to identity until centuries later, sexuality is what defines subjectivity in the case of women because it is the realm over which it is most difficult to establish male control. The pagan state prescribes reproductive sexuality for its women; the early Christian Church, chastity. Read together, then, Hrotsvit's plays reveal parallels between Church and state in their attempts to acquire power over female subjects. The ways in which the Romans project internal unrest in their state onto the dissident virgins is reminiscent of the treatment of the two prostitutes by the hermit. The hermits and emperors even use similar terminology to describe sexual dissidence: both sin and chastity are figured as illness to confirm the idea of the uncontrollable female body. Pafnutius presents Thais's enclosure as a physical cure of a 'sickness of both body and soul' to be cured by the 'medicine of contraries' (113). Hadrian describes the Roman Empire as 'infected everywhere by the mortal plague of the Christian sect' (125–6). While this representation is accepted by the prostitutes, who allow themselves to be silenced, the virgins show the categories employed by the Romans to serve the purpose of maintaining power, simply by refusing to adopt them. The 'weak' prostitutes are susceptible to flattery and violent threats alike, while the virgins are not affected by male persuasion, and their voices are heard until the end. The parallel behavior of Church and state is obviously not intended to cause our censure of both since the plays attach very different value judgments to these institutions. The conflicting nature of these representations of female martyrdom can be overlooked if one purely concentrates on the ways in which Hrotsvit's work comes out of monastic contexts. Instead, the complex structure of her creations, which involve so many mirrorings and reversals, is more than an aesthetically pleasing dramatic achievement. It enables us to think about the relations between men and women, institution and subject, power and perversion, and torturer and tortured in new, challenging ways.

Hrotsvit begins her 'Preface to the Dramas' with an apology for the depiction of illicit sexuality in her plays. She claims that the presence of sexuality in her work is inevitable, however, because of her model, Terence: 'being forced by the conventions of this composition / I had to contemplate and give a rendition / of that detestable madness of unlawful lovers and of their evil flattery, / which we are not permitted even to hear' (3). If nuns are not allowed to hear evil flattery, has Hrotsvit avoided transgression herself by reading Terence? Is her engagement with his plays not more transgressive than a passive consumption of them? In writing plays, is she not making other women in her religious community hear evil flattery too?[17] She goes on to defend her use of the Terentian model by pointing out that the presence of sexual seduction and desire in her plays is a dramatic means to a moral end: 'the more seductive the unlawful flatteries of those who have lost their sense, / the greater the heavenly Helper's munificence / and the more glorious the victories of triumphant innocence are shown to be, especially when female weakness triumphs in conclusion / and male strength succumbs in confusion' (3). By asserting that she is forced to dramatize illicit behavior by her model, but capable of converting pagan form into the glorification of God, Hrotsvit situates herself in a position of simultaneous inferiority and superiority with respect to her predecessor.[18] Similarly, while admitting that religious women are not permitted to contemplate sexuality, she writes that by giving sexuality a presence in her plays she has achieved further glorification of God.

This duality of voice accounts for the dazzling rhetorical complexity of the preface, which almost allows the reader to forget that Hrotsvit fails to remark on her graphic depiction of violence against female bodies. The disavowal and incorporation of sexuality is paralleled by Hrotsvit's radically divergent representations of torture. Precisely by virtue of these contradictions her plays enable various insights into constructions of gender, sexuality, and violence. At the same time, the recognition that her equivocation is an integral part of her artistic achievement can bring about a new appreciation of her plays. While the readers of the 'protofeminist' Hrotsvit tend to focus on *The Martyrdom of the Holy Virgins Agape, Chionia, and Hirena* and *The Martyrdom of the Holy Virgins Fides, Spes, and Karitas*, these plays are more generally seen as less effective dramatically than the hermit plays. For Sandro Sticca, as for many others, *The Fall and Repentance of Mary* is the best of her plays.[19] He considers the Roman plays flawed because of a lack of characterological depth and calls the virgins 'monsters of theological stability,' a phrase he finds apt enough to use it in two articles (1975 8 and 1979 137). Peter Schroeder, on the other hand, argues that *The Martyrdom of the Holy Virgins Fides, Spes, and Karitas* 'articulates most explicitly her proto-feminist themes,' but has difficulty analyzing *The Fall and Repentance of Mary* and *The Conversion of the Harlot Thais* (55). He ends up claiming that the men in the hermit plays are feminized and that femininity is therefore implicitly endorsed. Based on the anachronistic assumption that an author's work should be unified, critics of Hrotsvit have felt the need to focus on one set of plays at the expense of others. The realization that the work of the medieval woman writer is often marked by a duality of voice allows not only for a better appreciation of both the Roman and the hermit plays, but also for a dialogue with contemporary theoretical accounts of perversion and torture that attributes equal significance to the medieval text and the theory.

Endnotes

1 See A. Daniel Frankforter (311) and M.R. Sperberg-McQueen (49). For more examples of critics who see Hrotsvit as a protofeminist, see among others Demers, Schroeder, and Gold, in spite of her emphasis on ambiguity. Cf. McNaughton for a critique of Schroeder's use of the term 'feminist' for Hrotsvit. Medieval scholars like Sandro Sticca and Katharina Wilson have tended to read her work primarily in terms of its monastic and artistic context even if they point to the ways in which Hrotsvit tries to transcend the prejudicial notions of women in her day (Wilson 1988 and Sticca 1975 and 1987). In her essay entitled 'Impassive Bodies: Hrotsvit Stages Martyrdom,' Marla Carlson treats the plays as expressing different meanings in relation to different potential 10th century audiences. She argues against a reading of Hrotsvit's plays as subversive in gendered terms, emphasizing their compliance to and strengthening of the Ottonian regime and Imperial Church.

2 Few commentators have remarked on the contradictions. Charles Nelson reads the plays as characterized by duality. He gives a sympathetic account of the problematic position of the medieval woman writer, drawing conclusions that differ from mine. Nelson explains the contradictions by asserting that Hrotsvit's aim is to establish symmetry of power between men and women. She does this, he argues, by appealing to the doctrine that everyone was equal in salvation (the 'salvation theology of equivalence'). Nevertheless, Nelson concludes that Hrotsvit is ultimately 'undone' by the 'creation theology of subordination' of her religion (54, 47). Peter Dronke writes about the ambiguities in the plays and especially the preface, but his conclusions are reductive. In disregard of the political aspects of Hrotsvit's position as a female writer in the Middle Ages, he characterizes the contradictions in very unfortunate and frequently criticized terms as her 'weapon of literary coquetry': 'Her shape-shifting, her "weak little woman" pose, her headily exaggerated modesty-topoi, her diminutives, her graceful to-and-fro of affirmation and negation, can all be seen as in the service of that coquetry' (72).

3 Carlson asserts that 'Twentieth-century writings on torture, terror, and representation are largely inadequate to explain this staging, because Hrotsvit does not stage the body in pain' (474). In spite of the historical insight that her essay affords, it is clear that while the bodies of the virgins in two of Hrotsvit's plays may not be in pain, they *are* subjected to torture. Besides, the bodies of the prostitutes in the other two plays discussed here certainly are in pain. Carlson's use of the term 'ordeal' for moments of torture in these plays to posit a distinction between bodies in pain and bodies undergoing torture without suffering is enlightening. It should not prevent us, however, from seeing that the plays' representations of torture can be illuminated by and deepen our readings of modern work on the body in pain.

4 Several of Scarry's reviewers have remarked on her universalizing theory. See especially Peter Singer's comparison of Scarry's assumptions with the findings of Edward Peters in *Torture* (New York: Blackwell, 1985). Similarly, Susan Rubin Suleiman has argued, in an otherwise very positive review, that a number of Scarry's assertions on war do not agree with historical examples. The suggested failure of Scarry's theoretical notion of torture to live up to comparisons with actual cases does not change my argument because I place her work in dialogue with an artistic, equally idealized representation of torture. It should be noted that Scarry's work on torture is only a component of a much larger argument on the antithesis of pain and imagination as exemplary of 'the making and unmaking of the world.' As part of the negative half of the equation, the analysis of torture is crucial to the argument as a whole, however, and its significance is indicated by the fact that it takes up the first chapter of her book.

5   The Latin titles are *Lapsus et conversio Mariae neptis Habrahae heremicolae, Conversio Thaidis meretricis, Passio sanctarum virginum Fidei Spei et Karitatis,* and *Passio sanctarum virginum Agapis Chioniae et Hirenae.* It has long been critical practice to use the short-hand titles of the plays, *Abraham, Pafnutius, Dulcitius,* and *Sapientia,* but, as Peter Dronke has pointed out, the original titles refer to the female characters rather than the male protagonists of the plays and more recent work has begun to employ the correct titles (Dronke 294). I agree with David Wiles, who sees the renaming as a 'sign of male appropriation' (73) and have therefore chosen to use the original titles as translated by Katharina Wilson. Hrotsvit's name is spelled in many different ways (Hrotsvith, Hrotsvitha, Hroswitha, etc.); I follow Wilson's lead in this respect. All quotations from the plays and the 'Preface to the Dramas' are from Wilson 1989.

6   See Wilson's introductions to Hrotsvit's work for very different, aesthetically oriented discussions of the parallels and oppositions in Hrotsvit's plays (Wilson 1989 xv–xxii and 1984 36–7). See also Dronke on the elaborate symmetries that mark the entire oeuvre.

7   In *Discipline and Punish,* Foucault only briefly refers to the cell in modern penitentiaries as based on the monastic model, claiming that 'the disciplinary space is always, basically, cellular' (143). Mary and Thais can be seen as 'docile bodies' in the end, and a comparison of Hrotsvit's Roman and hermit plays would suggest that enclosure is a more effective, individualized form of punishment than spectacular torture in the marketplace. While in his earlier work, Foucault may have been guilty of the kind of 'othering' of the medieval period that still characterizes some new historicist criticism on the early modern period, in his later writings, he uncovers the many ways in which the 'pastoral' power of the Christian Church has informed modern, secular power relations. Cf. his essay 'The Subject and Power' (1982) and, for an account of the ways in which the medieval subject has been mistakenly treated as diametrically opposed to the early modern subject, especially in new historicist work, David Aers.

8   See Sticca 1975 for a brief account of the misogyny of influential religious writing of the period. He cites Aquinas's assertion that woman was 'a male gone awry' (6, quoted from *Summa Theologica* I, 92, Art. 1).

9   M.R. Sperberg-McQueen reads his presence as evidence of incest committed by Abraham, a reading that imposes modern criteria of realism on the text and attempts to provide a 'plausible' explanation for the presence of the mysterious other, who is overtly identified as the devil in the play. Mixing the discussion of the play with the legend of the 4th-century Maria, Sperberg-McQueen claims that 'on the evidence we have, the scenario I describe *could* have happened' (59) as if the play gives unproblematic, direct access to historical reality and serves a documentary rather than an artistic and religious purpose.

10 Caroline Bynum argues against the commonplace that medieval thinkers always conceived of the body as gendered female: 'Medieval ritual, practice, story, and belief made use of many binary contrasts, some of which corresponded with a male/female opposition. In formal theological and devotional writing, these contrasts often associated women with body and matter ... But symbolic patterns do not, of course, fit into only a single grid. ... Much of the serious work on medieval sources from the past fifteen years has shown us how polymorphous are medieval uses of gender categories and images' (16).

11 Marla Carlson gives historical, legal, and religious evidence for her assertion that, 'we can safely assume that Hrotsvit lived and wrote in a culture accustomed to reading bodily signs as evidence of divine intervention in the world' (478).

12 See Marina Warner's *Alone of All Her Sex,* especially chapter five, 'Virgins and Martyrs,' 68–78, and Elizabeth Robertson's essay 'The Corporeality of Female Sanctity in *The Life of Saint Margaret.*' Robertson modifies Warner's argument that torture of martyrs was sexualized, by adding the suggestion that desexualization of the female body is effected through suffering.

13 Scarry 14. The claim that torture is used especially by unstable regimes has been discredited by Peter Singer on the basis of historical information provided in Edward Peters's *Torture*.
14 One reviewer who has remarked very briefly on Scarry's oversight with respect to martyrdom is Michael Ignatieff, but the argument is not developed further.
15 The analysis of torture in Marla Carlson's essay on Hrotsvit agrees in some ways with mine in that she too notes the importance of representation to torture and the patterns by which the virgins triumph over their martyrs. However, she ultimately denies the subversive qualities of the Roman plays. In her focus on potential audiences for these plays, Carlson emphasizes the ways in which the plays strengthen and confirm the power of the Imperial Church and the Ottonian Empire. She concludes by attacking 'protofeminist' readings and arguing that 'what looks like subversion to a twentieth-century feminist can just as easily be read as a model for covert coercion designed to benefit those in power' (487).
16 While we are dealing with a dramatic rendition of the subversion inherent in spectacular punishment, Hrotsvit's plays dramatize what has been presented in Christian sources as historical reality. The Roman emperors of the days of Christian persecution normally excluded females and children under fourteen from torture, except in the limit-case of the Christian martyr. Chris Jones speculates, on the admittedly biased basis of Christian texts, that audiences would have responded favorably to female martyrs who held up under punishment: 'It was not the fact that women were tortured and died so painfully that caused surprise, but the fact that they could show themselves the equals of men in their endurance' (34).
17 The critical consensus has been that Hrotsvit's plays were most likely not performed but read aloud in public (Wilson 1989 xxvii–viii and 1984 40). But see David Wiles for the argument that this view of Hrotsvit's plays is the result of a 'patriarchal bias which holds that women are not likely to write for performance, particularly if their plays seem to be full of humour and violence' (73). Sue-Ellen Case points out that she was perhaps 'the first woman playwright to write for a community of women' (537). Barbara Gold emphasizes this possibility in her reading of Hrotsvit's work, while Marla Carlson expands the potential audience to include not only women at Gandersheim, but also Ottonian rulers and aristocratic women (both at court and in Gandersheim).
18 Barbara Gold emphasizes Hrotsvit's use of diminutives and self-effacement in her Preface, showing that it suggests 'self-conscious irony' and mock-exaggeration (51). Pointing to the repetition of some key words and phrases from the Preface in the plays, Gold sees the Preface in combination with the plays as a medium of self-expression.
19 Sticca 1975 13 and Wilson 1989 155–6. See also Sperberg-McQueen, who claims that '[t]his play is generally considered Hrotswitha's most successful dramatically' (56).

Bibliography

Aers, David. 'A Whisper in the Ear of Early Modernists; or, Reflections on Literary Critics Writing the "History of the Subject."' *Culture and History, 1350–1600: Essays on English Communities, Identities, and Writing*. Ed. David Aers. Detroit: Wayne State University Press, 1992. 177–202.

Burns, E. Jane. *Bodytalk: When Women Speak in Old French Literature*. Philadelphia: University of Pennsylvania Press, 1993.

Bynum, Caroline. 'Why All the Fuss About the Body? A Medievalist's Perspective.' *Critical Inquiry* 22.1 (1995): 1–33.

Carlson, Marla. 'Impassive Bodies: Hrotsvit Stages Martyrdom.' *Theatre Journal* 50.4 (1998): 473–87.
Case, Sue-Ellen. 'Re-Viewing Hrotsvit.' *Theatre Journal* 35.4 (1983): 533–42.
Demers, Patricia. '*In virginea forma*: The Salvific Feminine in the Plays of Hrotsvitha of Gandersheim and Hildegard of Bingen.' *ReImagining Women: Representations of Women in Culture*. Eds. S. Neuman and G. Stephenson. Toronto: University of Toronto Press, 1993. 45–60.
Dollimore, Jonathan. *Sexual Dissidence: Augustine to Wilde, Freud to Foucault*. Oxford: Clarendon Press, 1991.
Dronke, Peter. *Women Writers of the Middle Ages: A Critical Study of Texts from Perpetua (Ü 203) to Marguerite Porete (Ü 1310)*. Cambridge: Cambridge University Press, 1984.
Foucault, Michel. *Discipline and Punish: The Birth of the Prison*. Trans. A. Sheridan. New York: Vintage, 1979.
—— 'The Subject and Power.' *Michel Foucault: Beyond Structuralism and Hermeneutics*. Eds. H. L. Dreyfus and P. Rabinow. Chicago: The University of Chicago Press, 1982. 208–26.
—— 'Technologies of the Self.' *Technologies of the Self: A Seminar with Michel Foucault*. Eds. L.H. Martin, H. Gutman, P.H. Hutton. Amherst: University of Massachusetts Press, 1988. 16–49.
Frankforter, A. Daniel. 'Hroswitha of Gandersheim and the Destiny of Women.' *The Historian* 41.2 (1979): 295–314.
Gold, Barbara K. 'Hrotswitha Writes Herself: *Clamor Validus Gandeshemensis*.' *Sex and Gender in Medieval and Renaissance Texts: The Latin Tradition*. Eds. B. K. Gold, P. Allen Miller, and C. Platter. Albany: State University of New York Press, 1997. 41–69.
Ignatieff, Michael. 'The Truth About Torture.' Rev. of *Torture* by Edward Peters, *The Spectacle of Suffering*, by Pieter Spierenburg, and *The Body in Pain*, by Elaine Scarry. *The New Republic* 9 Dec. 1985: 28.
Jones, Chris. 'Women, Death, and the Law During the Christian Persecutions.' *Martyrs and Martyrologies. Papers Read at the 1992 Summer Meeting and the 1993 Winter Meeting of the Ecclesiastical History Society*. Ed. D. Wood. Oxford: Blackwell, 1993. 23–34.
McNaughton, Howard. 'Hrotsvitha and the Dramaturgy of Liminality.' *AUMLA* 80 (1993): 1–16.
Nelson, Charles. 'Hrotsvit von Gandersheim: Madwoman in the Abbey.' *Women as Protagonists and Poets in the German Middle Ages: An Anthology of Feminist Approaches to Middle High German Literature*. Ed. A. Classen. Goppingen: Kummerle, 1991. 43–55.
Robertson, Elizabeth. 'The Corporeality of Female Sanctity in *The Life of Saint Margaret*.' *Images of Sainthood in Medieval Europe*. Eds. R. Blumenfeld-Kosinsky and T. Szell. Ithaca: Cornell University Press, 1991. 268–87.
Scarry, Elaine. *The Body in Pain: The Making and Unmaking of the World*. New York: Oxford University Press, 1985.
Schroeder, Peter S. 'Hroswitha and the Feminization of Drama.' *Women in Theatre*. Ed. J. Redmond. Themes in Drama Vol. 11. Cambridge: Cambridge University Press, 1989. 49–58.
Singer, Peter. 'Unspeakable Acts.' Rev. of *The Body in Pain*, by Elaine Scarry and *Torture*, by Edward Peters. *New York Review of Books* 27 Feb. 1986: 27.
Sperberg-McQueen, M.R. 'Whose Body Is It? Chaste Strategies and the Reinforcement of Patriarchy in Three Plays by Hrotswitha von Gandersheim.' *Women in German Yearbook: Feminist Studies in German Literature and Culture* 8 (1992): 47–71.
Sticca, Sandro: 'The Hagiographical and Monastic Context of Hrotswitha's Plays.' Wilson, *Rara Avis* 1–34.

—— 'Sacred Drama and Comic Realism in the Plays of Hrotswitha of Gandersheim.' *The Early Middle Ages. Acta.* Vol. VI. Ed. W. H. Snyder. Binghamton: Center for Medieval and Early Renaissance Studies, State University of New York, 1979. 117–43.

—— 'Sin and Salvation: The Dramatic Context of Hrotswitha's Women.' *The Roles and Images of Women in the Middle Ages and Renaissance.* Ed. D. Radcliff-Umstead. University of Pittsburgh Publications on the Middle Ages and the Renaissance Vol. III. Pittsburgh: University of Pittsburgh Press, 1975. 3–22.

Suleiman, Susan Rubin. 'Misery Loves Creativity.' Rev. of *The Body in Pain*, by Elaine Scarry. *New York Times Book Review* 5 Jan. 1986: 20.

Warner, Marina. *Alone of All Her Sex: The Myth and the Cult of the Virgin Mary.* New York: Knopf, 1976.

Wiles, David. 'Theatre in Roman and Christian Europe.' *The Oxford Illustrated History of Theatre.* Ed. John Russell Brown. Oxford: Oxford University Press, 1997.

Wilson, Katharina M. *Hrotsvit of Gandersheim: The Ethics of Authorial Stance.* Leiden: E.J. Brill, 1988.

—— ed. *Hrotsvit of Gandersheim: Rara Avis in Saxonia?* Medieval and Renaissance Monograph Series VII. Ann Arbor: MARC, 1987.

—— ed. *Medieval Women Writers.* Athens: The University of Georgia Press, 1984.

—— trans. *The Plays of Hrotsvit of Gandersheim.* Garland Library of Medieval Literature Vol. 62, Series B. New York: Garland, 1989.

Chapter 2

Clothing Naked Desire in Marlowe's *Hero and Leander*

Cindy L. Carlson

Hero, the nun of Venus in Marlowe's *Hero and Leander* officiates in a highly decorated temple adorned with 'gods in sundry shapes,/ Committing heady riots, incest, rapes' (1.143-4) beneath the transparent glass floor. The temple itself is called by the townspeople of Sestos 'Venus' glass,' a mirror that reflects our own desires back to us as we gaze at the floor (1.142). In such a world of omnidirectional erotic desire, any sort of desire may appear equally possible, equally justified. Yet this poem, with its various erotic possibilities open to would-be lovers, particularly male lovers, presents itself to the reader, whether enthralled or shocked, as choices that are not to be made automatically on hetero-erotic presumptions. In fact, to the extent that the poem gives evidence of erotic preference, male-male homoeroticism is to be preferred to a male-female heteroeroticism that threatens the survival or well-being of the male lover. Hero, desirable to many men, offers a dangerous object of erotic pursuit to Leander because she is associated with her own glittering surface that repels even as it attracts, by the isolation of her vocation and dwelling, by the deaths she causes through her sacrificial rituals and by the self-sacrifices of her would-be lovers.

In the glass of Venus, all gods are gods below the surface; we tread on them, but they reflect us and our below the surface desires with, presumably, embarrassing accuracy. The gods shift shape as Jove makes love with Danae as rain, with Europa as a bull, and the mortals shift shape as they are pursued by the gods; when Ciparissus is pursued, he turns into a cypress. The gods turn away from marriage, with Mars pursuing Venus and Jove pursuing everyone as he avoids his sister-wife in favor of mortal women and Ganymede. Among the gods, love is pursued from a male perspective, with erotic objects fairly evenly distributed among males and females. The opening images, of Danae in a tower and Ganymede captured by Jove while he wanders from Juno's bed, are indeed mirrors of the mortals in the poem, Hero in her tower across the Hellespont and Leander pulled below the surface of the ocean as the ocean's god seeks to capture him as a Ganymede apparently wandering from the bed of Jove.

Surfaces

Hero and Leander revels in surfaces: clothing, decoration, and skin are all described with ecstatic attention to detail. In this respect both Hero and Leander are treated in similar fashion. Hero is described in a series of 'hyperbolic materializations' as 'Marlowe gives his attention to the unmoralized glitter of the surface itself' (Altieri 152). When the poem turns to Leander, 'Marlowe is insistent again upon surfaces at least as striking as Hero's' (Altieri 153). But the surfaces described are quite different and in different voices. Hero is described as extravagantly clothed in a narrative moment as the reader seems to see her walk through Sestos toward the temple of Venus to officiate there at a festival honoring Adonis. Leander is described as nude and in a language rich with metaphorical associations in an aside from the narrative – he is seen in a kind of revery of the narrator's that we may share, but the moment is not part of the narrative momentum of the story. Leander's nude body might be part of the back story, in every sense of the word, to the plot unfolded by the narrative present of the poem.

The poem opens with these two descriptive pieces, beginning with the fully clothed, draped, and veiled Hero. Her hair is the first item in the catalog and the reason given for Apollo's love for Hero, but the hair is covered by a veil reaching to the floor and anchored by a myrtle wreath. Everything else is a picture of artificiality from the embroidered scene on her sleeves that depicts a naked Venus failing to attract the erotic notice of a 'proud' and 'disdainful' Adonis, to the false leaves and flowers that adorn the veil itself (1.13–4, 19). The flowers deceive men and animals; her breath deceives the bees, her rhinestones remind one of diamonds, and water-powered mechanical birds twitter on her boots. Her beauty deceives Cupid into thinking that she is Venus, and it also blinds him, so he cannot see which is the god and which the nun (1.21 et seq.). No wonder Nature weeps because Hero takes more beauty than she leaves behind in her nun's vows of chastity (1.46–7), but she might also weep that Hero is so beautiful without the aid of nature, for art seems to have done most of the work. The description does not bother with Hero's heart, so stays on the surface, as critics have noted. But the surface is enough to supply erotic complexity because the surface creates and frustrates desire. Apollo appears to have loved her in vain, as he is wont to desire all mortal maidens. Where the disdainful Daphne in *Metamorphoses* turns into a laurel that may yet be appropriated by Apollo and Syrinx into a reed that he may play upon, Hero is left as she is, a glitteringly attractive and unwelcoming surface. Mortal men have desired her, been rejected, and bloodily 'slain' in front of her, or at least in front of her clothing, with the result that her blue kirtle is stained (1.15–6). There is no honey for the bees, no return of an eroticized maternal embrace. There is no diamond in the setting.

On the surface of the surface, the embroidered version of the tale of Venus and Adonis, Hero's rejection of seductive advances is mirrored by Adonis rejecting the overtures of a naked Venus. The surface decoration of Hero's sleeves may comment on whether she resembles more the frustrating Adonis or the frustrated Venus in her oxymoronic title of Venus' nun. The alluring surfaces present all that we may see of Hero; to the extent that the surface represents what sort of desiring heart might beat beneath the decoration, the evidence is, at best, ambiguous, perhaps a bit disturbing. Underneath the clothing, Hero, if she exists apart from her clothing, might not be so alluring to the bees, the slain lovers, the desiring Apollo. Nature might leave half the world in darkness simply to avoid seeing Hero's beauty as it is rather than as it seems. Nature's abandonment of half the world because of Hero's separation from Nature associates Hero with the inanimate technologies of allure. Hero's glittering surfaces mimic and depart from Nature's own fruitfulness. The allure of the artificial and unnatural hovers over her like her veil.

The Blazoned Male

The description of Leander serves as a sort of reflecting glass to that of Hero. The poem drops out of narrative mode into an erotic revery of the narrator who suddenly brings 'my rude pen' to the surface of the poem in the middle of the description in order to wonder at his pen's power to 'blazon forth the loves of men/ Much less of powerful gods,' not a problem heretofore with a seemingly omnipotent, remote narrator dealing with Hero as an object of mortal and divine desire (1.69–71).[1] The narrator speaks of 'amorous' Leander, but it is the poem that desires the boy, for Leander has, at this narrative juncture, not yet seen and fallen in love with Hero (1.51). Like Hero, he has a beautiful head of hair more worth a voyage of discovery made by 'vent'rous youth of Greece' than the Golden Fleece (1.58–9). Cynthia desires to embrace him, but apparently in vain. With Jove, the poem makes the immediate connection to Ganymede, but this cup bearer needs no other vessel than his body, for Jove would desire to have 'sipped out nectar from his hand' (1.62). Just as other blazoning pens tend to run out of ink when they reach the female genitalia, this blazoning pen turns rude and silent after having traced the 'heavenly path with many a curious dint/ that runs along his back' from his shoulder to his buttocks (1.68–9).[2] When the pen resumes again, the 'slack muse' has begun to sing of Leander's face as an object of universal desire for both men and women (1.72 et seq.). The narrator might urge Leander not to turn into Narcissus because he is so desirable that men who have rejected the love of women, like Hippolytus, would here want to banquet, sip nectar from his hand, taste the 'meat' of his body, but this Leander is figured as consumable object, not a rejecting one. Loving Leander's beauty is as natural as loving food to those hungry for it.

In the mirror, below the clothed surface, appears what some, who swear that Leander is a 'maid,' desire: the beautiful boy who is dressed as 'a maid in man's attire,' apparently his own body (1.83). On the surface, Leander is male, but under the surface of his body, he is a maid dressed as a man, or at least seems so to some of the men [and women?] who desire him. Others who know that he is a man desire him as one fit for 'amorous play,' suitable to be 'in love, and loved by all' (1.88-9).[3] Swearing by Leander's feminine face and knowing his masculine body appear to encompass the entire range of what one may desire. But what is really desired here? Is there any real confusion as to Leander's sex? If his body is his male attire, then the maidenly face is unlikely to mislead any of Leander's admirers. Whether the male body is the surface, underneath which is a desirable maiden, or whether the female face is a sort of surface to the male body below it, the male body, especially its back surface, is presented for universal admiration and desire. Considering the poem's interest in mirrors, we might pause to consider the attention paid to Leander's feminine face after the poem has toured his masculine body. As Anne Hollander has explained in her survey of Renaissance pictures that involve mirrors, the face is pre-eminently the concern of the reflecting mirror, especially the face that is created for the mirror. That reflected face is hardly able to be a truthful reflection, for '[l]ooking in the mirror is . . . traditionally supposed to mean looking at something taken for truth that is really false . . .; but the falsity in the mirror is somehow felt to be generated out of the viewer's own falsity – of heart, of soul, of intention' (Hollander 394). Here the falsity might be understood as a deceptive face/body union or as a union of face and body that is inconsistent. The image in the mirror is most typically the beholder's face, but a face arranged for view, not a 'natural' face at all.

Though Nature wept at the abundance of Hero's beauty, Nature is not weeping here, for Leander appears as a sort of horn of plenty who offers delights to all who see him. And the fulfillment of Nature here does not seem to be the desire that Leander engender children, as seems to be the case with the rejecting Hero, but the desire that Leander return the love so ardently given by all of his admirers. Because he is so loved by all observers, Leander should be in love. He should return the gaze of one of his many admirers (1.89). Insofar as Leander is like the erotically unawakened (to the desirability of women) Adonis and Hippolytus, he resembles the rough Thracian soldiers who are able to awaken to a world of desire through the beauty of men who are as beautiful as himself. The sophisticated, amusing world of love among men is the world offered to Leander through the blandishments of Neptune and the knowing, laughing, desirous voice of the narrator whenever his rough pen pauses to consider the beauty of Leander. The 'augmenting of physical beauty' that Gregory Woods ascribes to the actions of a love that is 'itself . . . an adornment, a kind of cross dressing in the aptness of the loved one's garb,' we might rather assign to the work of desire and seduction (72).[4]

Leander, the beautiful, the desirable, dresses or cross-dresses in that desirability that tends to code him as feminine. Though Leander is not yet an active player in the game of love, he does not appear to inspire or create disaster – no blindness, no would-be lovers slain during his blazoning. Loving him appears to be safe, even if rather exhausting, for his desirous observers. And, even though not yet a responsive object of desire, Leander's admirers, including the narrator, assume that he can and will become a vital lover.

The Naked Transvestite

When Leander, again nude, swims the Hellespont, he encounters Neptune, at once the god of the sea and the sea itself. Indeed, Leander doffs his clothing for the swim only after the 'rising billows' of the sea answer 'No' to his prayer for a dry path (2.152). Neptune's sea appears charged with erotic energy and activity both at its surface and in its depths where the mermaids 'sported with their loves' and play at refusing the riches and spoils of the sea and its wrecks (2.162–4). Once Leander dives into the sea, Neptune immediately takes him below the surface, thinking to steal Ganymede from Jove. Here Leander's male body appears able to deceive gods as to its divinity or mortality, but surely not as to its sex.

When Leander rejects what he conceives to be Neptune's advances made on the basis of feminine desirability and declares 'I am no woman, I' he brackets his statement as to what he is not with an assertion of 'I' and identity (2.192). But if 'I' is not a woman, what then is this 'I'? There can hardly be any doubt as to the sex of the body Leander would protect from what he assumes is a mistaken interest on the part of Neptune. As Holmes remarks, 'Leander interprets himself as he imagines Neptune to see him, forgetting that, to be a transvestite, one must sport a more complex costume than bare skin' (161). Yet Leander's feminine face along with his nude beauty may still call for some explanation, for his nudity is a sort of costume. Hollander invites her readers to see that pictured nudes are, in fact, in costume: 'An image of the nude body that is absolutely free of any counter image of clothing is virtually impossible. Thus all nudes since modern fashion began are wearing the ghosts of absent clothes – sometimes highly visible ghosts' (85–6). Leander's nudity is desirable and desired, clearly, by Neptune and the sea he governs, but it comes clothed with an apparently ambiguous gender. Recall his feminine face, his lovely skin. This nude 'clothing' makes Leander desirable in his 'Ganymede' outfit, the lovely boy available to a god's seduction or abduction. Even the life-preserving bracelet given to him by Neptune figures Leander as transvestic, for the bracelet was formerly worn by Helle, a daughter fleeing parental restriction who has drowned in the Hellespont and given the sea that Leander swims in her name. The bracelet recalls the nun's ring given to Leander by Hero, so that both these circlets signifying preservation and loss come to Leander as feminine adornment.

Because Leander's knowledge of love is drawn from what he has read, not what he has experienced, in a world of hetero-normative texts, he imagines the existence only of male-female love affairs, pursued through words, not actions. Neptune has been reading, too, but in a world of homoerotic discourse and supplemented by a number of seductive and violent episodes in his past experience. From this reading in the worlds of artful seduction, both Neptune and Leander appreciate what the nude costume might mean, even though they construct slightly different readings of that nude body. Their desires are shaped by artful literary presentation and, perhaps, by the quite artful blazoning of Leander that the poem 'paints' of the nude boy.

> A sense of 'natural' nakedness in actual life is trained more by art than by knowledge; people tend to aspire to look like nudes in pictures in order to appear more like perfect 'natural' specimens. The unclothed costume, when it is intended to be looked at – by an intimate, a camera, an audience, or in a mirror – is subject to current standards of nude fashion. Its 'natural' gestures and postures of the head, neck, and shoulders, of the spine and legs, will be worn according to this mode, in correct period style . . . People without clothes are still likely to behave as if they wore them, and so 'natural' nudity is affected by two kinds of ideal nudity – the one created by clothes directly and the one created by nude art, which also depends on fashions of dress. Clothes, even when omitted, cannot be escaped. (Hollander 87)

Leander's style, as the text indicates when it points out his desirability in female or male guise, partakes of both female and male attributes, even when he is nude. His blazoned body is male but is addressed through the very existence of the blazon as a feminine body to be desired by a male in a series of seductive parts available for the appreciation of the male gaze and pen. Even nude, Leander does not escape his feminine [dis]guise. If we were inclined to imagine that the nude, natural body can tell us only one thing about gender, this poem can enlighten us, even as Neptune attempts to augment Leander's store of erotic knowledge both from his own experience and his own extensive reading in pastoral.

Disrobing Hero

While Leander appears frequently without clothing, whether in the narrative or in the mind's eye of the narrator, Hero seems to consist of her multiple layers of clothing and, perhaps, not much else. The erotic thrill of reading the love scene in *Hero and Leander* with all of its Ovidian notes has a final payoff in the 'contemplation of the girl's nakedness (which takes place *après coup* in *Hero and Leander*)' and in Marlowe, as well as in Ovid's *Amores*, this disrobing of the desired girl is the 'true center of interest' of the text (Koppenfels 130). In light of Leander's nude desireability, the disinterested reader might be inclined to desire a description of Hero as an additional center of interest. Both poets make a practice of leading their readers to expect more than any single poem is quite prepared to reveal, whether of the sexual encounter or the desirable nudity of the girl. So, just as Ovid in *Amores* I.5 does not quite describe the act of love that he has led his readers to envision, Marlowe does not quite reveal a fully naked Hero after she and Leander have made love. As Hero tries to sneak out of the bed, putting her 'naked' foot to the floor, Leander clings to her in such a fashion that she slips 'mermaid-like unto the floor' where 'One half appeared, the other half was hid' (2.312,16, 17). The bedclothes still hide Hero from our and Leander's view. With the dawn, Hero's blushes reveal her 'all naked to his sight displayed' even though there has been no narrative to set her free of the bedclothes. In any case, the word 'naked' serves as the sole reward for the reader, whatever the possessive pleasure that Leander experiences in viewing Hero, more intense than the pleasure of Dis regarding his golden treasure (2.326).[5] What has been under the glittering surface now shines forth in a line of poetic declaration, but as soon as the sun that comes up might let the reader share Leander's gaze, the poem suddenly ends as a feminine Night takes her ugly self away in 'anguish, shame and rage'(2.333).

No blazoning here, for the word 'naked' must provide all the erotic thrill for the reader. The body that cannot truly be seen is Hero's and, indeed, its very existence has been in question ever since the elaborate description of her clothing. In Leander's first attempt to seduce Hero, though the narrator calls him a 'sophister,' his arguments tend toward demonstrating the nothingness of the female body and its integrity (1.197). In arguing for the bliss of sexual union, Leander claims that 'One is no number; maids are nothing then' (1.255), a single nothingness that apparently does not afflict men, including the virginal Leander himself.[6] To Hero's claims to protect her virginity, Leander opposes a theory of virtue that does not just minimize the value of virginity; it eliminates virginal virtue entirely:

> This idol which you term virginity
> Is neither essence subject to the eye,
> No, nor to any one exterior sense,
> Nor hath it any place of residence,
> Nor is 't of earth or mould celestial,
> Or capable of any form at all.
> Of that which hath no being, do not boast;
>
> Things that are not at all, are never lost. (1.269–76)

Through the series of negations, repeated insistently, Leander eliminates the virtue of virginity along with any bodily or spiritual place for its existence. If it does not exist in any place, it does not exist at all. If the rhetorically innocent might have supposed that virginity's place might be the female body, the interpolation of Mercury's erotic adventures puts the female body and its 'places' into question. When the god seeks 'To eye those parts which no eye should behold,' his shepherdess lover runs away and uses Mercury's desire against him as a means to bargain for immortality (1.408). Those parts might exist, but cannot be seen.

Indeed, they cannot be easily found by the innocent Leander in his first embraces with Hero. Marlowe rings the changes on the word 'it' which stands in for both the sexual experience that Leander craves and the bodily part he is attempting to find as he struggles with the coyly reluctant Hero (2.71–5). Yet this 'it' cannot be named or described, as though the poem shares with Leander his ignorance of the female body and the possibilities of erotic experience. Under the clothing that Hero has forbidden Leander to touch at their last parting (1.344), is a kind of no-man's land. To the extent that Hero's body exists, she has vowed it into non-existence, or, perhaps, nun-existence. If the narrative tone partakes of Hero's coyness, knowing 'it,' the secret knowledge and space that presumably every ignorant lover wants to know, then the readers are made complicit with the narration's knowingness and must settle for the 'it' that indicates a love that need not speak its name among such erotic sophisticates. In either case, the female body remains unexplored, undescribed, absent from the text that is presumably much concerned with Hero's physical desirability.

The text, most frustratingly, may not reveal to its reader what the reader most wants to know. This text experiences sudden modesty or incapacity at what could have been, to the frustrated reader, its most telling moments. The narrator's pen grows slack just as it reaches, or approaches, the apparent erotic goal of Leander's buttocks and anus. The 'it' that Leander desires but cannot find or practice is veiled under the pronoun. The nude Hero is pronounced to be naked, but is never fully described. As Leander breaks his bed treaty and grapples, soldier like, with Hero's body, the text notices Leander's handhold on the globed breast of Hero, but the completed act of love is, again, treated as something that readers of this poem must already know about: to make love is like entering the garden of the Hesperides 'Whose fruit none rightly can describe but he / That pulls or shakes it from the golden tree' (2.299–300). Even this image of heroic adventure may strike an odd note as an image of a man making love to a woman, for while the garden itself might be a female sort of space, the tree with fruit to be pulled or shaken off seems a phallic and masturbatory image. The text seems to suggest an action to the erotically interested reader who desires more knowledge, but that is not knowledge to be gained by reading alone. The text practices the coquettish chastity that it accuses Hero of deploying against the innocent Leander and far more successfully. While Leander finally knows Hero fully, we can never know the erotic secrets the text withholds. The text acts like Hero in her first embrace with

Leander. Hero appears to grant Leander's every desire as 'She, seeming lavish, saved her maidenhead' by 'a kind of granting' letting Leander approach close to the goal, but then 'Like to the tree of Tantalus she fled' (2.76, 73, 75). The text promises the reader full partnership in the text's own erotic knowledge and experience, but acts like the tree that pulls the fruit from Tantalus, not the tree in the Hesperides that yields to the hero who simply takes what he wants.

And even if the text spoke fully and clearly, if it became bold where it now retires into coy modesty, the reader would learn little, perhaps no more than Leander has learned through his reading: enough for witty discourse, far too little to become a lover and seducer in practice. The knowingness of the text, its jokes with Leander and the reader, create a reader already knowledgeable, for every time the reader laughs at the text or responds with erotic interest to it, the text makes the reader a co-conspirator, one who already has access to the garden and the trees therein, or one who is willing to pass as though s/he already had that knowledge. Any true modesty and innocence must be put aside to read *Hero and Leander*, but the text will not enlighten the ignorant reader. The text coyly retires behind our own willingness to seem modest while allowing ourselves to be seduced into laughter or into desire. Like Hero, the reader probably uses only half his or her strength against the manifold blandishments of the text. The innocent reader might resemble Leander in the water with Neptune, unable to hear what offer is being made. Leander rejects Neptune because he insists that he is not a woman. When Neptune's response indicates that Leander's reading might have prepared him to understand that a woman might not be necessary for what Neptune has in mind, Leander appears to ignore or simply not to hear the invitation of the God. His own hurry to arrive at Hero's tower may be sufficient reason for Leander's immunity to another kind of invitation to play. But Leander's ignorance has been a source of comedy for this poem, so the reader is not encouraged to identify with that ignorance. Instead, the reader has been encouraged to see along with the narrator and with Neptune a full range of erotic possibilities, to respond to every invitation reflected in Venus' glass, even if none of these loves ever reveal themselves fully at the stage of the invitation. Reading the invitation in the text, in this text, is only the first step.

Hero and Desire

In a world of male desire, desire that directs its attention to both men and women, Hero can seem a strange erotic object, not at all the obvious choice for a Leander just beginning his erotic career. Hero, other than the 'beldame' who is said to attend her, is the only woman in the narrative present of the story. Venus, Danae, Phaedra, and Mercury's unnamed mortal girl appear in the poem as asides, as allusions, but no woman other than Hero acts in the narrative. Her actions, whether walking toward the temple dressed in full and strange regalia, sacrificing doves, bantering with Leander, or submitting to his increasingly expert advances, the narrative couches in language that alludes to violence, both toward women and toward men. Love is certainly not full of pity where relations with Hero are concerned, though Neptune might, on occasion, show pity to the reluctant Leander.

Just as the nun's costume and function connect Hero with nothingness or an unnamed 'it' that cannot be fully known, the same costume and function connect her with bloodiness and death. Her kirtle is stained with the blood of denied lovers; she herself makes the silver altar run with the blood of sacrificed turtledoves; her embroidered sleeves recall the frustrations of Venus and the impending death of Adonis. While Marlowe ends his poem before the death of Leander and the suicide of Hero, he opens the poem by accusing the Hellespont of blood guilt in the matter of lovers' deaths and closes the poem with an angry and bereft Night plunging down in fury to the lower regions. Leander wears the bracelet of a drowned girl, drowned in the very Hellespont that he crosses in order to make love to Hero. Hero and Leander may form part of a series of distressed and fated lovers; indeed, the Mercury digression indicates that the Fates are murderously jealous of lovers, just as Neptune's thrown, and recalled, weapon figures the murderous jealousy of the gods who are, temporarily, frustrated in love. Amid these distressing images of fate and death, Hero's unique position as a woman who acts, and is acted upon, in the narrative present of the poem is strikingly ambivalent.

If the kirtle stained with blood is part of the nun's habit adopted by Hero, the blood stands as a substitute for the blood shed upon loss of virginity. The kirtle indicates that the blood that Hero has refused to shed in a consummated love must then be shed by others, the frustrated lovers who have pursued the nun who has renounced love and the turtledoves sacrificed to Venus. Just as Leander will remonstrate with Hero over the appropriateness or possibility of a vow of chastity as a rightful ritual of Venus, the blood shed by and upon Hero throws the value of her chastity into question.

Hero's own sexual desires also interrogate her vows. At the moment of finishing the sacrifice, Hero looks up to the congregation and instantly falls in love with the already enamored Leander. This exchange of the desiring gaze preserves the kirtle from Leander's blood, but does not spare Leander himself the battles of seduction. In the pursuit of Hero, Leander encounters not a true naif, but a coy defender of what the narrator insists she wants to lose, even as she 'cuts him off' at his first rhetorical advance (1.196). Even so, it is she who invites Leander to 'Come thither' to her dwelling, the all-too-suggestive tower, that they may play at more interesting games than her usual pastimes of playing with swans and sparrows sacred to Venus or speaking to her dwarfish female servant (1.357). It is one of many instances when Hero's speech simply slips past what she might have intended to say and so betrays her or when speech is simply duplicitous, for the narrator is sure that her 'no' means 'yes.'

At times, the narration seems to absolve Hero of responsibility in love and death. When she invites, in a verbal slip, Leander to her isolated tower, she prays that she might keep her vows of chastity, but Cupid/Love rejects those prayers in a fit of anger. Enraged, he shoots her with the arrow of love, wounding Hero so grievously that she cries tears, tears that turn into pearl jewelry for Cupid to wear. Love's own plea for a continued relationship for Hero and Leander is, in turn, rejected by the Fates. In this passage, Hero is a victim of the exigencies of both love and destiny, absolved from breaking her vows, given sympathy for the suffering she will endure for love. Elsewhere, the narrative convicts her of playing a duplicitous part as she seems to deny Leander's attempts at seduction while painfully acceding to them. Indeed, her coyness becomes part of her attraction for Leander. She drops her fan that Leander might pick it up; when he is to visit her the first time, she is ready ahead of time and has the board spread and the door open. She wishes, though 'not from heart,' that he might leave her alone (2.37). She saves her maidenhead through a struggle that makes her into a tease like the trees that torment Tantalus in the underworld even though she initially 'throws' herself into an embrace with the lover she desires and denies (2.46). Only Leander's innocence delays the 'sacrifice' that Hero here is willing, and not willing, to make (2.48).

When the two lovers consummate their passion on Leander's second visit to the tower, Hero opens the door dressed in a translucent gown and in mock fear hides herself in her bed. Leander's rhetoric as he wheedles his way into bed is at least as sophistic as his first arguments against virginity, but Hero now agrees to take him into bed for the express purpose of warming a poor young man naked and nearly drowned. She may resist being seen, but yields the fortress of her body

> because Treson was in her thought,
> And cunningly to yield herself she sought.
> Seeming not won, yet won she was at length,
> In such wars women use but half their strength. (2.293–6)

The narration shows Hero some sympathy, for 'love is not full of pity (as men say),' but more like a hunt in which the hunter will wring the fluttering bird's neck with his own hands (2.287). Yet even this passage casts doubt on who is the hunter and who the prey. When Hero dives down into her bed covers to hide herself, she is compared to Diana hiding herself from the gaze of Actaeon. That absolutely chaste goddess has no trouble hunting the hunter and making Actaeon the victim of his own hunting hounds. As long as she resists Leander, Hero plays the harpy, spoiling what she cannot consume. She is not so much conquered in the erotic battle as she plays the part of being taken while striving to yield.

This language of violence, though Hero herself is not, finally, shown to be a victim of it, has implications for Leander. Relations between men and women seem to come freighted with issues of dominance and rape. Neptune, though a god who has a violent sexual past, shows mercy to Leander. He does not kidnap the boy, does not rape him, does not even try too hard to seduce the single-minded object of his affection. His violent impulses are all recalled before they do damage. In contrast, Hero wears the kirtle stained with the blood of frustrated lovers, she kills the doves as part of her priestly function, her distance as an object of desire will kill Leander in the story that the reader is familiar with as s/he reads Marlowe's version that ends differently. Her threat to well-being is more apparent than is Neptune's. In the alluded-to stories, Venus and Hippolyta love men who refuse love at their own peril. Even Mercury's shepherdess has designs above her station. Where Jupiter has no trouble introducing his Ganymede among the immortals, the shepherdess's request leads Mercury to a world of frustrated, vengeful, old women who foolishly believe his flattery and then attempt vengeance when it proves false.

Finally, the very unknowability of the female body remains the most ominous threat to male well-being. Neptune may well smile as Leander declares, 'I am no woman, I,' for he sees and appreciates Leander's nude beauty as Leander swims alongside the god and through the God's element. In contrast, women's bodies remain obscure; their clothing a strange barrier of what might be underneath their protective and confusing folds. The shepherdess runs away when Mercury attempts to discover, visually, a new way to love. While the shepherdess might willingly consent to make love, she does not submit to visual inspection. Hero, delighted and terrified to see a naked man at her doorstep, wears an alluringly translucent gown, but soon hides herself in the bed. Even after she has made love with Leander, she cannot quite be seen. As she tumbles out of bed, the bedclothes wrap around her, making her appear like a terrestrial mermaid, the one who might, in a later poet's formulation, drown us as she awakens us.

The Female Transvestite

The very inscrutability of the female body renders it strange in this poem, renders it dangerous or unsatisfying as an erotic object choice. Hero's body, heavily attired in kirtle, sleeves, buskins, and veil is, itself, in tranvestic disguise. Only the veil reads as unambiguously feminine attire. As Bruce Smith has shown in discussing Marlowe's 'Passionate Shepherd,' the beloved is offered a 'kirtle,' among other gifts, and none of those gifts read as necessarily for a female recipient.[7] She processes to the temple in such array as part of her ritual function, so that 'kirtle' is likely to partake of the definition offered in Smith's text: 'a robe of state' (91). If so, then the blood thereon is part of the ritual effect to be evoked in her audience. When Michael Bristol contrasts the social order made manifest and apparently triumphant in ritual procession, he also notes that the carnevalesque takes over procession as a form in order to mock the established order through:

> the wearing of borrowed and misappropriated costumes to generate rude, foolish, abusive mimicry of everyday social functions ... Travesty ... manifests itself in role- and status-reversal of several different kinds. Identity is made questionable by mixing of attributes – code-switching – or by grotesque exaggeration. Guise, that is, customary appropriate garb or social integument, is permitted to mingle with *dis*guise and the will to deception.[8]

Her clothing and her manner partake of both guise and disguise in a way that confuses clear gender delineation. Even the innocent Leander seems quite aware of the oxymoronic title 'venus's nun' that Hero bears, with its implication of both renunciation and whorishness.[9] Hero's modesty also partakes of disguise in a willingness to betray the fort of her own body to the invader who would conquer it. In her own desires, in her own priestly function, Hero combines both the guise and the costume that disguises. As such an ambiguous figure, Hero is the disorderly choice for Leander, in modern terms, the perverse choice, not likely to promise much satisfaction, at least to one regarding her from the poem's playful, and distrustful, point of view.

Hero's body remains mysterious because her bloody kirtle and veil participate in carnivalesque travesty. Her transvestic appearance, then, bespeaks 'the degree to which *all* women cross-dress as women when they produce themselves as artifacts' (Garber 49). The artificiality of Hero's appearance has been insisted upon from the beginning of Marlowe's poem and even the ending that produces the 'naked' Hero in name but not description tends to preserve the artificiality rather than dissipate it in nude revelation. Her coyness partakes of the same artificiality, in seeming to preserve her chastity; to insist on her vows of chastity, she, in fact, achieves her desire to make love with Leander, to become servant to his saint.

Hero's destabilizing 'thirdness,' to borrow Garber's formulation, throws into question the rightness or inevitability of Leander's choice of Hero as an object of his seductive powers. In arguing for the thirdness of transvestitism, Garber insists that she is not talking about a third sex or sexual orientation, but about 'a mode of articulation, a way of describing a space of possibility. Three puts in question the idea of identity, self-sufficiency, self-knowledge' (Garber 11). In setting gender categories in play, Marlowe could not simply make the homoerotic passages between Neptune and Leander seem amusing and justified by Leander's well-described beauty, he had to make the heteronormative seem strange by showing Hero as the artifactual woman, in both clothing and nature. In doing so, he does not simply reveal Hero as a typically misogynistic creation of Renaissance poetry, the one who says 'no' while meaning to indicate 'yes,' but also as 'masculine' in clothing, in some of her attitudes. While that very masculinity can be read against her, and is, it also throws her essential nature into doubt, as does the unknowability of the body beneath the clothing. Judith Butler picks up on a similar notion arising from the gender parody of transvestism:

> The notion of gender parody defended here does not assume that there is an original which such parodic identities imitate. Indeed, the parody is *of* the very notion of an original; ... gender parody reveals that the original identity after which gender fashions itself is an imitation without an origin. To be more precise, it is a production which, in effect – that is, in its effect – postures as an imitation. (138)

Hero and Leander creates Hero both as a kind of clothed vacancy and as a collection of feminine attributes drawn from familiar stereotypes: she is beautiful yet unknowable, she is chaste but unchaste, she is desirable but she is deadly. In either situation, Hero 'imitates' a woman where there is no original, real woman to be found. While Leander might be read in a similar fashion, for he is masculine in beauty, but also feminine in beauty, seductiveness, and innocence, his lovely nakedness might make him seem more 'natural,' or real than Hero, even if that naked beauty is drawn from the frequently performed and imitated form of the blazon of female beauty. The playfulness of the poem has worked to destabilize the reality of both figures, but has worked to preserve the desirability of Leander for the reader.

For if Hero is the strange choice, Leander is surely the obvious choice to the [mostly male] readers the poem seems to create. He is the easy choice to understand, the easy choice to appreciate, however shy he may be of wooing. He even has greater chastity than Hero, refusing what he genuinely does not understand, rather than seeming to refuse what she affects not to understand. He would be the trustworthy choice because his innocence is real, not manufactured, just as his beauty, even if celebrated artfully, arises from nature. He is the 'natural' choice and Nature revels in him, leaving out the tears shed by Nature over Hero and the self-destructive fury of Night over Hero. The reader may safely enjoy his beauty, attached as it is to both male and female standards of delight. Where Hero seems unmoored from the feminine, Leander seems full of the best qualities of both genders. Where Hero seems dangerous to know, Leander seems available to love and seduction without danger for the man who desires him. He is the safe and orderly choice, even while he retains his erotic promise. Hero, in contrast, offers so many barriers of difficulty and danger to her admirers, that she is the erotic choice that is disorderly, a perverse turning away from the promises of life and love.

Endnotes

1 Here, my reading of the poem departs from Altieri's who claims that Marlowe rejects as a poetic technique the 'speaker as a self-regarding subject experiencing the paradoxes of love' (154). The rude pen of the speaker/writer that suddenly seems weak with desire or reverence in the poetic task of blazoning Leander's naked body, and weak only after having enjoyed Leander's body and its poetic associations thoroughly, creates a narrator who sometimes feels a personal interest in the poetic objects his pen has limned.

2 See, for example, Philisides' song in the third book of *The Old Arcadia*; this blazon has enough energy to document both front and back of the 'unkind mistress' (207), but elides her genitalia:

> Her belly there glad sight doth fill,
> Justly entitled Cupid's hill;
> A hill most fit for such a master,
> A spotless mine of alabaster,
> Like Alabaster fair and sleek,
> But soft and supple, satin-like,
> In that sweet seat the boy doth sport.
> Loath, I must leave his chief resort;
> For such an use the world hath gotten;
> The best things still must be forgotten. (209)

This duty to forget 'best things' when a poem speaks publicly may afflict the narrator of *Hero and Leander*. In the alternative, his erotic energy may be in question. Pyrocles has the advantage of making love to Philoclea while remembering Philisides' song as a screen and as a sop to the reading audience. Sir Philip Sidney, *The Countess of Pembroke's Arcadia (The Old Arcadia)*, Katherine Duncan-Jones, ed. (Oxford: Oxford University Press, 1985)

3 Here I differ with M. Morgan Holme's argument that understands those who swear to Leander's 'feminine' facial beauty as ignorant of his male body (159). Those attracted by the feminine face need not necessarily differ from those who desire the male body. If the reader knows from the blazoning of the nude Leander that Leander is male and a fit object for desire, surely these other admirers who have no other existence than as audience for the same blazoning may know as much or as little about Leander as we do.

4 Where Woods sees that Leander 'cross-dresses' in the beauty of the beloved and thus may be apprehended as feminine, I'm not sure that the timing here works, for Leander has been described as possessing a female beauty before his first embraces with Hero. Perhaps the love that augments and cross-dresses is one that cross-dresses the beloved – the one who is desired or is to be seduced may be automatically feminine. The one who is gazed at, is blazoned is cross-dressed by desire. Woods himself notes this tendency when he remarks that most of Marlowe's desirable boys are 'generally seen either in fancy dress or in drag, and it is this adornment that shows they are either beloved already, or available to be loved' (81). The great exception, the naked boy playing Diana in *Edward II*, is cross dressed 'only by the most sophisticated, symbolic criterion' because Diana's beauty must be seen in the nearly naked boy (81). His nakedness, indicates Woods, would hardly disguise his physical sex, but his desirability, his Diana-like qualities, turn him into a figure of naked transvestism, clothed only in his own desirability and desired by a sophisticated theater audience. The tone of *Hero and Leander* is similarly sophisticated, inviting the reader to admit or feign an Ovidian level of erotic sophistication in admitting and, presumably, visualizing the desirability of the continually naked Leander.

5   Here we might recall the nature of treasure under the surface, with Neptune's sea nymphs refusing the gifts of buried treasure at the bottom of the sea or Pluto regarding his subterranean wealth.

6   When Irigaray asks, in *This Sex Which Is Not One*, 'Must this multiplicity of female desire and female language be understood as shards, scattered remnants of a violated sexuality? A sexuality denied?' she admits that these questions are not easily answered. Her response, in terms of women's understanding of themselves, might also respond to Leander's sophistry, for 'the exclusion of a female imaginary certainly puts woman in the position of experiencing herself only fragmentarily, in the little-structured margins of a dominant ideology as waste, or excess, what is left in a mirror invested by the (masculine) subject to reflect himself' (30). The excess, these fragments seem crucial to the poem's and Leander's experience of Hero, the inhabited costume of Venus' nun.

7   Bruce K Smith, *Homosexual Desire in Shakespeare's England: A Cultural Poetics* (Chicago: University of Chicago Press, 1994). In the erotic sensuality of the gifts offered to the beloved, 'What could there be in this vision of delight to indicate any differences in status between wooer and wooed?' (92).

8   Michael Bristol, *Carnival and Theater: Plebeian Culture and the Structure of Authority in Renaissance England* (New York: Methuen, 1985) p. 65. While I do not want to argue that Marlowe's elegant epyllion partakes of rudeness, I do want to note the poem's gleeful puncturing of stereotypes: Leander is more innocent than Hero, Neptune is more merciful in love than Leander, and Hero exists in a conflation of 'code-switching' accessories – her kirtle, her tower, her knives at the altar.

9   See Marjorie Garber's discussion in *Vested Interests: Cross-dressing and Cultural Anxiety*, (New York: Routledge, 1992) where she discusses the transvestite nun who is a man beneath the nun's habit:

> The third space – the space of thirdness – is simultaneously demarcated, filled, and emptied out by the phantom nun – the nun (or 'none') that calls into question categories of males and female, Catholic and Protestant, English and French, gay and straight [and I would add, in a Renaissance text, chaste and libidinous]: in Wallace Steven's words 'nothing that is not there and the nothing that is.' That the story of the transvestite nun is so often tinged with a suspicion of hysteria indicates not only the subtextual misogyny and/or homophobia that marks these particular instances, but also a more general and pervasive fear of transvestism *as* a powerful agent of destabilization and change, the sign of *un*groundedness of identities on which social structures and hierarchies depend. (223, emphasis in original).

Marlowe is not, I think, homophobic in this poem, though he may be misogynistic, but the interest in destabilizing gender, sexual roles, and sexual decorum of all kinds is certainly present.

Bibliography

Altieri, Joanne. '*Hero and Leander*: Sensible Myth and Lyric Subjectivity.' *John Donne Journal* 8 1–2 (1989) 151–166.

Bristol, Michael. *Carnival and Theater: Plebian Culture and the Structure of Authority in Renaissance England*. New York: Methuen, 1985.

Butler, Judith. *Gender Trouble: Feminism and the Subversion of Identity*. New York: Routledge, 1990.

Comensoli, Viviana. 'Homophobia and the Regulation of Desire: A Psychoanalytic Reading of Marlowe's *Edward II*.' *Journal of the History of Sexuality*. 4 #2 (1993): 175–200.
Garber, Marjorie. *Vested Interests: Cross-dressing and Cultural Anxiety*. 1992. New York: Routledge, 1997.
Hollander, Anne. *Seeing through Clothes*. 1975. Berkeley: University of California Press, 1993.
Holmes, M. Morgan. 'Identity and the Dissidence it Makes: Homoerotic Nonsense in Kit Marlowe's *Hero and Leander*.' *English Studies in Canada* 21 2(1995): 151:69.
Irigaray, Luce. *The Sex Which Is Not One*. Catherine Porter with Carolyn Burke, trans. Ithaca: Cornell University Press, 1985.
Koppenfels, Werner von. 'Dis-covering the Female Body: Erotic Explorations in Elizabethan Poetry.' *Shakespeare Survey* 47 (1994): 127–35.
Lerner, Laurence. 'On Ambiguity, Modernism, and Sacred Texts.' *On Modern Poetry: Essays Presented to David Davie*. Vereen Bell and Laurence Lerner, eds. Nashville, TN: Vanderbilt University Press, 1988. 133–44.
Logan, Robert A. 'Perspective in Marlowe's *Hero and Leander*: Engaging Our Detachment.' *'A Poet and a filthy Play-maker': New Essays on Christopher Marlowe*. Kenneth Friedenreich, Roma Gill, and Constance B. Kuriyama, eds. New York: AMS Press, 1988. 279–92.
—— 'The Sexual Attitudes of Marlowe and Shakespeare.' *University of Hartford Studies in Literature* 19 2–3 (1987): 1–23.
Milne, Fred L. 'Love-Strife and Night Motifs in Christopher Marlowe's Hero and Leander.' *Journal of Evolutionary Psychology* 17 3–4 (1996): 219–29.
Smith, Bruce K. *Homosexual Desire in Shakespeare's England: A Cultural Poetics*. Chicago: University of Chicago, 1994.
Woods, Gregory. 'Body, Costume, and Desire in Christopher Marlowe.' *Homosexuality in Renaissance and Enlightenment England: Literary Representations in Historical Context*. Claude J. Summers, ed. New York: Haworth Press, 1992.

Chapter 3

Seductive Confession in Mary Shelley's *Mathilda*

Susan M. Bernardo

> We seduce with our death, our vulnerability, and with a void that haunts us.
> – Jean Baudrillard, *Seduction*

Mary Shelley's *Mathilda* is itself an instance of literary repression. Though she wrote the tale in 1819, it was not published until 1959. One of the reasons for the work's lying unpublished for so long was her father, Godwin's, objections to its subject as 'disgusting and detestable,' despite the fact that Mary Shelley created *Mathilda* as a rewritten version of her story 'Fields of Fancy' to try to raise money to help her father (Sunstein 175). As the editor of the 1959 publication, Elizabeth Nitchie, states: 'Highly personal as the story was Mary Shelley hoped that it would be published, evidently believing that the characters and the situations were sufficiently disguised. In May of 1820 she sent it to England by her friends, the Gisbornes, with a request that her father would arrange for its publication' (vii). Many writers have approached *Mathilda* through the lens of Shelley biography, as Nitchie's comments suggest; however, my approach will take a different direction. In revisiting Mary Shelley's repressed text, I will align it with Charles Perrault's 'Peau d'âne' ('Donkey-skin'), a fairy tale that deals openly with the theme of father-daughter incest. In viewing Shelley's text with the help of Perrault's I am concerned with the redefinition of incest through narcissism and monogamy as they intersect with the workings of desire and seduction. Mathilda actually entwines notions of her own identity with her father's as she narrates, which implicates her as a creator in the game of desire, rather than as its innocent victim.

Mathilda as the writer/controller of narrative, engages in an act of seduction by initially refusing to reveal her secret and then by revealing it in a way that keeps it cloaked from Woodville, her one friend, until after her physical absence in death. This avoidance of revelation leads William Brewer to see Mathilda as 'logophobic,' though she narrates her own tale (396). Her continual play with absence/presence as she first isolates herself from her father (after his profession of love – a love which was nourished by both her mother's and Mathilda's absences) then from humanity in general, makes her more than a simple protector of secrets. Indeed, her handling of the situation marks her as, as she rightly says, blameworthy. I depart from Kate Ferguson Ellis and Anne K. Mellor here since both see Mathilda as a victim ('Subversive Surfaces' 228 and *Mary Shelley: Her Life, Her Fiction, Her Monsters* 199, respectively). Unlike her seventeenth-century counterpart, the Princess of Perrault's 'Peau d'âne,' Mathilda does not recover from the possibility of incest by seeking and finding a suitable male companion; instead she nurses a strange desire in the absence of her father, just as he had done after her mother's death. Neither Mathilda nor her father initially understand that physical distance will not kill desire, but fuel it. Death, then, is the ultimate 'attraction.'

Though at first it seems that Mathilda becomes the object of her father's lust because she reminds him, uncannily, of her mother, the situation becomes more complex. Her resemblance to her mother is a part of the problem, but the resemblance is not complete. The narrative tells us that Mathilda has noticeable traits of both her parents. Shelley's portrayal of incest is born both of loyalty to the deceased beloved (monogamy) and narcissism. Incest becomes a desire turned inward as well as outwards to the defamiliarized absent object of desire. Consummation would be utterly impossible in this view since it would mean, essentially, self-destruction. That self-destruction occurs, as Baudrillard says of seduction (97), cannot destroy the power of seduction itself – it only augments it, as Mathilda continues the solipsistic/narcissistic tradition she willingly inherits from her father. His death is consummation for him and the prolonging of desire for her.

Their entire relationship prepares each one for the linking of their eventual fates. Her father's first sighting of her as she floats towards him over the water wraith-like, dressed in white, charges the meeting scene with notions of the mother's shroud. In a real sense her father's love for her exhibits his loyalty to her mother whose memory he has not effaced though he has wandered for sixteen years. In fact, in an attempt to become other or go beyond the reach of the dead woman and the living child, he even changed his name (*Mathilda* 181). Mathilda, likewise, has been estranged even from the estate of her biological parents. The aunt who raised her brought her to an isolated area of Scotland. Indeed, this aunt will not even allow Mathilda to travel to England to reunite with her father – it is he who must make the trip to Scotland. They meet, as it were, on 'neutral' ground. The problem is that there is no such plot of land or emotional space for these two.

When her father takes Mathilda to London his desire for her grows. Her potential availability, signaled by the approach of eligible suitors, makes her all the more desirable and causes him to be more and more disturbed by his desire. Her interpretation of his London moods – that he is somehow displeased with her – is not far from the truth. The more she seems separate from him, the more his desire for her strengthens. It is easier, in other words, to desire Mathilda because she has grown up without him – easier for him not to see her as his actual daughter – and because he has spent sixteen years trying to escape a snare that he knew would bind him

Perrault's 'Peau d'âne' similarly presents the father with death and loss that leads directly to the desire for his daughter. However, the Perrault story provides the support of society and a stance that incest is improper and to be avoided as Donkey-Skin (what the Princess is called for most of the story), on advice from her fairy godmother, flees her father's kingdom and ends up with a Prince whose desire is inflamed through his voyeurism as he spies Donkey-Skin in her royal attire while she admires her own beauty in a mirror. He becomes the younger, acceptable version of male desire as she again becomes the object of his gaze. That she also gazes at herself reintroduces narcissism into the scopic moment; but Donkey-Skin symbolically controls her Prince as she slips her ring into a cake she bakes for him (Lewis 813). He, predictably, then seeks the woman whose hand can wear the planted ring. Donkey-Skin has succeeded in reinscribing, through her culinary exercise, the site of desire. She moves past her father's improper desire by associating with peasants and by taking on herself punishment, exile and servitude in order to escape her father and find a suitable lover. Her father's desire has prepared her – in a tangible sense in the form of the three magnificent dresses he had made for her as she tried to put him off with amazing requests – to attract and return the attentions of a Prince. Her father's desire, furthermore, was authorized by his Queen whose dying words bound him to take another wife only if he could find someone else who equaled her beauty. Clearly, the Queen may be dead, but guarantees her ability to compete with any other woman for her husband's affection. This placing of the originary blame on the mother leaves the father free to come back to his senses by the end of the tale and finally act out the fate his wife had willed for him: to stay faithful and celibate, in other words, to die to sexual desire as soon as the object of his desire dies.

Mathilda's father's desire has no such verbalized prompting, nor does he appear capable of moving beyond his attachment to his newly-met daughter. Woodville, who befriends Mathilda after her father's death and during her self-imposed isolation, also cannot become the new love interest for Mathilda whose fidelity to her father and her insistence on emotional self-flagellation continue and actually grow in the exercise of creating her own narrative. Mathilda so mirrors her father that at the news of his death she says that she 'sank lifeless to the ground; and would that then all been at an end!' (214), repeating the physical image of his suicide.

Mathilda is expert at nursing her own desire even while she is under the watchful, frigid eye of her aunt. In contrast to the musical instruction she receives on the harp in an attempt to make her more like her aunt who also played the instrument, her musical practices lead in another direction: 'I often addressed it [the harp] as my only friend; I could pour forth to it my hopes and loves, and I fancied that its sweet accents answered me . . .' (*Mathilda* 185). Mathilda here indulges in speaking to herself, of enlarging and forming her own desires. Her imagination has as its idol her 'unhappy, wandering father.' She feeds her desire for a reunion with him by looking at a miniature of him, copying out his last letter and reading it many times, and finally creating what she calls her 'favorite vision':

> that when I grew up I would leave my aunt, whose coldness lulled my conscience, and disguised like a boy I would seek my father through the world. My imagination hung upon the scene of recognition; his miniature, which I should continually wear exposed on my breast, would be the means and I imaged the moment to my mind a thousand and a thousand times. (185)

Clearly, Mathilda does everything she can to link her own future happiness to the idea of her father and goes so far as to imagine herself as a boy in order to be free to seek him and to be more like him. She also speaks of her time with her father as life in 'an enchanted palace, amidst odours, and music, and every luxurious delight . . .'(190). The connection between Mathilda's powerful imagination and seduction becomes even clearer as Baudrillard explains: 'To seduce is to die as reality and reconstitute oneself as illusion. It is to be taken in by one's own illusion and move in an enchanted world' (*Seduction* 69).

The father she encounters later in the narrative seems to be all her imaginings, spurred on by his portrait, could have wished. She, in turn, becomes a creature of his desire/mind when he sees her. She says 'my father has often told me that I looked more like a spirit than a human maid' (187). From this point on Mathilda's status as perfect bearer of her own and her father's desire grows. Her physical similarity to her dead mother is reinforced when an old servant of her father's family says 'You are like her although there is more of my lord in you' (195). Though the remark is embedded in a discourse that centers on the servant's concern for her father, whose mood has been grim, it reminds the reader of Mathilda's earlier fantasy of becoming a boy ('there is more of my lord in you'). Rather than becoming her father's helper and companion, Mathilda actually repeats his path in life. She blames herself for his death because she pushed him to admit his guilty love and thus drive them apart. She gets another letter from him before his suicide in which he makes a play for the role of guiltiest. Each of them wants the role and, of course, each succeeds in creating it for him/herself. Both father and daughter live in the land of fantasy and emotion. Mathilda had planned to flee from him, as he had fled from her over grief at the loss of her mother, and she falls severely ill after his death (215). She later stages her own death by disappearing from her guardian's house. To make the link with her father more complete 'it was believed from the letters that I left and other circumstances that I planned that I had destroyed myself' (219). Though Harpold sees Mathilda's desire for death as a way of preparing 'for her eventual identification with the mother' (60), Mathilda's insistent mirroring of her absent father indicates otherwise.

She becomes the self-ordained, self-created voice of guilt and death. Her preparation for the role of narrator of her own demise began with the loss of her mother. Maternal absence is absolutely essential to Mathilda's desires. As Baudrillard says, 'true seduction proceeds by absence' (108). Her entire narrative is an extended play with absence as she delays reporting the horrible utterance that she insisted on and which shattered (at least temporarily) her happy life with her father. Her narrative tries desperately to cover over the wound of speech, to reinstate the silence and mystery of her time with her father and even the time prior to their meeting. As Ford states, 'power also resides in what is not named' in the text (65), though Mathilda recognizes this only after the breach between her and her father. Mathilda's seclusion and feigned death become maneuvers that bring her some degree of renewed happiness, not only because she doubles her dead father thus bringing him back even in his absence, but also because being alone fuels desire anew through writing and imagination.

The relationship between Mathilda and her father becomes perverse not because incestuous desire exists, but as Baudrillard claims because the desire, the potential incest, is articulated and thus revealed (*Seduction* 127). This point becomes clearer when we return to 'Donkey-Skin' and realize that the political, verbal nature of the king's desire, the setting up of a game of desire with the three dresses, had actually created the perverse possibility that the Princess might marry her father, thus putting a public stamp on incest. The unspoken desire would be potentially far more intense and less perverse. Without being measured against a norm, incestuous desire exists in its own world. When seduction becomes perversion it is 'monotonous and interminable,' 'theatrical and complicit' (128). Mathilda's story, to a modern reader, appears to employ theatricality when we recall her fantasy of dressing like a boy and seeking her father. This episode, as well as both her own and her father's reactions to his declaration of love for her (she locks herself in her room and plans to flee, he flees and kills himself) and her almost ghostly appearance when she does meet him, push the situation to extremes. These extremes are what Mathilda tries to reshape, rename and reinvest in her narrative account. 'Language returns to its secret seduction despite all the efforts to uncover and betray it in order to make it signify', (80–81) states Baudrillard. Mathilda's attempts to gain control over the situation, thus, can only end in the validation of the seduction of incest.

Both Mathilda and the Princess in 'Donkey Skin' take over the game of seduction after the father loses his place in it or is absent from it. Donkey-Skin, as mentioned earlier, uses all she has learned from her experience and finds and attracts an appropriate love object, while Mathilda uses narrative to replay the scenes of her desires and fears. Donkey-Skin, importantly, does not rely on language, but rather on looking in her approach to the Prince. The most significant looks in the tale occur when there are apparent barriers to the view. As Perrault's text archly states, '*Par hasard il [the Prince] mit l'oeil au trou de la serrure*' which leads to his pleasure: '*En la voyant reprendre haleine, / Tant il est comblé de plaisir*' (Perrault 67-8). It is apparent that Mathilda, too, has learned that distance and absence are particularly important in maintaining intensity of emotion as she does her best to keep the sympathetic Woodville at arm's length. She makes certain that though he knows she is ill, he is unaware that she is dying and thus will not hurry back to her. Though in the early part of her story she identifies Woodville as the person likely to read the pages she writes, in Chapters IX and X she begins to relate his history and the tale of how they met as though Woodville is not the primary reader. She also speaks of him in the past tense: 'The name of my friend was Woodville' (*Mathilda* 223). She retells his life history as she had her father's – beginning with events that predate her personal knowledge of him, but that set him up as one who grieves for the loss of a beloved woman. In telling Woodville's story she extends her father's presence in the text since his and Woodville's woes are similar. The only difference is the cause of death of Woodville's Elinor – rather than dying of childbirth, she dies of fever.

Indeed, Woodville and Elinor are more analogous to her father and herself than Mathilda sees. Her fascination with Woodville's sorrow is thus actually self-reflexive. Like Woodville and Elinor, Mathilda and her father never consummate their love. Like Elinor Mathilda dies as a potential bride: 'In truth I am in love with death; no maiden ever took more pleasure in the contemplation of her bridal attire than I in fancying my limbs already enwrapt in their shroud: is it not my marriage dress?' (244). Being in love with death, of course, brings Mathilda closer to her father.

Genres and Desires

The structure of the narrative Mathilda presents furthermore plays a game of life/death and seclusion/inclusion. She makes repeated allusions to the secret of hers and her father's desires before she actually reveals the mystery. In the opening chapter she claims 'My fate has been governed by necessity, a hideous necessity' (176); at the end of Chapter III she enigmatically says 'But, no, my tale must not pause; it must be as rapid as was my fate' (190), though the reader does not get clarity until two chapters later. She acts like a writer of gothic fiction who makes a conscious effort to create tension, suspense and readerly expectation, thus creating a writerly seduction. The use of seclusion and flight also associates her narrative with gothic fiction; but Mathilda becomes both the villain and the victim. Most gothic fiction, too, centers on perversions or threats to domestic harmony. Radcliffe's *Mysteries of Udolpho* and Walpole's *The Castle of Otranto* are two prominent examples. It is pertinent to note that according to Mary Shelley's *Journal* she had read Mrs. Radcliffe's *Udolpho* in 1815 (92). Interestingly, in Walpole's *Castle of Otranto* the loyal daughter, whose name is Matilda, is stabbed to death by her father who intended to kill Matilda's lover, Theodore. Mathilda's tale also draws on the language of sentimental literature and confession. Thus, the tale presents the reader with a hybridization of fictional genres that mirrors the complication of incest with monogamy, identification and narcissism.

Mathilda's narrative shares with the gothic a love of secrets and their ultimately sudden discovery or uncovering. The elaborate descriptions of her emotional states that link her story with sentimental fiction become part of the technique of writerly seduction. While interesting the reader she engages in a game of narcissistic confession and delay. The real purpose of her confession is not to seek resolution or absolution for herself, but to immortalize her desire beyond the confines of her physical existence. Why else would Mathilda claim at the prefatory outset of her story 'that I am about to die and I feel happy – joyous' (175)? She describes herself as the isolated young woman of a gothic tale as she opens her own tale, but instead of the dreary castle with arcane passageways, trap doors and bizarre portraits, she inhabits 'a lone cottage on a solitary, wide heath' (175). Indeed all the settings in the story show the reader a singular young woman. Even her time in London she describes in a way that does not create any sense of the bustle and crowd. She focuses instead on time spent with her father and studying.

When she and her father visit the house he had lived in with her mother, the trap of desire her narrative describes is undergirded by references to other texts. Her father significantly changes his mind about allowing her to read to him from Dante as her mother had. When he leaves the choice to Mathilda she reads from Spenser's *Faerie Queene*, Book II. Both Dante's *Divine Comedy*[1] and Spenser's text focus clearly on temptation, sin and human failings. In the case of Spenser's Sir Guyon the temptations to excess are everywhere, so that Mathilda's reading choice cannot have helped settle her father's nerves or lessened his torment. As the knight of Temperance, Guyon provides a counter example to anyone who would give in to seduction. Spenser also tells us that Guyon needs a helper (the Palmer) because he is sometimes overconfident. At the end of Book II Guyon says: 'See the mind of beastly man, / That hath so soone forgot the excellence / Of his creation, when he life began, / That now he chooseth, with vile difference, / To be a beast, and lack intelligence' (xii, 87). Mathilda's text choice does not take her father's mind off his problems. Uncannily she helps prepare the way for the succumbing to emotional temptation. Though Mathilda speaks of how troubled she is by her father's odd moods, she ironically continues to feed those moods.

Beyond her reading of Spenser as a snare to her father, we encounter her belief in superstition or in supernatural intervention and signs which further emphasize her tale's involvement with gothic. When she goes after her father, certain because she knows him and herself that he will try to kill himself, she designates a tree as a bearer of meaning. She addresses the servant who travels with her: 'Mark, Gaspar, if the next flash of lightning rend not that oak my father will be alive' (213). Of course, the lightning reduces the tree to ashes and Mathilda has a witness to her link with the supernatural universe. Her story in this scene claims the supernatural as complicit in events. Her creation of the symbol exhibits her control over events as she continues to follow her father's last steps. Again she mirrors him after learning of his death as she faints (214). She plays two roles in the narrative of the loss of her father: she is the desire from which he tries to flee and the marker of his absence. Though he physically escapes, she uses the gothic strain here to keep him and incestuous desire alive. Significantly, she does not ever say that she sees her father's corpse. Instead she reports '. . .a cottage stood beside the path; we knocked at the door and it was opened: the bed within instantly caught my eye; something stiff and straight lay on it, covered by a sheet; the cottagers looked aghast' (214). This odd description gives the reader a door that opens through no verbally apparent agency, a covered *object* and terrified cottagers rather than a direct encounter with her dead father. His death is very much a verbal construct rather than a visual, physical event, for as Mathilda says at the start of the next chapter: 'I often said to myself, my father is dead' (215) and remarks that she is troubled at feeling 'no horror.'

She determines to keep the tension of seductive incest alive as she plots to sever herself from society and normal human comfort, thus signaling her complicity with the dead father's desire. Instead of embracing the standard gothic conclusion of the freeing of a younger generation through the demise of the troubling patriarch, Mathilda describes herself as feeling like Job in his suffering; but hers is a suffering she chooses to create and prolong. She utters a prayer whose language gestures toward a divine Father, but is aimed at her own dead parent: 'Oh, beloved father! Accept the pure heart of your unhappy daughter; permit me to join you unspotted as I was or you will not recognize my altered semblance' (218). She has twisted the situation now as she fears his rejection of her. She earlier, of course, had rejected his declaration of love so her prayer acts to place her in the position her father had formerly occupied.

It is in passages like the one just quoted, furthermore, that Mathilda's language becomes the language of sentiment. Her feelings are the continual topic of her narrative whose events act as props to her emotional opera. Her focus on emotion is essential to maintaining the illusion that Baudrillard identifies as integral to seduction. Though she sets up her text as a confession, she lacks the conventional motivation and the improving conversion that confessions usually include. She attributes her need to tell her story to two different and contradictory impulses when she claims that she writes to explain her situation to Woodville and claims to be a blameless victim of fate (176) and when she claims in the final chapter that the writing has brought her some joy and that she looks forward to being again with her father. She describes herself as both innocent and blameworthy, unlike the speakers of confessions who tell of their sins in order to guide others in making better choices and to seek forgiveness for those sins. Mathilda's moral universe, because it is ruled by the powerful absent father and the incestuous attraction between them, casts her as both an actor in the drama of her life and a cause of the events that unfold. Her very interesting use of memory in telling her tale highlights the father's centrality to the degree that her own experience comes to us mingled with her father's life and woes. Unlike the penitent who confesses, furthermore, her only conversion is the one that happens when her father, at her insistence, declares his love for her. All the actions that follow from this point, as I have shown earlier, show us a young woman committed to replicating her dead father's trajectory of loneliness, desire and illusion. Inasmuch as Mathilda's narrative takes the shape of a confession, then, it is an anti-confession that allows the self-identified penitent not only to remember the troubles that she has been through, but to guarantee the continuance of the strong desire that her father's solitude and her own create and nurture.

Mathilda's talking of her own death aligns well with ongoing seduction, for as Baudrillard claims:

> Perhaps death is always incestuous – a fact that would only add to its spell . . . The great stories of seduction, that of Phaedra or Isolde, are stories of incest, and always end in death. What are we to conclude, if not that death itself awaits us in the age-old temptation of incest, including *in the incestuous relation we maintain with our own image?* (69)

What Mathilda's telling finally presents the reader with is a complex story of desire that feeds on absence and death. The powerful secret that Mathilda reveals is not as much the point of her narrative as her recreated memory of her feelings toward the idea of her father, the illusory paradise she creates through her conjurings of his image, and the ultimate attraction of dissolution that will reinvest her solitary life with renewed connection to her fondest imaginings. Rather than being the victim of fate or circumstance, Mathilda becomes the agent of incestuous, narcissistic seduction who makes the unfortunate mistake of perverting the enchantment by forcing her father to utter words of love. Her task in writing of her life is truly the task of re-enchanting desire. Even at the end of her story she reinvests her death with mystical meaning as she stresses that she dies in May: 'It was May, four years ago, that I first saw my beloved father; it was in May, three years ago that my folly destroyed the only being I was doomed to love. May is returned, and I die' (246). That the significant month is May, the time of year when all is renewed and romantic love often begins, acts as a lover's gesture. Death, for Mathilda, her own or her father's, becomes the ultimate seduction as it provides for immortality of desire and the continued play of absence that moves her narrative.

Endnote

1   Mary Shelley was certainly reading Dante at about the time she was writing *Mathilda*. In August of 1819 Mary Shelley reports in a letter to Maria Gisborne: 'I write in the morning – read latin till two when we dine, – then I read some English book and two cantos of Dante with Shelley.' (*Letters* Vol. 1, 104)

Bibliography

Baudrillard, Jean. *Seduction*. trans. Brian Singer. NY: St. Martin's Press, 1990.
Brewer, William D. 'Mary Shelley on the Therapeutic Value of Language.' *Papers on Literature and Language* 30, 4 (Fall 1994): 387–407.
Ellis, Kate Ferguson. 'Subversive Surfaces: The Limits of Domestic Affection in Mary Shelley's Later Fiction.' *The Other Mary Shelley: Beyond Frankenstein*. eds. Audrey A. Fisch, Anne K. Mellor and Esther Schor. New York: Oxford University Press, 1993. 220–34.
Ford, Susan Allen. '"A name more dear": Daughters, Fathers, and Desire in *A Simple Story, The False Friend*, and *Mathilda*.' *Re-Visioning Romanticism, British Women Writers, 1776–1837*. eds. Carol Shiner Wilson and Joel Haefner. Philadelphia: University of Pennsylvania, 1994; 57–71.
Harpold, Terence. '"Did you get Mathilda from Papa?": Seduction Fantasy and the Circulation of Mary Shelley's *Mathilda*.' *Studies in Romanticism* 28 (Spring 1989): 49–67.
Lewis, Philip. 'Food for Sight: Perrault's "Peau d'âne."' *MLN* 106 (1991): 793–817.
Mellor, Anne K. *Mary Shelley: Her Life, Her Fiction, Her Monsters*. New York: Routledge, 1989.
Nitchie, Elizabeth. 'Introduction.' *Mathilda*. Mary Shelley. Chapel Hill: University of North Carolina Press, 1959; pp. vii–xv.
Perrault, Charles. 'Peau d'âne.' *Contes de Perrault*. Paris: Éditions Garnier Frères, 1967. 57–75.
Shelley, Mary. *The Journals of Mary Shelley 1814–1844*. eds. Paula R. Feldman and Diana Scott-Kilvert. Baltimore: The Johns Hopkins University Press, 1987.
—— *The Letters of Mary Wollstonecraft Shelley*. Vol. 1 ed. Betty T. Bennett. 1980. Baltimore: The Johns Hopkins University Press, 1991.
—— *Mathilda*. *The Mary Shelley Reader*. eds. Betty T. Bennett and Charles E. Robinson. New York: Oxford University Press, 1990.
Smith, Johanna. *Mary Shelley*. NY: Twayne, 1996.

Spenser, Edmund. *The Faerie Queene*. eds. J.C. Smith and E. de Selincourt. *Spenser Poetical Works*. Oxford: Oxford University Press, 1979.
Sunstein, Emily W. *Mary Shelley: Romance and Reality*. Baltimore: The Johns Hopkins University Press, 1989.

Chapter 4

Villette and the Perversions of Feminine Identity

Eleanor Salotto

In this essay, I argue that Lucy Snowe's narrative in *Villette* is uncanny inasmuch as Charlotte Brontë formulates a model for a reading of the feminine subject as perverse – as not adhering to the rules of the game of feminine identity, and thus Brontë illustrates the transgressive quality of the 'I' as never being centered originally – identity rests on a series of representations which one inhabits. And in her rewriting of the feminine 'I,' she engenders one that is uncanny, one which cannot be pinpointed definitively. What makes Lucy Snowe's narrative so uncanny is that there are no clear markers with which to read her, thereby demonstrating Brontë's refusal to situate woman as an ideal fixed marker. Brontë splinters the notion that one text defines woman: by announcing woman's status as a text already written, she allows for a perverse counterwriting, which negates a discrete placement. *Villette* charts new territory for feminine autobiography in that it focuses on the dynamics of a radical disjunction between the 'I' and the representational images used to stand for that 'I.'

The multiple origins of a woman's life, which Brontë emphasizes in picturing the 'I' as a series of representations, constitute a starting point for an analysis of feminine subjectivity. As I argue below, Brontë positions woman as a series of conflicting and contradictory images; and in beginning the autobiography of Lucy Snowe with the life of Paulina Home, Brontë uncovers woman's place in discourse as the object of the male gaze. After this move in the opening chapters of *Villette*, however, she charts new territory for the 'I.' In doing so, she brings to the forefront the idea of the uncanny, which is continually involved in a dynamic between the familiarity and the strangeness of woman's place in representational plots.

By interpreting *Villette* as concerning the contestatory nature of identity, we can envision new placements for women in the structure of masculine discourse. *Villette* opens with scenes of representation in which Lucy describes Paulina Home as the object of the gaze. The opening chapters constitute a series of tableaus about feminine identity: Polly is compared to an Odalisque (88), and in a primal scene of representation, '[Graham] caught her up with one hand, and with that one hand held her poised aloft above his head. She saw herself thus lifted on high, in the glass over the fireplace' (75). This scene involves several gazes: Graham's, Lucy's, Polly's, and the reader's. This passage presents a mirror image where the feminine subject looks into the mirror and sees not only herself, but herself being looked at. This scene is reminiscent of the positioning of woman in the patriarchal economy of language, where woman occupies the place of the other in masculine discourse. Polly, in effect, sees herself through Graham's eyes. She is that remainder, that lack, which ensures masculine subjectivity; his 'I' is shored up by his representation of her. In including this scene of representation encased in Lucy Snowe's autobiographical account, the text highlights woman's specular relationship to language. Polly in this passage is frozen in the frame of the mirror.

Lucy Snowe, however, begins her task of rewriting this dynamic of feminine representation by tampering with masculine discourse. She does this by splintering the image of woman and offering in its place not a coherent identity, which would reflect back a masculine 'I,' but one that is marked by disjunction and disequilibrium. After Miss Marchmont's death, Lucy describes the image of herself in the mirror: 'I saw myself in the glass, in my mourning-dress, a faded, hollow-eyed vision' (96). As Lucy moves from the image of Polly in the mirror seen above, she views a faded image that does not correspond with the centered image of the viewer and viewed, where the masculine viewer's subjectivity is ensured. If the eyes are the guarantor of subjectivity, in that the eye in the mirror confirms the coherent image, then the description of Lucy's eyes as hollow helps to problematize the notion of a corresponding coherent 'I.' The hollow 'I' sets the stage for a rewriting of the 'I' by uncovering the eye's place in the specular economy of gendered subjectivity. The text exposes the image in front of the mirror: it is hollow because it refuses to reflect back the image of wholeness, which the mirror image traditionally guarantees. Positioned between two mirror images of woman – one that is created for her and one that reflects the hollowness of that vision – Lucy opts for the latter but not without repercussions for her narrative formulation of the 'I.' Hollowness leads us to consider the falsity of an already-existing image of woman. By disturbing the representational dynamic of wholeness, Lucy's narrative hinges on the uncanny, which reveals the contradictory location of a feminine autobiographer as she grapples with creating a new image of woman in the existing discourse.

A discussion of the uncanny will set the stage for an analysis of the text's perversion of the feminine 'I.' Several critics of *Villette* discuss the uncanny in relation to the appearance of the nun who signals Lucy's repressed feelings.[1] The nun, according to these critics, reveals herself at heightened moments in the narrative when Lucy is torn between reason and imagination. As an example, the nun makes her first appearance after Lucy receives a letter from Dr. John. This letter occasions feelings of happiness and pain in Lucy. At this moment, she sees 'in the middle of that ghostly chamber a figure all black or white, the skirts straight, narrow, black; the head bandaged, veiled, white' (325). Mary Jacobus underscores the uncanniness of the nun when she writes: 'She [the nun] is the joker in the pack, the alien, ex-centric self which no image can mirror – only the structure of language' ('The Buried Letter' 51). Jacobus describes the overdetermined symbolization that the nun evokes. This symbolization is equivalent, Jacobus maintains, to language's inability to posit full reference. Christina Crosby proposes that 'the nun is metaphorically representative of Lucy's fragmented self, first inside, then outside: inside when Lucy is racked with internal conflicts, outside when she is more in control of herself' (705).[2] While these two critics have contributed greatly to a psychological reading of the novel, I want to shift the focus from the nun as a representation of Lucy to the uncanniness which inheres in the narrative structure of *Villette*. It is my hypothesis that the text is uncanny at the level of its plot structure; that is to say, as Lucy fashions her 'I', she is haunted by the remnants of a woman's life in narrative. Doubling prevails in the structure of the plot; Lucy Snowe begins her life with the biography of another woman, Paulina Home.

What does beginning the narrative of one's life with another's life mean for the study of women's lives in autobiography? My analysis of *Villette* differs from Gilbert and Gubar's – who, in *The Madwoman in the Attic*, claim that women must shatter the image they see portrayed hanging in the gallery of patriarchy – in its insistence on preserving the doubleness in both the subject and plot structure. As Lucy Snowe begins this process of creating a new image of woman, her text remains haunted by images of women. Particularly relevant in my analysis of *Villette* will be the following question: what happens when one looks into the mirror of autobiographical representation and sees a double or hybrid figure which calls forth the uncanny?

Before turning to *Villette*, a brief commentary on Freud's essay on 'The Uncanny' will set the stage for the argument.[3] He begins his essay with the linguistic usage of the word '*heimlich*' or canny. He gives various definitions of *heimlich*; it is that which belongs 'to the house' (222); it is that which is familiar and not strange. Significantly, Freud comes across an ambivalence in the denotation of the word; *heimlich* comes to mean also that which is 'concealed,' and 'kept from sight' (223), Thus, he establishes the doubleness inherent in the word *heimlich*; it simultaneously stands for the familiar and the not familiar. He implies that the word contains a double signification, which paves the way for an analysis of the doubleness of the plot structure in *Villette*.

Freud relates the uncanny to infantile psychology; he explains that 'everything which now strikes us as 'uncanny' fulfills the condition of touching those residues of animistic mental activity within us and bringing them to expression' (240–1). The uncanny, therefore, is 'in reality nothing new or alien, but something which is familiar and old-established in the mind and which has become alienated from it only through the process of repression' (241). The uncanny represents a model of ego formation of the individual. The individual as he or she enters the laws of society represses the past, whether of the individual or of the race. Thus, for example, primitive beliefs in ghosts give way to religion. For Freud, the healthy individual represses infantile memories of the individual and the race: memories surface as the uncanny when an impression or memory revives the repressed material.

It remains clear that the uncanny is related to the infantile stage of human development. The uncanny represents that which, as Schelling phrases it, 'ought to have remained hidden but has come to light' (quoted in Freud 241), reminding the individual of a former existence, or a former state of things. What would be the result of applying what Freud articulates about the life of the individual and the uncanny to the life of women in literature, to narrative models for lives? That is to say, women's lives in autobiography in the nineteenth century represent the fledgling stage of the elucidation of women's plots; to what extent are women's narratives uncanny, given the model of the uncanniness of plots which I have set forth?

The question which seems to haunt the narrative is: why does Lucy Snowe begin the autobiography of her life with another woman's life, Paulina Home's? The first three chapters of *Villette* center on Lucy's telling of Paulina Home's entrance into the home of the Brettons. Lucy finds out about Paulina's arrival when she sees additions to her furniture in her bedroom. She describes that 'in a corner [appeared] a small crib . . . [and] a tiny rosewood chest' (62). These items lead her to articulate her first spoken words in the text: 'Of what are these things the signs and tokens?' (62), to which a servant replies, 'A second guest is coming' (62). This scene represents Lucy looking into the mirror of her text and seeing another image. Something is not quite right in this representational practice, making the resultant narrative uncanny. Paulina functions as the sign and token for the 'other,' 'the second guest,' who will layer over the representation of Lucy's life. Lucy tells her story through another's story; it is as if her story cannot be named as yet, something is missing, no signs and tokens exist for which she can write her story. The compulsion to repeat, which is central to an understanding of the idea of the uncanny, is reflected in Lucy's beginning her story with Paulina. This manifests Lucy's desire to restore the stability of the sign, which is related to the familiarity of plots in nineteenth-century fiction.

Women have traditionally been encased in plots not entirely of their own making. In the eighteenth century, as Nancy K. Miller has pointed out, the only plots available to women were the marriage plot and the death plot. Lucy Snowe figures women in plots in her narrative through images of boats and steersmen.[4] In chapter four, she writes:

> I will permit the reader to picture me, for the next eight years, as a bark slumbering through halcyon weather, in a harbour still as glass – the steersman stretched on the little deck, his face up to heaven, his eyes closed: buried, if you will, in a long prayer. A great many women and girls are supposed to pass their lives something in that fashion; why not I with the rest? (94)

While Lucy figures herself as a boat, she is led by the steersman. This passage constitutes an inscription of woman's place in narrative plots; she is steered by the narrator who controls the forward movement of the plot. This narrative positioning is one of equilibrium; nothing disturbs the tranquillity of the woman as a static image. Everything in the passage represents that which is *heimlich* or familiar to the home of women's plots: the phrases 'slumbering,' 'halcyon,' and 'a harbour still as glass,' attest to the image of woman as a sight to be looked at; she is the recipient of the metaphorical gaze of the steersman; she does not activate the gaze. The 'harbour still as glass' corresponds to a mirror image where one sees her reflected image, as reflected by the steersman.

This image of the slumbering woman, however, quickly gets overturned in the text by the figure of Lucy who must drive her own plot. Similarly, the storm at the end of the novel signals the rewriting of woman in a plot that reflects equilibrium. As I will argue below, the storm forecasts the tension inherent in Lucy's steering of her own plot and the marriage plot's threat of containment. A passage in the middle of the text returns to the image of the boat and its navigator. Lucy speculates on the difference between her life and that of Louisa Bretton:

> The difference between her and me might be figured by that between the stately ship, cruising on the smooth seas, with its full complement of crew, a captain gay and brave, and venturous and provident; and the life boat, which most days of the year lies dry and solitary in an old, dark boat-house, only putting to sea when the billows run high in rough weather, when danger and death divide between them the rule of the great deep. No, the 'Louisa Bretton' never was out of harbour on such a night, and in such a scene: her crew could not conceive it; so the half-drowned life-boat man keeps his own counsel, and spins no yarns. (254)

Again, we are presented with an image of a woman who is guided by a crew; implicitly Louisa Bretton is steered though the mechanism of plot. The life-boat, however, makes its own way through the disequilibriums of plot, as figured by the woman going off the course of the prescribed narrative of a woman's life which is 'safe' and 'smooth.' The life boat begins its course, its narrative course, as I am suggesting, only when 'the billows run high in rough weather,' signaling the transgressive quality of the narrative which is in danger of capsizing. This image of drowning and possible death suggests the problematics of representing the other or the perverse image of woman, which goes against the image of the stately ship. Lucy begins the passage by referring to the difference between herself and Louisa Bretton: Louisa Bretton is the stately ship and Lucy is the life boat.

But the language in the passage splinters apart, reflecting the profound split inherent in the woman who creates, Lucy Snowe, and the language in which she must articulate that creation. The life boat man does not have a story to tell. In effect, this is as a result of the crew not being able to conceive of being out on the seas on such a stormy night. Brontë makes the connection clear here: a story requires consensus. It requires fitting in to always already agreed upon models of reality. Silenced by not having a readable story to tell, the life-boat man in effect occupies a limbo-like place where he wafts between remaining silent and speaking. This is the position of Lucy in the text. Also, the gender slippage in the passage which alternates from Lucy to the life-boat man reflects a language that strives to encapsulate a woman's reality. Would one conceive of a life-boat woman? Is there a language with which Lucy can articulate her desires?

This doubling of the image of woman leads us back to the realm of the uncanny, where Lucy occupies the position of woman, even though she also exists outside of it. Plot, for Lucy Snowe, becomes a *locus suspectus,* an uncanny place. This idea is most readily observable in the text's inability to escape from representations of women: they haunt the text. Struggling to remain inside the narrative plots for women, Lucy begins her narrative with the story of another woman, who represents a typical account of a woman's life in the home. Paulina Home stands for that which is *heimlich* (homelike or familiar); Lucy portrays Paulina's acquiescence to what characterizes the home: 'One would have thought the child had no mind or life of her own, but must necessarily live, move, and have her being in another: now that her father was taken from her, she nestled to Graham, and seemed to feel by his feeling: to exist in his existence' (83). Similar to the images of the women being guided by the steersmen, Polly emblematizes the life of a woman, who exists not in herself, but as the mirror of man's feeling.

Why, then, is Lucy obsessed with Paulina's image, with representing her?[5] Lucy's narrative runs the risk of remaining static; images of women who do not possess the power to look remind her of her place in the social order. Lucy gazes into her plot; but that look entails a loss of footing in the world of the familiar. The uncanny for Lucy involves entering a narrative world where there is no discrete path marked out. At any moment in the text – and this is what makes her narrative so uncanny – she is confronted with the abyss, that unexplained strangeness that has no explainable origins, such as the figure of the nun.

This recurrence of the same thing, a crucial aspect in Freud's discussion of the uncanny, surfaces in the plot in *Villette,* which, in a sense, stages its own return to the lives of women in narrative. As Lucy wishes to originate her own story, she is drawn back continually to the representations of other women's lives. What makes the other plots frightening to her is that she may be forced to repeat them, and indeed the opening of her text obsessively returns to other plots of women. Her narrative is thus uncanny; as it struggles to move forward, to assume its own course, it is haunted by the past of a woman's life. Thus, the narrative of *Villette* becomes uncanny by its involuntary repetition; as Freud describes it, 'involuntary repetition . . . forces upon us the idea of something fateful and inescapable' (237). Representations of other women produce an uncanny text; 'the uncanny is that class of the frightening which leads back to what is known of lost and old familiar' (Freud 220). The text's harking back to the image of an 'ideal' woman, Paulina Home, represents its uncanny struggle with a familiar place for women in narrative plots. The text returns to the familiarity of woman's plots and Lucy's fear and dread of being encased in this plot. Lucy begins her autobiography with Paulina, which suggests a compulsion to repeat the narrative of the life in the home; the narrative is haunted by the images of woman in the culture. Lucy confronts the gaze headlong, but the gaze for women is lifeless, reflecting a masculine look.

The uncanny in *Villette* announces itself in an oft-quoted passage used to describe the duplicity of Lucy Snowe. She relates regarding Paulina: 'I Lucy Snowe, plead guiltless of that curse, an overheated and discursive imagination; but whenever, opening a room-door, I found her seated in a corner alone, her head in her pigmy hand, that room seemed to me not inhabited, but haunted' (69). Clearly, Lucy's feelings are overdetermined; Paulina experiences profoundly the temporary loss of her father, but what fuels the choice of Lucy's words to describe the room as being haunted by Polly's grief? Her grief must remind Lucy of something in her own life. Mary Jacobus has argued convincingly that Polly acts out Lucy's loss in the opening chapters: the loss of Graham Bretton and her family.[6] I want to shift this focus, however, and argue that Lucy's displaced grief is a narrative retrospective one, in the sense that through Paulina, Lucy encounters someone who, paradoxically, is foreign and familiar, distant and close, totally estranged, unknown, and at the same time strangely recognizable and known. The haunting that Lucy experiences in the room translates into her initially having to occupy the space of Paulina's plot. It is Polly, then, who sparks the uncanny into action as she acts out the life of a woman. The representation of her provokes an anxiety in Lucy; she does not quite fit the *heimlich* image produced by Paulina.

This image of Paulina is closely associated with an inanimate object: Lucy defines her as looking 'a mere doll; her neck, delicate as wax, her head of silky curls, increased . . . the resemblance' (64). Similarly, Paulina is envisaged as 'an Odalisque, on a couch' (87). These images intimate the static quality of traditional representations of women in narrative. Lucy in her narrative cannot start out entirely from the position of the uncanny, which would place her outside the model of available plots for women; she begins from the *heimlich*, which paradoxically calls forth the uncanny because of the doubleness of the image of a woman's life: in the home and out of the home, which describe Paulina and Lucy respectively.

Freud describes the image of the double as reflecting a self-preservative instinct. He speculates that the 'immortal' soul was the first 'double' of the body' (235). The double signals the function of primary narcissism, in that it preserves the image in the other, but the double paradoxically moves towards ambivalence, and, according to Freud, 'From having been an assurance of immortality, it becomes the uncanny harbinger of death' (235). *Villette* suggests that Paulina is Lucy's double.[7] At one point, in a scene with her father, during which Polly is particularly restrained, Lucy says that she wishes Polly 'would utter some hysterical cry, so that I might get relief and be at ease' (71). Later on, Lucy 'wonder[s] to find my thoughts hers: there are certain things in which we so rarely meet with our double that it seems a miracle when that chance befalls' (361). At the beginning of her narrative, Lucy identifies herself with Polly, establishing the division in her self. Lucy experiences ambivalence about telling her plot, so she plays it safe by using the image of woman which would repeat back to her a canny feeling. Freud postulates about the identificatory relationship between the subject and her double: 'The subject identifies himself with someone else, so that he is in doubt as to which his self is, or substitutes the extraneous self for his own' (234). This idea works in *Villette* in the following way: in telling her story Lucy reverts to a traditional narrative plot for woman; in a sense, she has not completely separated herself from this plot. But this *heimlich* feeling crosses over into the uncanny because Paulina images the harbinger of death for the plot of Lucy's life.

Brontë creates in Lucy a character who does pervert the narrative of a woman's life, but she confronts dread and horror before the image of Polly. If woman is always-already constructed, then, in a sense she does not exist in the symbolic order. As Lucy puts it regarding Paulina, 'herself was forgotten in him' (82). Thus, the image of Polly threatens death for Lucy. Polly represents the non-narratable; there is no story to tell, for her story has already been told. Lucy must look and grapple with the static image represented by Polly.

Before Lucy can dismantle the created image of woman, she confronts these already existing images. Claude Levesque relates about narrative self-fashioning: 'To tell one's story is to consort with the terrifying' (quoted in *The Ear of the Other* 72). Initially, for Lucy, narrating her story means facing the ghostly images of women; the narrative movement in the text suggests that these images seek to create her in their image. Lucy views the ghostly presence of Paulina, the cultural ideal, the woman who pricks herself continually while sewing but still remains 'silent, diligent, absorbed, womanly' (73). Paulina's pet name is Polly; she is doomed to parrot her master's words. The following dialogue between Polly and Mrs. Bretton confirms her linguistic mimicry:

'What is my little one's name?'

'Missy.'
'But besides Missy?'
'Polly, papa calls her.' (64)

In the opening of *Villette*, Lucy looks into the cultural mirror, similar to Lacan's mirror stage, and sees an image of the Imaginary, the whole and centered Paulina. Underlying that image is Lucy, the displaced subject, but in order for Lucy's narrative to progress, she must struggle with Paulina's image.

Lucy, in returning to Polly in her autobiography, contends with past images of women in order to exorcise them. In that return, however, Lucy fears being captured by the double. In negotiating her narrative enterprise, Lucy runs the risk of being claimed by the image of Paulina. Anne Hollander reminds us of the pictorial quality of representation when she writes of the mirror that it 'remains a picture, inextricable from the representational style of its moment' (416). Hollander describes how images are framed by the discourse of what it means to be a subject before the mirror captures the illusion of the image. She indicates that the mirror image is actually engendered by the cultural ideal. Thus, when one looks into the mirror, one sees an image of desire: in effect, what one is supposed to look like.

Polly engenders the uncanny as Lucy animates a new image of woman. Lucy's narrative initially runs the risk of closure or death; it is only because her ship capsizes that she has a story to tell. She relates: 'Picture me then idle, basking, plump, and happy, stretched on a cushioned deck, warmed with constant sunshine, rocked by breezes indolently soft. However, it cannot be concealed that, in that case, I must have fallen over-board, or that there must have been a wreck at last' (94). Polly inspires the uncanny in Lucy because of the primitive fear of the dead (metaphorically, in *Villette*, the deadness of woman's plots) associated with the uncanny. Freud explains: 'Most likely our fear still implies the old belief that the dead man becomes the enemy of his survivor and seeks to carry him off to share his new life with him' (242). The plot of Lucy's life cannot entirely put to rest the images of women from which it originated. While the plot moves away from the canny plot of Paulina, there exists a concurrent feeling of nostalgia for the *heimlich*. This may serve as a protective mechanism, for Lucy laments the disequilibrium effected by the changes in her life: 'It seemed I must be stimulated into action. I must be goaded, driven, stung, forced to energy' (97). The opening chapters simultaneously mourn and move away from the plot of past images of a woman's life.

The doubleness of a woman's life in narrative plots is perhaps most startlingly displayed on the title page of *Villette*, where the name Currer Bell appears as the author of the text and '*Jane Eyre, Shirley*, etc.'[8] The name Currer Bell is a ghostly presence in the text, serving as a reminder of woman's place in narrative discourse: she is a cipher in that discourse, for in a sense, she cannot be named. This erasure of the name signals the uncanny. By doubling the name, Brontë returns to a male name, a familiar place, which will evoke a feeling of the familiar for readers. Paradoxically, the assumption of the pseudonym suggests both the canny and the uncanny. Writing from the position of a masculine and feminine subject, Brontë doubles the authorial self. The double, Currer Bell, while allowing Brontë the freedom to write, also haunts the narrative in the guise of Paulina, who carts back Lucy to her home, the place in which Robert Southey would have women remain; his advice to Brontë was: 'Literature cannot be the business of a woman's life, and it ought not to be. The more she is engaged in her proper duties, the less leisure will she have for it, even as an accomplishment and a recreation' (quoted in Gaskell 173). In *Villette*, Graham Bretton echoes Southey's view when Lucy reports that he 'judged [Vashti] as a woman, not as an artist; it was a branding judgment' (342). These statements constitute a splitting of the subject in *Villette*, where Brontë writes a contradictory text about the feminine subject.

It is no accident that the novel is entitled *Villette* rather than *Lucy Snowe*. Brontë, in choosing the name of a town rather than that of her protagonist, attests to woman's entry into a symbolic order which by its very ordering displaces her. The title of the text demonstrates woman's inability to escape her social construction; the feminine is produced within a particular system of gender representation. Further, the name Villette resembles, particularly in the pronunciation, the French word *fillette*, signifying a little girl. The feminine subject is rendered as diminutive, as secondary. The first paragraph of the text establishes the placement of woman in the symbolic order:

> My godmother lived in a handsome house in the clean and ancient town of Bretton. Her husband's family had been residents there for generations, and bore, indeed, the name of their birthplace – Bretton of Bretton: whether by coincidence, or because some remote ancestor had been a personage of sufficient importance to leave his name to his neighborhood, I know not. (61)

The passage describes the importance of tradition and the name which bears that tradition. The emphasis is on the husband's family and his ancestors. By opening the text in this way, Brontë establishes woman's secondary place in the social law that prizes the male name.

But the text perverts the social order by rewriting the rules of the language game. In this connection, Brontë's choice of a surname for her character attests to her means of tampering with language and its social implications. We know that Brontë initially settled on the name Lucy Frost for her protagonist but then decided upon the surname Snowe.[9] The words 'frost' and 'snow' hint at the frozen language of the plot of Paulina Home. This spatial location of the life in the home hampers narration. The names Frost and Snowe recapitulate the difficulty the woman autobiographer has in articulating her plot; she runs the risk of her plot freezing her in the language which she necessarily must speak. The name Snowe also signifies the blank subject who will be written upon.

Brontë's changing of the name from Frost to Snowe demonstrates, however, an obfuscation in a straightforward reading of the name as reflective of a woman frozen in the home. The denotation of snow is solid precipitation and frozen particles of water vapor. The meaning of 'to snow,' however, is to cover, shut off, or close with snow. Lucy tells her readers parenthetically of her memories of the past: '(for I speak of a time gone by: my hair which till a late period withstood the frosts of time, lies now, at last white, under a white cap, like snow beneath snow)' (105). Her use of the word 'snow' to describe her hair can lead to a speculation on her hiding beneath the cover of patriarchal language. That is to say, Lucy conceals the traditional 'I' and puts in its place a new signifier which refuses to stay in its proper place. This new meaning of the name scatters the name; the burial of the 'I' beneath snow leads to a creation of an 'I' that will rewrite the meaning of frost.

The foregoing establishes the doubleness inherent in the uncanny. While the opening of the text signals mourning for the plot of past images of woman, simultaneously, the opening chapters move away from the idea of the home. Like the creature in *Frankenstein*, Lucy does not have a home: She asks: 'What prospects had I in life? What friends had I on earth? Whence did I come? Whither should I go? What should I do?' (107). These questions revolve around the search for origins and for a temporal movement in time, or a plot. Lucy knows that the origins of a woman's life are always already inscribed. Late in the text, M. Paul asks Lucy whether she is home-sick and she replies: 'To be home-sick, one must have a home; which I have not' (452). At the surface level, she speaks of not having a familial home, but the statement has resonant implications for plot: not being in the home quickly becomes the structural condition of a woman who writes a narrative plot of autobiography. Not encased in the home, she can position herself in several spaces.

Existing outside the home, Lucy exposes the home for what it is; she perverts the rules of the house.[10] As we remember from the text, Lucy is closely associated with the figure of the nun 'whom a monkish conclave of the drear middle ages had here buried alive, for some sin against her vow' (172). The passage demonstrates that the idea of transgression or perversion figures into the uncanny; the uncanny encompasses that which 'ought to have remained . . . secret and hidden but has come to light' (Schelling, quoted in Freud 224). Lucy unearths the secrets of representation about a woman's life and brings them to light; in this sense, her narrative is uncanny because of its transgression of cultural prohibitions about narrative self-representation. She disrupts the unity of the law of narrative representation; the underside of the feminine pulses through her narrative, attesting to an otherness to the definitions of the subject imposed by the symbolic order. Gender identity in *Villette* and Lucy's representation of it thus becomes a modern telling of the uncanny; the more Lucy tries to relate her experience it remains closed off to definitive interpretation. Brontë settles on making woman perverse: the uncanny image of woman prevails as the narrative moves on.

Lucy reveals woman as the nun – the no one in representational practice; that is to say, she uncovers what lies behind the veil of the nun and finds a figure, to which several meanings attach.[11] The nun signifies the figure in the legend: she stands for Lucy's repression, and she also represents de Hamal who is a cross-dresser. This multi-signification evokes the shifting place of woman in discourse; no one meaning attaches to her. Significantly, Lucy tears apart this representation; she exposes the figure as figure. She tells us that she 'rushed on the haunted couch ... [and] tore her up – the incubus! I held her on high – the goblin! I shook her loose – the mystery! And down she fell – down all round me – down in shreds and fragments – and I trode upon her' (569). Tearing apart the 'truth' value of representation, Lucy shatters the unilateral meaning of woman in discourse. Revealing the image of woman as a stand-in for the woman, she disturbs the meaning of woman in narrative plots. She cannot represent the 'real' woman in her narrative, for this 'real' woman is a fiction.

In order to move away from the presentation of a *heimlich* or a 'real' woman, Lucy wears a narrative veil; therefore, she cannot be read: her narrative remains uncanny by its opacity. She does not translate for the reader; the French language that M. Paul uses to describe her is untranslated. In her words, 'the reader will excuse my modesty in allowing this flattering sketch of my amiable self to retain the slight veil of the original tongue' (178). The French language erects a fog over the surface presentation of Lucy's 'I.' It plays on the limits imposed on translating the 'I' into a literal meaning. In enclosing her remarks under the cover of the veil, the French language, Lucy reveals language to be innately foreign to her project of self-representation. There is no definitive 'I' behind the veil of subjectivity that can be translated. Screening herself, Lucy speaks to the problem of representing herself in a language system from which she is alienated. Adopting the metaphor of the mask, she disguises herself, thereby playing out the difficulties in articulating the homeless plot which has not yet been written. Several characters in the text try to read her, but Lucy has the last word about the other characters' views of her when she says of Graham Bretton: 'He might think, he might even believe that Lucy was contained within that shawl and sheltered under that hat; he could never be certain for he did not see my face' (555). She hides her face, representative of the 'I,' and remains outside the realm of the representable.

One of the ways in which Lucy perverts a straightforward reading of woman is by shattering the sequence of the sentence which would place woman definitively into an ordered, fixed moment in time. Opting for homelessness in the narrative sentence, which refuses to posit an ending, she disturbs temporality in her text. Splintering the sentence, she creates a double text. This disequilibrium in the plot sequence is revealed most startlingly in the double ending of the text, where the text conjures up a shipwreck and the death of M. Paul, Lucy's betrothed, but then Lucy creates an alternative vision:

> Here pause: pause at once. There is enough said. Trouble no quiet, kind heart; leave sunny imaginations hope. Let it be theirs to conceive the delight of joy born again fresh out of great terror, the rapture of rescue from peril, the wondrous reprieve from dread, the fruition of return. Let them picture union and a happy succeeding life. (596)

This double ending signals the presence of the uncanny in the text: it is as if Lucy writes a conclusion under the mark of Currer Bell which would valorize the love plot terminating in marriage and happiness, the traditional course of a woman's life; simultaneously, she writes an ending under the signature of her own name which depicts an ending where the ambition plot succeeds.[12] But together, the double conclusion denies a temporal reading of the subject; there are possibilities for alternative readings. By means of the double ending, Lucy fractures the traditional life of a woman, producing an alternative 'truth.' The narrative's splintering of narrative temporality remains uncanny. If Lucy does not inscribe a coherent closure, she remains continually wandering, the aberrant signifier who transgresses the rules of the home.

Now I would like to complicate the argument about Lucy's move to begin the story of her life with Paulina Home. In focusing on the multiple origins for a woman's life, inscribed and yet to be written, in Paulina and Lucy's lives respectively, Brontë shifts the meaning of woman as a static 'sign and token'; the multiple origins present at the beginning of the text signal an unwillingness to posit woman in any one particular home. The feminine expresses the play of difference which cannot be elided. The uncanny thus comes to represent the sheer proliferation of language surrounding the term 'woman' which attempts and fails to define or name. Reflecting on the problematics of beginnings and endings for women, Brontë places woman in a continual present. The uncanny causes a disruption of the symbolic, and this disruption in *Villette* leads to a refiguration of the concept of the subject. Lucy's subjectivity does not stay in place; it remains multiple and shifting. If language acquisition represents the entry into the symbolic where meanings cohere according to a strict system of binary identification, then *Villette* may be said to confound categories of binary thought.

To further the idea of the uncanny, it is fruitful to turn now to the uncanny as the disruption of the symbolic, where the symbol supposedly represents the name. Lucy opens her fictional autobiography insisting on the metaphor of the screen: in beginning her story with Paulina's, she explores the subject as if it were another identity. A passage in the text will elucidate the shifting role of the subject in the eye/I specularity. Lucy observes Graham Bretton and he sees her looking at him through a mirror; 'his notice was arrested, . . . it had caught my movement in a clear little oval mirror fixed in the side of the window recess – by the aid of which reflector madame often secretly spied persons walking in the garden below' (163). This passage signals the shifting view of the eye/'I' as it is apprehended through reflections, veiling a direct apprehension. Lucy follows a similar narrative practice in presenting the 'I' though a screen: a theatrical backdrop so to speak, where character cannot be seen directly but where it is viewed though various shifting reflections.

By disclosing one's subjectivity as another's, Brontë composes a multivocal text, where feminine identity is not enclosed. In beginning the narrative with stories of woman in the culture, Brontë emphasizes that a multiplicity of origins exist for a woman's life, thereby denying one unique model of subjectivity. Concerning origins, Helene Cixous has observed: 'The origin is a masculine myth: I always want to know where I come from' (quoted in Rubenstein 3). This myth of masculine origins, which implicitly wants to pit the speaker as the originator of his discourse, has a different meaning for woman's texts. Women know from where they originate; their origins are in representations about them. The text illustrates that there is no discrete subjectivity, only representations. In beginning the story with Polly, Brontë sets forth the idea that at the place where definitive origins are supposed to exist, multiple origins are found. This fluidity in the presentation of subjectivity suggests the subversiveness of Lucy's text. By opening her story with another's, she implies that at the basis of subjectivity, another subjectivity exists. In *Villette* the subject becomes a ghostly signifier, haunting the novel in its many guises, never attaching concretely to a definitive signified.

Late in the narrative, Lucy says of Madame Beck: 'Her habitual disguise, her mask and her domino, were to me a mere network reticulated with holes' (544). Lucy speaks of detecting what lies underneath the mask of Madame Beck. But Lucy's text reveals that what exists behind the veil of character is the masquerade. She masquerades in the text and performs identity as a network reticulated with holes. Her disguise in the text is not very different from Madame Beck's 'mask' and 'domino.' Screening herself, Lucy exposes subjectivity as riddled with gaps and inconsistencies that cannot be covered over. The 'I' will be masked, and she adopts the screen to hide her identity. At one point in the text, she prefers to sit in the shade, explaining, 'I kept rather in the shade and out of sight, not wishing to be immediately recognized' (292). And later, at the fete, she wears a straw hat, about which she relates: 'I only took the precaution to bind down the broad leaf gipsy-wise, with a supplementary ribbon; and then I felt safe as if masked' (551). Lucy's hiding in the text leads to the following exchange:

> Ginevra: 'Who are you, Miss Snowe?'. . .
> Lucy: 'Who am I indeed? Perhaps a personage in disguise. Pity I don't look the character . . .'
> Ginevra: '[Y]ou must be a cool hand.' (392–3)

Lucy's use of the words 'personage' and 'disguise' reveals that subjectivity is apprehended through veils and disguises. Lucy's words comment on the motif of disguise which operates in the text to obfuscate the 'I': a deliberate strategy which attests to the multiple personages behind the veil of subjectivity.

This codification of the self behind the trope of the screen marks Lucy's illegibility. Several characters in the text would like to find the definitive marker for Lucy Snowe; numerous gazes seek to contain her. As an example, Madame Beck observes Lucy on the first night of her arrival in Villette. Lucy feigns sleep and Madame Beck 'studied me long . . . I dare say she sat a quarter of an hour on the edge of my bed, gazing at my face' (131). Similarly, numerous characters wish to read and define Lucy; she relates about their interpretation of her:

> What contradictory attributes of character we sometimes find ascribed to us, according to the eye with which we are viewed! Madame Beck esteemed me learned and blue; Miss Fanshawe, caustic, ironic, and cynical; Mr. Home, a model teacher, the essence of the sedate and discreet: somewhat conventional perhaps, too strict, limited and scrupulous, but still the pink and pattern of governess-correctness; whilst another person, Professor Paul Emanuel, to wit, never lost an opportunity of intimating his opinion that mine was rather a fiery and rash nature – adventurous, undocile, and audacious. (386)

Lucy, however, gives her readers clues on how to read her when she articulates: 'He [Graham Bretton] might think, he might even believe that Lucy was contained within that shawl, and sheltered under that hat; he could never be certain for he did not see my face' (555). Hiding her face, the site of the 'I,' she cannot be interpreted in a unilateral way. Brontë indicates that reading the 'I' in the text for a definitive interpretation is futile; Lucy's 'I' will shift places and meanings.

Brontë's illegible handwriting is analogous to her encoding of the self in indecipherability. Writing in such a small hand, from the beginning of her writing career, she uses the metaphor of illegibility to obfuscate meaning. In a story entitled 'The Secret,' she writes in such a small hand that the characters are impossible to read. Elizabeth Gaskell relates:

> I have had a curious packet confided to me, containing an immense amount of manuscript, in an inconceivably small space; tales, dramas, poems, romances, written principally by Charlotte, in a hand which it is almost impossible to decipher without the aid of a magnifying glass. (111–12)

Writing for Brontë disguises meaning and signals the illegibility of the feminine subject. Existing behind the veil of writing, the subject can disturb the notion of presence on which the idea of autobiography has rested.

The figure of the nun can shed light on the figuration of identity in *Villette*. In the text, characters express a desire for the nun to be a sign of something: as we have seen above, she is at various times thought to be the ghost of the actual nun who died for a sin against her vow, a representative of Lucy's heightened imagination, and De Hamal. But underneath the veil, the nun is a figure of sheer illegibility and opacity; she exists by virtue of the symbol. She is a succession of stories, emptied of substance. Underneath the veil, nothing is there, as is revealed when Lucy tears apart the figure of the nun.

The nun replicates Lucy's absent subjectivity; behind the imaginary fullness of the veil, there may indeed be no one coherent image shoring up the rifts in the subject. Concurrently, Lucy wears the veil of subjectivity in autobiographical practice, attesting to the overdetermined status of woman as sign. What lies underneath the veil of her subjectivity is the uncanniness of herself as not truly there; she remains elsewhere. Lucy and the nun are associated when Ginevra writes in her letter to Lucy, 'The nun of the attic bequeaths to Lucy Snowe her wardrobe. She will be seen in the Rue Fossette no more' (569). But the nun as symbol does resurface in Lucy's narrative practice as the sign for her character hiding behind the veil of subjectivity. This idea is most readily observable in her description of the fete, which occurs immediately preceding the scene with the nun. At the fete, she observes that 'the night's drama was but begun . . . the prologue was scarce spoken: throughout this woody and turfy theatre reigned a shadow of mystery; actors and incidents unlooked for, waited behind the scenes: I thought so: foreboding told me as much' (556). This scene duplicates Lucy's writing of herself as an autobiographical subject. She moves through the procession of subjectivity, but another scene will rewrite the previous scene. Her drugged state suggests an alternative consciousness, one that is not easily articulated into an existing discourse which has no markers to represent her subjectivity. The nun continually refers to another signification: the legend, Justine Marie, de Hamal, and Lucy. At the place where signification is supposed to reside, multiple significations exist: the nun embodies a missing center. The uncanny surfaces in the text, in language which tries to posit identity for Lucy Snowe but ultimately fails.

Another way that Brontë deploys a discordant feminine subject is in her use of present-tense narration. It is my contention that Brontë uses time to pervert a logical ordering of the self through the sentence of time. The importance of Lucy's structuring of her 'I' in narrative temporality can be made clear if we turn to the valorization of temporal distinctions in autobiography. Several critics of autobiographical texts privilege the mode of retrospection. As Roy Pascal explains: '[I]t is his present position which enables him to see his life as something of a unity, something which may be reduced to order' (9). One adduces that unification of the self through narrative time is an aesthetic marker of autobiography. George Gusdorf expresses a similar view: 'Autobiography . . . requires a man to take a distance with regard to himself in order to reconstitute himself in the focus of his special unity and identity across time' (35). Gusdorf describes the importance of retrospection – of being able to read and interpret an earlier self. These two views construct the self as whole and harmonious; the autobiographer reformulates the self through an interpretation in time.

In *Villette*, however, the movement of the self through time is treated differently.[13] Lucy's narrative exhibits a lack of temporal distinctions. Following Miss Marchmont's death, Lucy relates to the reader: 'About this time I might be a little – a very little, shaken in nerves' (103). The wording is curious: she does not write, 'I might have been' or 'I was shaken in nerves'; rather, she chooses the present tense.[14] The time of the narration is coextensive with the time following Miss Marchmont's death, producing a disorientation in the reader's sense of narrative time. At the climax of the novel, Lucy alternates between present and past tense narration. When she leaves Madame Beck's to go to the fete, she relates: 'I know where a board is loose, and will avoid it. The oak staircase creaks somewhat as I descend, but not much: – I am in the carre' (548). And on her return to the Rue Fossette, she narrates:

> [A]s I enter it, for the first time, the sound of a carriage tears up the deep peace of this quarter. It comes this way – comes very fast. How loud sounds its rattle on the paved path! The street is narrow and I keep carefully to the causeway. The carriage thunders past, but what do I see, or fancy I see, as it rushes by? Surely something white fluttered from that window – surely a hand waved a handkerchief. (568)

Lucy, in her narrative time, breaks the sequence of a straightforward temporal perspective: by writing portions of her narrative as if they were taking place in the present, she collapses a pattern of order and significance. Why does Lucy shatter narrative temporality?[15]

As I have argued above, Lucy tries to escape from the plots which have sought to contain and define women through a narrative time which freezes them in the male gaze. Thus, her tactic of not conforming to a linear model of the self through time suggests a novel way of reading the feminine subject. In this connection, Toril Moi explains Kristeva's notion of female subjectivity and temporality:

> [F]emale subjectivity would seem to be linked both to *cyclical* time (repetition) and to *monumental* time (eternity), at least in so far as both are ways of conceptualizing time from the perspective of motherhood and reproduction. The time of history, however, can be characterized as *linear* time: time as project, teleology, departure, progression and arrival. This linear time is also that of language considered as the enunciation of a sequence of words. (Introduction to 'Women's Time' 187)

Kristeva establishes the connection between the cycles of the body and the narration of the sentence. Thus, woman's narrative time is cyclical, while man's narrative time is ordered and finished. Problematizing sex as the causal link accounting for the difference in masculine and feminine narratives will provide a more complex reading of the origins of subjectivity in narrative. In *Villette*, temporality is disturbed, but this does not originate from the sex of the female protagonist; rather, it stems from woman's place in narrative plots. That is to say, providing Lucy Snowe with narrative agency will allow us to position her as disturbing the dynamic of a linear plot, thereby demolishing the accepted patterns of order and significance. Her homelessness in narrative plots is transferred to the reader; she does not want him or her to feel at ease in her narrative plot.

Lucy presents the reader with broken fragments of a story, intimating a fragmentation of narrative consciousness. The shift between the story of Paulina in the opening chapters to Lucy's story, and the shifting plot and character emphases throughout the text, attest to a model of subjectivity not based on the masculine model of arrival and departure. The collapse of temporal order in the telling of the self suggests a subjectivity not bound to conventional notions of order in autobiography. The present-tense narration demonstrates the continual making of the feminine self in narrative time which traditionally has sought to contain her.

Fredric Jameson writes of the postmodernist collapse of temporality, intimating that in postmodernist works often there is a difficulty in temporal organization, a 'problem of the form that time, temporality and the syntagmatic will be able to take in a culture increasingly dominated by space and spatial logic' (71). But time for women in autobiographical narratives has always presented a problem in that they have traditionally been positioned outside the time of narrative by their lack of access to the forms of narrative. For woman's autobiography in the nineteenth-century, there is, in a sense, no temporal model of a life; life has been traditionally in the home. As we have seen, plots for women in the eighteenth-century typically revolve around marriage and death, as Nancy K. Miller has pointed out. Lacking a model for a woman's life other than domestic consciousness, Lucy exhibits a problem with time in her autobiography.

Jameson goes on to elaborate a formulation of schizophrenia as it relates to temporality. He describes schizophrenia as a 'series of pure and unrelated presents in time' (72). Further, he explains a breakdown of temporality in which the 'present suddenly engulfs the subject with indescribable vividness, a materiality of perception properly overwhelming, which effectively dramatizes the power of the material – or better still, the literal – signifier in isolation' (73). By her narrative practice, Lucy snaps the links of meaning crucial to a complete ordering and understanding of the self. She creates an unrelated self in time. As a result, personal identity does not reside in the sentence.[16]

This idea is an important one for feminism. While the masculine subject has traditionally defined his being through time, through his access to the plots which mark his position in time, the feminine subject traditionally did not have access to this privileged location. Remaining outside of this placement of the subject's ordering his life in time, Brontë's model of subjectivity shows that any attempt to unify the self in time implies a masterful reading of the self which would fix it.

Women traditionally have been cordoned off in the time of masculine narratives; examples in *Villette* appear at the art gallery, where women's lives are reduced to stages in the series of portraits entitled 'La Vie d'une Femme,' which depict woman in a sequence of linear, fixed moments in time: she is first a 'Jeune Fille,' then a 'Mariée,' next, a 'Jeune Mère,' and finally a 'Veuve.' This series indicates that a woman's life is formally mapped for her; concurrently, she is doubly enclosed by the pictorial frame and the narrative frame of the names which mark her as following a prescribed course. Not possessing agency, she is relegated to names which describe her in relation to others: she is a married woman, a young mother, and a widow.

Lucy fragments temporality in *Villette*; that is the movement of the self through time, effecting a questioning of the composite formation of identity and memory. Outside of the time of history, and deprived in a certain sense of temporal consciousness (existence in time), woman in *Villette* does not occupy a space in time of the master narrator who presents a unified subject and story. Similarly, retrospection in narration implies a mastery of the past, a reading of it in a unilateral way. Retrospection involves translating the subject in time, but Lucy does not disentangle temporality for the reader.

Alienated from the sentence, which would bind her in time, Lucy writes an uncanny version of temporal perspective. She does not stay on the line of the sentence. Just as she relates her plot to a life boat in stormy waters, contrasting herself to the cruise ship sailing on calm waters, her sentences go off the course of narrative time. She inverts many of them, disrupting traditional order. 'Me she had forgotten' (82) is one example.[17] By the use of inversion, the text challenges modes of syntactic representation which focus on an ordering of the self through time. Her fluid narratorial gaze, which does not fix meaning, allows signification to spread out over a temporal continuum.

Lucy's text ends with present-tense narration; temporal energy reveals present possibilities. 'And now the three years are past: M. Emanuel's return is fixed. It is Autumn; he is to be with me ere the mists of November come. My school flourishes, my house is ready' (595). In the last paragraph of the novel, however, she relates in the past tense: 'Madame Beck prospered all the days of her life; so did Père Silas; Madame Walravens fulfilled her ninetieth year before she died. Farewell' (596). In the latter example, the characters are encased in the past tense, the sentence of time; but Lucy's present-tense narration suggests future possibilities. Beginning and ending her narration with characters other than herself, she suggests that she cannot be bound in a narratorial frame.

Not only does the text shatter the subject's temporality but it also fractures the movement in plot from equilibrium, disequilibrium, to equilibrium. Tzevan Todorov explains: 'An 'ideal' narrative begins with a stable situation which is disturbed by some power or force. There results a state of disequilibrium; by the action of a force directed in the opposite direction, the equilibrium is re-established' (111). But Lucy's text begins in a state of disequilibrium, on the radical disjunction between her 'I' and Paulina's, and ends on a note of disequilibrium: on the text's refusal to posit a definitive ending. The novel's embrace of disequilibrium suggests the unstable positioning of woman in narrative discourse; additionally, it also implies the shifting of the sign of the 'I.' Lucy will remain in a state of disequilibrium or flux.

We are now in the position to speculate on woman's narratives and the uncanny. If woman is by her place in the social order alienated from language, then necessarily her words will be alien and foreign to her. But this is not to be viewed negatively. Rather, woman can position herself through narrative as not accepting the placement which she has been assigned. In a sense, by breaking with narrative temporality, she undoes feminine sexuality and reveals it for what it is. She adopts consciously the radical discontinuity of the woman who will not be fixed in time. She acts the part, but her narrative meaning remains elsewhere. And the parts start to fragment, revealing an inanimate object. Lucy collapses a unified representation of herself. The *unheimlich* signifies the inability to attach meaning; the uncanny for woman's plots then revolves around woman crossing the threshold of the construction of feminine identity which has no fixed meaning.

Endnotes

1   See Jacobus and Crosby.
2   For a brief discussion of the uncanny, see Tanner, who claims, 'Lucy is everywhere not-at-home, and this constantly produces that feeling of the ... "uncanny" as described by Freud' (12).
3   For critiques of Freud's essay, see Todd, 'The Veiled Woman;' Cixous, 'Fiction;' Jones; and Hertz. Todd concentrates on what Freud has repressed in his text: 'The central figure of woman in many of his examples and the related theme of seeing and being seen' (521). Cixous focuses on the 'undecidable nature of all that touches the unheimliche' (526). She maintains that Freud fails in his attempt to write a categorical interpretation of 'The Sandman' as representing castration anxiety. Jones calls for an alternative reading of the uncanny – for 'a post-Freudian psychoanalytic account of 'Der Sandmann' which does less violence to Hoffmann's text than Freud's, does more justice to aggression and gives less prominence to sexuality' (98). Hertz in his insightful biographical reading of Freud's essay speculates on the triangular relations in Freud's life; namely, among Tausk, Salome, and Freud. This relationship influences his reading of the oedipal triangulation in 'The Sandman' among Coppelius, Nathanael, and Clara and among Coppola, Nathanael, and Olympia.
4   See *The Faerie Queene*, Book Two, for a related image of a woman being guided in a craft. Phaedria has a boat 'Withouten oare or pilot it to guide' (II.vi.3). Spenser writes:

> And running to her boat with outen ore,
> From the departing land it launched light,
> And after them did driue with all her power and might ... (II.xii.7–9)

Additionally, Tennyson's 'The Lady of Shalott' continues the image of the woman in a boat who does not navigate her own course:

> And as the boat-head wound along
> The willowy hills and fields among,
> They heard her singing her last song,
>   The Lady of Shalott.

5 Carlisle views Brontë's beginning the story with Paulina's life as an instance of Lucy's reticence; also, 'It illustrates what Lucy knows to be the basic structure of human relationships: emotional bonds are forged by the pressure of a woman's great need, and they are inevitably disrupted by 'fate' or a man's fickle indifference' (272). Nancy Sorkin Rabinowitz argues, however, that 'as she refuses to tell us what the beginning of her life was like, or how it ends for her, Lucy allows us to imagine that she has led the life of other women, the heroines of other novels' (250–51).

6 Jacobus writes: 'Paulina's grief – that of the abandoned child cast among strangers – has in any case already acted out Lucy's' (44).

7 Patricia S. Yaeger argues that 'early and late in *Villette*, Polly Home represents Lucy's sweet, immature, male-obsessed double' (20).

8 Susan Snaider Lanser discusses the historical practice of women authors adopting male pseudonyms. '[W]hen an authorial voice has represented itself as female, it has risked being (dis)qualified. It is possible that women's writing has carried fuller public authority when its voice has not been marked as female' (18). Similarly, Elaine Showalter argues that 'One of the many indications that this generation saw the will to write as a vocation in direct conflict with their status as women is the appearance of the male pseudonym' (19). Also, Brontë's letters reveal the stigma attached to the female name when she writes: '[W]e veiled our own names under those of Currer, Ellis and Acton Bell . . . because . . . we had a vague impression that authoresses are liable to be looked on with prejudice' (quoted in Gaskell 285–6). I agree completely with these views; however, I am interested in pointing out the doubleness that the name evokes in *Villette*.

9 In a letter, Brontë writes: 'I am not leniently disposed towards Miss Frost; from the beginning I never meant to appoint her lines in pleasant places' (Shorter 284).

10 See, for example, Drucilla Cornell, who writes: 'As Barbara Johnson reminds us, when we write of women everything is out of place, and it is precisely this displacement of gender difference, that potentially inheres in the writing of women, that is celebrated' (73).

11 Eve Kofofsky Sedgwick in her discussion of the veil in the gothic novel claims: 'It is in the insistence of this constitutive struggle, and the attenuated versions involving the veil and habit rather than the countenance itself, that the Gothic novel makes its most radical contribution to the development of character in fiction' (263).

12 On the ending, Rabinowitz argues: 'M. Paul has to die . . . not to destroy Lucy Snowe but to prevent her taking second place to him. If he were to come back, Brontë would not have succeeded in creating a new plot for a woman's life' (252). Similarly, Lawrence argues that 'Lucy succeeds as a headmistress and writer, in the space provided by Paul's absence' (99). While Litvak contends: 'Brontë . . . at once kills him off and brings him back alive, playing the game of *fort/da,* not only with this newly crowned monarch, but also, outrageously, with her own authoritarian father, who pressed her for a 'happy' ending' (489). Similarly, Jacobus claims that 'The entire novel, not just its ending, bears the marks of this compromise – between Victorian romance and the Romantic Imagination, between the realist novel and Gothicism' (54).

13 Janice Carlisle argues that Lucy 'ignores one of the prominent themes of midcentury autobiography by flatly refusing to acknowledge the cost of retrospection' (267); while Tony Tanner contends: 'Rather than summarize incidents from the comfortable security of her position as a retrospective writer, she re-creates the moment by moment anxiety or excitement or panic she experienced, thus drawing the reader into the incomplete experience itself rather than handing over a safely bound statement of it' (46).
14 One might very well argue that the historical present tense is a common usage in prose narrative. I take the tack, however, that Lucy's use of the historical present tense at certain moments of her narrative suggests a counter narrative to reading the self in time.
15 I mean to suggest here a fracturing of time, which is equated with schizophrenia. In *The Madwoman in the Attic,* Gilbert and Gubar discuss Lucy's 'schizophrenia' and point to the split between restraint and passion and reason and imagination in her narrative (403). As will become clear, I argue for the schizophrenic temporal perspective of Lucy's narrative.
16 See Frederick Jameson, who explains the construction of personal identity as it relates to the construction of the sentence:

> [P]ersonal identity is itself the effect of a certain temporal unification of past and future with the present before me; . . . such active temporal unification is itself a function of language, or better still of the sentence, as it moves along its hermeneutic circle through time. If we are unable to unify the past, present and future of the sentence, then we are similarly unable to unify the past, present and future of our own biographical experience or psychic life. (72)

> See Margot Peters' insightful study on Charlotte Brontë's style. She claims that Brontë's use of inversion bespeaks a 'taste for distortion, a certain contrariness, a delight in negativeness, and reversal that can be called perverse' (57). Other examples of Brontë's use of inversion in *Villette* are 'Some fearful hours went over me: indescribably was I torn, racked and oppressed in mind' (231) and 'In debt, however, I was not' (103).

Bibliography

Brontë, Charlotte. *Villette.* New York: Penguin, 1979.
Carlisle, Janice. 'The Face in the Mirror: *Villette* and the Conventions of Autobiography.' *Critical Essays on Charlotte Brontë.* Ed. Barbara Timm Gates. Boston: G. K. Hall and Co., 1990. 264–87.
Cixous, Helene. 'Fiction and its Phantoms: A Reading of Freud's *Das Unheimliche* (the "uncanny").' *New Literary History* 3 (Spring 1976): 525–48.
Cornell, Drucilla. *Transformations.* New York: Routledge, 1993.
Crosby, Christina. 'Charlotte Brontë's Haunted Text.' *Studies in English Literature* 24 (1984): 701–15.
Freud, Sigmund. 'The Uncanny.' *The Standard Edition of the Complete Psychological Works of Sigmund Freud,* Vol. XVII. Trans. James Strachey. London: The Hogarth Press, 1955.
Gaskell, Elizabeth. *The Life of Charlotte Brontë.* New York: Penguin, 1979.
Gilbert, Sandra M. and Gubar, Susan. *The Madwoman in the Attic: The Woman Writer and the Nineteenth Century Literary Imagination.* New Haven: Yale University Press, 1979.
Gusdorf, Georges. 'Conditions and Limits of Autobiography.' *Autobiography: Essays Theoretical and Critical.* Trans. James Olney. Ed. James Olney. Princeton: Princeton University Press, 1980.

Hertz, Neil. 'Freud and the Sandman.' *The End of the Line: Essays on Psychoanalysis and the Sublime.* New York: Columbia University Press, 1985. 97–121.
Hollander, Anne. *Seeing Through Clothes.* New York: The Viking Press, 1978.
Jacobus, Mary. 'The Buried Letter: Feminism and Romanticism in *Villette.*' *Women Writing and Writing about Women.* Ed. Mary Jacobus. New York: Barnes and Noble, 1979.
Jameson, Frederic. 'Postmodernism, or the Cultural Logic of Late Capitalism.' *New Left Review* 146 (July–August 1984): 53–92.
Jones, Malcolm V. '"Der Sandmann" and "the uncanny": A Sketch for an Alternative Approach.' *Paragraph* 7. (March 1986): 77–101.
Kristeva, Julia. 'Women's Time.' *The Kristeva Reader.* Ed. Toril Moi. New York: Columbia University Press, 1986.
Lanser, Susan Snaider. *Fictions of Authority: Women Writers and Narrative Voice.* Ithaca: Cornell, 1992.
Lawrence, Karen. 'The Cypher: Disclosure and Reticence in *Villette. Tradition and the Talents of Women.* Ed. Florence Howe. Chicago: University of Chicago Press, 1991.
Levesque, Claude. 'Autobiography.' In Jacques Derrida, *The Ear of the Other: Otobiography, Transference, Translation.* Trans. Peggy Kamuf. New York: Schocken, 1985.
Litvak, Joseph. 'Charlotte Brontë and the Scene of Instruction: Authority and Subversion in *Villette.*' *Nineteenth-Century Literature* 42 (March 1988): 467–89.
Miller, Nancy K. *The Heroine's Text: Readings in the French and English Novel, 1722–1782.* New York: Columbia University Press, 1980.
Pascal, Roy. *Design and Truth in Autobiography.* New York: Garland, 1985.
Peters, Margot. *Charlotte Bronte: Style in the Novel.* Madison: University of Wisconsin Press, 1973.
Rabinowitz, Nancy Sorkin. "Faithful Narrator' or 'Partial Eulogist': First-Person Narration in Brontë's *Villette.*' *Journal of Narrative Technique* 15 (Fall 1985): 244–55.
Rubenstein, Roberta. *Boundaries of the Self: Gender, Culture, Fiction.* Urbana and Chicago: University of Chicago Press, 1987.
Sedgwick, Eve Kosofsky. 'The Character in the Veil: Imagery of the Surface in the Gothic Novel.' *PMLA* 96 (255–70).
Shelley, Mary. *Frankenstein.* New York: Penguin, 1985.
Shorter, Clement. *The Brontë's: Life and Letters.* 2 vols. London: Hodder and Stoughton, 1908.
Showalter, Elaine. *A Literature of their Own: British Women Novelists from Bronte to Lessing.* Princeton: Princeton University Press, 1977.
Spenser, Edmund. *The Faerie Queene. The Complete Poetical Works of Edmund Spenser.* Boston: Cambridge, 1908.
Tanner, Tony. Introduction to *Villette.* New York: Penguin, 1979.
Tennyson, Alfred. *Selected Poetry of Tennyson*: New York: The Modern Library, 1951.
Todd, Jane Marie. 'The Veiled Woman in Freud's *"Das Unheimliche."*' *Signs* 11 (Spring 1986): 519–28.
Todorov, Tzvetan. *The Poetics of Prose.* Trans. Richard Howard. Ithaca: Cornell, 1977.
Yaeger, Patricia. 'Honey-Mad Women: Charlotte Brontë's Bilingual Heroines.' *Browning Institute Studies* 14 (1986): 11–35.

Chapter 5

Abjecting Freud: Masculinity, Maternity, and Perversion

Deborah Caslav Covino

The concept of the abject has come into prominence through Julia Kristeva's 1980 *Powers of Horror: An Essay on Abjection*. Briefly, the abject is the body of indefinite boundaries that excretes waste products and exudes fluids: feces, urine, pus, semen, vomit, and menstrual blood. The abject body horrifies because it disturbs the subject-object split upon which subjectivity seems to depend: Is my excrement I or other? My inside or my outside? An indication of my body's growth, or its decay? A sign of health, or contamination? Abjection as a verbal form refers to the casting off of the abject body with its vile contents, and threatening meanings.

Politicizers of the abject have extended Kristeva's concept beyond the personal body, to the social arena, viewing the racial other, the homosexual, and the woman as abject entities. A central contribution to this tendency is the *Abject Art* exhibition that appeared at the Whitney Museum of American Art in 1993, and associated abjection with fleshly scenes of waste, fragmentation, nudity, and dismemberment. The exhibition features what is arguably a companion piece to Kristeva's *Powers of Horror* – Judy Chicago's *Menstruation Bathroom* (1972) – as a definitive portrait of abjection (Figure 5.1). Confronting us with an overflowing mound of bloodied menstrual pads, thus placing its emphasis on the abject woman, the photograph shows us what is ordinarily trashed and forgotten.

Perhaps no individual in this century has been more responsible for the maintenance of the 'menstruation bathroom' as abject than Sigmund Freud, especially in his construction of an Oedipal conflict in which the body of woman is the odd man out.[1] Freud's theories of feminine sexuality serve to reinforce male difference from the castrated woman. Freud argues that boys, and later men, view the woman's vagina as a site of mutilation. The woman excluded from phallic pleasure, because of her hollow genital, is personally threatening because she embodies this dreaded and despised state of deprivation. In a brief essay on the Medusa's Head, Freud contends that the Medusa, a symbol of the castrated and castrating woman, does not just terrify men, but really acts as a reminder that men do not share the Medusa's bereft physical form: men become '*stiff* with

Figure 5.1 Judy Chicago, *Menstruation Bathroom*, installation from *Womanhouse*. © Judy Chicago, 1971.

terror' at the sight of the Medusa; the phallus grows hard in the face of (petrifying) womanhood ('Medusa's Head' *Works* 18.273).

In order to fully censure Freud's abjection of the female and the concepts of perversion it enfranchises, I turn to an early, famous piece of 20th-century abject art, Arshile Gorky's *The Artist and His Mother* (Figure 5.2). With reference to Kristeva's concept of the abject, I read Armenian-American Expressionist Gorky's art as a rebuke of Freudian Oedipal constructions of the mother, that posit her as a primary abject of the social and cultural orders. Gorky's later, abstract dreamscapes have provoked consideration of him as a painter of the unconscious, and *The Artist* remains a striking representation of mother-son relations, which interpreters have lent decided Freudian significance.

This is the case with Jack Ben-Levi's reading of Gorky's *Artist*, which is my touch point here both because it is a singular instance of sophisticated critical attention to the painting, and because it maintains the presence of a Freudian paradigm for social-sexual perversions even as it confronts the Freudian denigration of homoerotic love; thus, Ben-Levi remains on some level a Freudian masculinist. And, as I will propose more briefly, so does Kristeva. It is Kristeva, however, who also provides us with the critical vocabulary that allows us to read the plight of the feminine against Freudian models of perversion.

It was Freud's view that male identification with femininity, especially the maternal feminine, is a man's most loathsome fear, and that to hold such an identification is to engage in the worst of masculine perversions. In Freud's theories of sexuality, a woman is, in the male psyche, a horrifying castrator, a type of grotesque that registers male dread of the feminine. These ideas are part of an enduring misogynist history. Culturally and historically speaking, the mother's body has long been considered defiled, ruptured, and unclean. The Levitical taboos establish the birthing woman as impure, while ancient Greek medical theories posit her as a mutilated form (Laqueur 4–16). Indeed, Kristeva's *Powers of Horror* posits the mother's body as the entity, or form, in tension with which masculinity comprehends itself. The maternal body of blood and rupture, pain and expulsion is masculinity's *primary abject,* a site of both psychological repudiation and legal prohibition, as *the* body from which all cultural taboos – primitive and civilized – derive.

However, Kristeva's is not a fully constructionist analysis; that is, she allows instead for a 'natural' view of the status of women, in particular, the status of women as abject.[2] *Powers of Horror* correctly confesses the alliance of the abject and maternal grotesque, but there is for Kristeva, as there was for Freud, good psychological and biological cause for repudiating the mother: it is to escape the horrible vacuity of the womb, and to achieve mature subjectivity through entry into the symbolic, an order of words, reason, and conduct that is the sole jurisdiction of the masculine. By espousing the constructionist view, I do not deny the

Figure 5.2 Arshile Gorky, *The Artist and His Mother.* Ailsa Mellon Bruce Fund. © 2000 Board of Trustees, National Gallery of Art, Washington.

widespread horror of the abject body – a body of indefinite boundaries and waste products – about which Kristeva speaks, but observe that the common anxiety about physical threat, dissolution, and death is actively projected, by prevailing discourses, onto the bodies of women, rather than inherent to those bodies. Within a Freudian paradigm, then, men urgently construct themselves as other than the cavernous, castrating, expelling, birthing, nursing body of the mother, the body out of control.

Begun in 1926 and finished in 1934, Gorky's *Artist*, a striking representation of mother-son relations, is based on a 1912 photograph of Gorky and his mother, intended for Gorky's father, who had left the family in Armenia and emigrated to America to avoid conscription into the Turkish army. The painting and the photograph are very different from one another.[3] In the painting, the mother is decidedly more sour, more angry, the boy more puzzled, his body curving away rather than touching hers, his tender gift of flowers disintegrating into indecipherability. Under the gaze of the 'absent' father, the mother is disappearing angrily into a flat whiteness, while the boy's orientation is uncertain: he seems both drawn toward the mother and shrinking from her.

In order to address the family dynamics in this painting, and elucidate the nature and limits of masculine perversion, I unfold Gorky's vision of abject femininity against the background of Freud's theory of the Oedipus complex: the painting tells the melancholy story of a lost mother, abjected from the Freudian Oedipal triangle that locates male maturity in the repudiation of her and the embrace of the father; and of a son struggling under the gaze of the father to determine the nature of his bond to his mother. I accept Jack Ben-Levi's proposition that Gorky's painting suggests a 'troubled Oedipal triangle,' yet I do not feature, with him, the boy's repressed homoerotic desire for the father. While I do not deny that this content may exist, nor even that his theory may complement my own, I nonetheless occasionally contend with Ben-Levi. Viewing the boy's wary and pensive expression as a symptom of spoiled affection for the mother, I foreground resistance toward, rather than desire for, the father. My reading – which holds that Gorky's painting depicts a child unhappily initiated into a world of abjected and distressed women – seeks to disturb rather than to uphold male bonding fantasies, and recommends the bonding of sons to mothers. To that extent, I favor reconstituting masculinity as (what Freud would have considered) 'perversion.' The reader should bear in mind that what follows does not insist on a particular reading of Gorky's painting; instead, it is a self-conscious move to hold Freud's theories in conspiracy with a certain set of cultural significances oppressive to women. In this sense, my reading acts as a strategic complaint.

The Artist and His Mother

Lips pursed, nostrils flaring, eyes so wide and bulging that the irises imbue the whites, the mother in Gorky's painting affronts us with a prodigious face. The woman in the 1912 photograph is not so defiant, nor so angry; a bit impatient, irritable perhaps, but in a more vulnerable way. Where Ben-Levi sees in the painted mother's face, 'self-certainty,' 'resoluteness,' and 'intense authority' (17), I see disturbance, displeasure, defensiveness: symptoms of psychic unease. Why, if the son and mother pose to reconnect with the father, does the mother look so grim? While it is true that solemnity is a trope of early posed photographs, it is also true that Gorky intensifies this solemnity years later.[4] Does the later, painted portrayal reveal something about the artist's changed perception of the woman attending him in the photograph? In 1918, six years after the photograph, Gorky's mother died of starvation in her son's arms. Had she grown more incensed in his view, between the time of the photograph and the painting's inception? Perhaps in retrospect of her sad and ultimately lethal abandonment by the father? Perhaps her fate had become more offensively real to the son once he had reunited with the father in America, following the mother's death.[5] These are questions that remain unaddressed in Gorky scholarship, but our mentioning them here serves to posit a likeness between the photographed mother and that of her painted sister: within the psychic organization of Freud's Oedipal triangle, both women are abject.

We are drawn into the painting by certain Freudian elements – a boy agitated, tenderly susceptible, under the simultaneous watch of mother and father – and so we are prompted to consult the theory that attends our vision. The Oedipal period, as constructed by Freud, is one in which lost objects play an important role. In the *Interpretation of Dreams* (*Works* 4–5), Freud argues that the young boy, pricked by nascent genital stirrings, unleashes his erotic impulses on the mother, making her an object of desire. In several later works, Freud develops his theory of the Oedipus complex, arguing that the complex is resolved through castration anxiety.[6] Erotic attachment to the mother is eventually overcome, when the boy discovers that the mother is 'castrated,' and begins to associate the possibility of his own emasculation with his erotic attachment to her.[7]

According to Freud, a general horror and disdain for the castrated woman fosters the child's need to separate himself from the mother, who belongs to this class of emasculated persons. The boy in the throes of Oedipal love has two choices: he may either spurn the father in favor of the mother, or opt to be bonded to him in enamored identification. Desire for the mother means exile from the community of men, a form of social emasculation. In *Totem and Taboo* (*Works* 13), Freud writes an etiologic tale of patricide, incest, and the first social prohibition, which dramatizes his theory of the Oedipus Complex: in the beginning, there was a violent and jealous father who hoarded all the females to himself, and drove away his growing sons. One day, the excluded and resentful brothers murdered the father, and took his women to themselves, including their own mothers. After a time, the sons were overcome with emotion: grief for the absent father, and remorse and guilt for the crime committed against him. Such emotion, however, is self-interested. Hostility against the father was displaced by the will to ensure personal safety: 'In thus guaranteeing one another's lives, the brothers were declaring that no one of them must be treated by another as their father was treated by them all jointly. They were precluding the possibility of a repetition of their father's fate' (146). *Totem and Taboo* explains, in fleshly terms, the stakes of son to father solidarity: both life and limb are at stake so long as the boy remains erotically attached to the mother. In response, the sons renounced their villainy, condemned patricide, and denied themselves the available women.

In addition to ensuring personal safety, the male-to-male bond also serves to reinforce male difference from the castrated woman. Freud argues that boys, and later men, view the 'castrated woman' as a mutilated creature, excepted, because of her hollow genital, from phallic pleasure, and personally threatening because she embodies this dreaded and despised state of deprivation.[8] The boy, then, abandons the taboo and abhorrent mother/woman, and substitutes identification with the father.

Ben-Levi (consulting Freud and Judith Butler) features the father, not the mother, as the boy's lost object.[9] He argues that heterosexual identity cannot entirely eliminate traces of an earlier bisexual history. Gorky's painting, he says, remembers this forgotten story of repression. Ben-Levi sees a boy who manifests ambivalence toward a paternal gaze that represents both the threat and the appeal of a forbidden and forgotten love (25). Persuading us to see in the boy a melancholia of sexual identity, in which the absent father names the boy's loss, his repression of an originary homoeroticism, Ben-Levi underwrites the Oedipus complex's stipulation that the mother is a means – through her abjection – of producing and reproducing male bonding rights. Observing that the artist is inscribed in the painting on two levels, as son and as painter, he asks, *Did [Gorky] want to be his own father?* (22). This question not only implicates Freud's claim that solidarity with the father is a normal and necessary part of the Oedipus complex's dissolution, but also emphasizes the father-son bond to the virtual exclusion of the mother-son bond, though the latter is the conspicuous subject of the painting.

I, too, read the painting with reference to lost objects, but argue that the boy's 'perversion' is to be understood with reference to the mother. For the post-Oedipal boy, both parents are, in a sense, left behind. While I acknowledge that the heterosexual institution militates against originary bisexuality, I fail to see that this content is foregrounded in Gorky's art. Ben-Levi notes that, depending on whether we identify with mother or father, the mother either comes forward or recedes. If the mother recedes, then 'a hint of awakening eroticism' for the father is revealed on the part of the now foregrounded boy (20).[10] Why, I would ask, does the boy emerge only when the *mother* recedes? Why not when the *father* recedes, absenting himself again from the family circle? According to Freud's theory of the 'complete' Oedipus complex, discussed in *Totem and Taboo* and *The Ego and the Id* (*Works* 19.3–68), a child's orientation to both parents is ambivalent, because of original bisexuality. But in this theory of double ambivalences, a boy's negative feelings are destined to fall more to the side of the mother (the castrated woman), positive feelings to the father, in whom the boy finds his own likeness. The loss of original love for which figure, then, remains the more unresolved? That for the father, with whom the boy ultimately reunites? Or that for the mother, the permanent scapegoat for the boy's lost pleasures and freedoms? Ben-Levi says that mother and son are complicit in a move to abject the father from the family triangle (19). A problem with this reading is that the son is not complicit with the mother. On the contrary, he appears divided from her. Clutching the flowers to himself, he mostly keeps his distance, holding one arm tense, curved away, inclining one foot outward (toward the door?) Mother and son are a kind of unit, confined side by side within the father's field of vision, but the boy's orientation to the mother, as he positions himself within the frame, is strained, resistant, self-conscious. Thus, childish ambivalence toward a *mother* is the foregrounded subject of Gorky's painting; ambivalence toward the father, toward the 'camera,' is also its subject, but this content remains behind the scenes, more fully repressed. To Ben-Levi's observations concerning repressed male homoeroticism, I would add, in consultation with Freud, that males who are bonded to the father also repress their identification with femininity. I have no interest in maintaining heterosexual relations here, but what is conspicuous in the painting is not the boy's relation to a beloved father, but to the presence that gazes upon him and his mother. In this presence, the boy is reticent, uncomfortable, the fingers of the hand nearest his mother disappearing. Also, the flowers lose their definition. *Do they wilt?* The boy is, as Ben-Levi says, guarded, but I would add, with immediate reference to the mother. He perceives some threat, but what this threat is remains to be discovered.

In the photograph, who fixes the subjects in the camera's field of vision? To suit his reading, and despite his admitted awareness of evidence to the contrary,[11] Ben-Levi offers an interpretive 'fantasy,' in which the father doubles as photographer, and the setting is the family home. This forced construction of an Oedipal triangle in which all members are literally present requires Ben-Levi's wrenching of the photograph's evidence; he states, for instance, that the mother and son look casual, and that the scene has the marks of an impromptu event, setting aside the fact that, as Spender notes, 'there was nothing casual about a portrait photograph in those days' (29). However, Ben-Levi does allow us to posit the roles of home and father more responsibly. The photo is a piece of 'home,' sent to the departed father; and, in a motivational sense, the father is the 'photographer,' the one who calls the shot, the one who constructs the scene. Ben-Levi says that mother and son disregard the intrusion of the camera's (father's) eye (19), but the painting (if not the photograph) shows us that the opposite is the case: they are fully aware of this eye, positioning themselves in relation to it with intense regard. Mother and son are obsessed with this eye: she meets its inspection squarely, her own eyes fixed exactingly on her observer; she communicates her displeasure to him; the boy looks partially away, evading the onlooker's gaze, yet remains aware of it.

Perhaps the boy in the painting has not fully left the pre-Oedipal 'womb' of non-distinction between self and mother. Restraint from her had been less imperative lately, in the father's absence. And now, with the father's 'return,' he is prompted to ask again, 'How do I orient my body? Toward my mother, or away?' The painting, commenced some twelve years after the photograph, is itself a kind of 'photograph': of the unconscious content of its original. I am reminded that Freud spoke of Shakespeare in his 15 October 1897 letter to Fliess in the same way that I now speak of Gorky. He said that, 'his [Shakespeare's] unconscious understood the unconscious of his hero [Hamlet]' *Works* 1.265). Thus, Gorky (unconsciously?) recapitulates an unconscious moment in the boy's earlier history of son-to-mother relations, a time, perhaps late in the Oedipal phase, when the boy had loitered between the abjection he thought he must enact, and the love he first felt for her. At age eight, the boy is, in Freud's terms, in his 'latency period,' which means not only that he has supposedly placed physical experimentation and erotic cathexes on hold,[12] but also that he has already internalized the demand that he abject the mother. But could it be that, in the father's absence, desire for the mother has been rekindled?[13] This primal splitting – between attachment and repudiation – we see reconstituted, then, as the father makes his reentry into the picture. Under the watchful eye of the paternal gaze, self-consciousness, the boy's sense that he courts an illicit desire, is reborn. Gorky freezes this Oedipal moment.

Freud had theorized that the resolution of the boy's complex is optimal. The boy achieves a strong sense of moral justice from the threat of punishing castration, as well as a salutary bond with the rest of the male population, with the father at its head.[14] Castration anxiety – the dread of the abject woman – serves him well in his goal to realize his manhood. Ben-Levi is not wrong to suggest that this son-father bond has an element of homosexuality in it. The salutary effect for the son, of bonding with the father, is primarily the son's inscription into the ranks of the brotherhood, a membership whose benefits include male priority over the female in both political and physical terms. While it may be the case that entry into the heterosexual order diminishes the boy's bisexual range, it is also the case that this change accords him many compensations, whose affirmative properties we have been listing.

The boy's erotic split from the mother, however, presents him with a complexity that is masked by Freud's celebration of the boy's healthy outcome. On the one hand, he is compelled by the heterosexual order to abject the mother; on the other hand, this same order demands that he reclaim her in the form of a new woman, to whom erotic attachment is permissible. Freud explains, in *The Ego and the Id*, that the boy must lose the object (the mother), but keep the aim (mature sexual desire for women). The object-aim theory observes that, when objects of desire are thwarted, substitutes will be supplied. At first, and in some ways permanently, this substitute will be the father; however, specifically sexual cathexis is to be transferred, following the latency period, to a woman who is not the boy's mother. The pertinent question is whether one can ever really give up the object so long as one preserves the aim. According to Freud himself, the answer is no. In 'Female Sexuality' (*Works* 21.223–46), he claims that the boy's rejection of the mother is extended to all later female relations: '[L]eft over in men from the influence of the Oedipus complex is a certain amount of disparagement in their attitude towards women, whom they regard as being castrated' (228). Or, as Gregory Zilboorg puts it, this disparagement is 'also directed against the very woman that man approaches sexually' (91). Because the boy cannot transfer his desire to another woman without some residue of the repudiating relation remaining, abjection of (the body of) the mother remains incomplete. Love displaced by fear and disdain will be always a future part of his relations with other women; feelings for the original object are conveyed into the new desire.[15] In a sense, then, the heterosexual male re-embraces 'the mother' each time he attaches erotic interest to a woman. Because he reclaims the repudiated object – in effect repossessing her each time he takes her body back into his own – he lives in a perpetual state of abortive abjection.[16] And, not immaterially: since the reincorporated woman is a castrated woman, he is faced with the titanic contradiction of having to love what he (consciously or unconsciously) knows to be unlovable. The post-Oedipal (heterosexual) male, then, undergoes a kind of psychic rupture, in which he must abject woman only in order to love her again.

We may read the symptoms of this bifurcation in the bodies of Gorky's subjects: 'castration anxiety' is manifest in the boy as bodily equivocation. Head, shoulders, arms, and feet all atilt, he vacillates (in the presence of the father) between the maternal and paternal sites of identification. The mother, by contrast, seems fixed in place. Ben-Levi rightly points out that the boy's space is the more three-dimensional. I propose that this ambivalence ultimately redeems him, that his fuller dimension is the physical expression – the symptom – of his assumption that his own fate may be as yet undecided. His range of motion sets him apart from the mother's unyielding form. She is a figure of lost dimension. Her fixedness is an expression of the damnable nature of her maternal situation. She registers, through physical stasis, the unchangeability of her fate: to be produced and reproduced, in the arena of both familial and social gender relations as one of only two possible women; either she is the nurturing, asexual 'good mother,' or the whorishly sexual woman, who incites male sexual longing, and onto whom men displace their sexual anxiety. In this connection, Freud's choice of the Medusa as the image of womanhood is revealing: the object of male desire and horror both, she reflects Freud's own bifurcated orientation toward women. If women are robbed of their three-dimensional identity by unfavorable characterizations of their sex and subjectivity, such as we find in Freud, then we might expect to see the psychic products of their abjection recorded in their faces, bodies, gestures. The mother has not the luxury of the boy's tenderness, his contemplative attitude. Her permanent inscription as the castrated woman (body of horror, body without desire) is read in the resolute pique of her face. Her own disappearing hands convey the depth of her loss: *do not touch*, they say.[17] Gorky's mother is not a woman blockading a boy's yearning for his father. She is mourning a son whom she will soon have to abandon to the paternal order. She is angry, because her son will be compelled to abject her from the family triangle of affections.

There appear varieties of confrontation with the father in Gorky's work. Besides the son's ambivalence and the mother's pique, we might consider the artist's own orientation toward this father. Gorky dedicates *The Artist and His Mother* not to his mother, but to his father. The dedication, then, is a kind of turning *toward* the father, though not a sentimental turning, but an ironic one instead. Gorky – the son, the artist – did not get along well with his father once the two were reunited in America. Gorky and his mother were subjected to much suffering – fear of genocide by the Turks, hunger, displacement – after the father's departure. The artistic capability that Gorky's mother had supported and nurtured in her son went unappreciated by his father, who wanted Gorky to take up some more practical, reliable work.[18] That the painting is, however, a sentimental dedication to the mother is supported by a number of historians. Jim Jordan, for example, asserts that the painting was 'to memorialize forever the beautiful mother, Lady Shushanik, who died of starvation in the young Gorky's arms in 1919' (53). Melvin Lader argues that her untimely death had made her something of a martyr in Gorky's mind, and suggests that the artist took the subject of the Virgin with attendant figures as his model for the painting (1984, 101). Finally, in several letters to his sister Vartoosh, Gorky extols the late Lady Shushanik's artistic sensibility, referring to her in one particularly reverential correspondence as the 'queen of the aesthetic domain' (2 November 1946; Mooradian 299). Because the painting enhances the 1912 photograph, amplifying the mother's irritability and the son's unease, I understand Gorky's dedication of it to his father as an effort to show him the ordeal of the Oedipal asylum. Lader supposes that when Gorky encountered again the photograph in America, 'it must have rekindled his already strong feelings for his deceased mother and revived memories of the hardships the 'fatherless' Adoian family had endured' (97). By formally dedicating the painting to his father, then, Gorky invites his attention to the disturbing content of the work. It is as if he says, 'Look on us. See what you are implicated in.' Ben-Levi argues that the painting places the father's *absence* under critique:

> Gorky's painting never stops dwelling on an interminable antagonism between mother and son. The very process of struggle between them counteracts the repressive closure by which the battle could be finished and forgotten. No father is in sight to facilitate such an ending; his absence may be the painting's most important point after all. (30)

Besides vilifying the mother as the obstacle to Oedipal closure, this interpretation buttresses Freud's contention that the father figure must be the desirable and desired one, the valued object, whose absence generates a longing that Freud associates, in *The Ego and the Id*, with 'the higher nature of man' responsible for the birth of religion, morality, sociality, goodness, sublimation, and material production (35). But if desire for the *father* brings out all that is best in us, then what of *mother*-longing? Under Freud's paternalist interpretation, it is *explicitly* debased, made perverse; in Ben-Levi's *implicitly* so. Gorky's painting shows us this debasement. The boy in the painting shrinks from his mother not because he perceives her anger, but because he knows he can do nothing to appease it. *The Artist and His Mother* may be read as the artist's way of reversing these events, of appeasing the dead mother by witnessing her fate. It is, then, an icon not of love, but of grievance. Gorky materializes an antagonism between mother and son not because the father is departed, but because he has come to call.

Kristeva and/against Freud

As Kristeva's work on abjection shows, there can be no compelling theory of womanhood that does not confront abjection in general, and the abject mother in particular. Saying this, I want to note that Kristeva is subtly complicit with Freud in her connection of mature subjectivity with the repudiation of the mother's body:

> [T]he symbolic light that a third party, eventually the father, can contribute helps the future subject, the more so if it happens to be endowed with a robust supply of energy drive, in pursuing a reluctant struggle against what, having been the mother, will turn into an abject. (*Powers* 13)

At the same time that she diminishes, even degrades, the role of the mother in the subject's psycho-emotional development, Kristeva posits the mother's body as the residual *chora* in the psyche that can disrupt the symbolic order:

> Let us ... not speak of primacy but of the instability of the symbolic function in its most significant aspect – the prohibition placed on the maternal body (as defense against auto eroticism and incest taboo). Here, drives hold sway and constitute a strange space that I shall name, after Plato (*Timaeus* 48–53), a *chora*, a receptacle. (*Powers* 14)

Here, the early intimacy between mother and child is productive of a heterogeneous, biologically-driven language, a desirable alternative to the symbolic order, with its tendencies toward structure and regulation, and its distaste for the body.

Ambivalence toward the mother notwithstanding, the power of Kristeva's abjection remains as a critical lens revealing the horror of the dissipating body. Yet we note that because Kristeva does not insist upon dispelling the symbolic status of the father figure, she does not fully disallow the reading of sons and mothers that Freud enfranchises. Kristeva too, then, is partly subject to our general caution about the positing of psychological origins and drives that maintain exclusive social relations: As long as the heterosexual decree that males reject the feminine remains in place, male-to-female sexuality will remain an alternative kind of perversion: an ineffectual effort to 'love' the refused other.

Endnotes

1. Karen Horney is perhaps Freud's most powerful early critic. Her work repeatedly points out the ways in which Freud roots his psychology of desire in anatomy and biology, rather than in the cultural dichotomy that devalues the feminine maternal and idealizes the masculine paternal (see especially 'Response to Freud,' from *New Ways in Psychoanalysis*). Embracing Horney's basic premise that biology and psychology are never separate from cultural constructions of the body, and in concert with the more current follow-ups to this position (e.g., Butler, Cixous, Deleuze and Guattari, Haraway, Irigaray, Lacan, and, arguably, Kristeva), I view Freud's theory as a cultural artifact that both produces and reproduces the symptoms it describes. In this position, I argue as a body critic who reads Freud's myth as a *grammar*, rather than an *anatomy* of fear and desire.
2. Kristeva's ambivalence about the abject status of women in general, and mothers in particular, has concerned some feminists, who view her penchant for appreciating male literary artists as an additional retreat from solidarity with women. See especially Grosz 66–68, 78.
3. The photograph is reprinted in Spender, 29. The Gorky estate would not grant permission for reproduction of the photograph for this essay.
4. Besides a chalk drawing, another version of the painting exists. It is thought to have been completed in 1936, and is owned by the National Gallery of Art. Most scholars agree that the Whitney version is the authoritative one, however, given its greater aesthetic resolve (Lader 97).
5. As Stephen Spender notes, Gorky's mother died as she was dictating a letter to his father, reiterating 'her wish never to leave Armenia' (47). Once he settled in America, Gorky remained estranged from his father, never telling his immediate family or friends that his father was alive (Spender 338).

6   See, for instance, 'The Dissolution of the Oedipus Complex' (*Works* 19.173–182), 'Some Psychical Consequences of the Anatomical Distinction Between the Sexes' (19.248–60), and 'The Infantile Genital Organization' (19.141–48).
7   In 'On the Sexual Theories of Children' (*Works* 9.205–26), Freud argues that the fear of castration is conditioned not only by verbal threats from parents who discover their sons engaging in masturbatory play, but also, in large part, by the boy's discovery that castration seems to have been actually carried out on members of the female sex.
8   See especially, 'Some Psychical Consequences of the Anatomical Distinction Between the Sexes.'
9   In *Feminism and Psychoanalytic Theory*, Nancy Chodorow argues that the father's primacy and over-value is rooted in the fact that he has traditionally been 'absent,' removed from the immediate familial space far more often than the mother, whose presence tends the domestic scene with greater constancy (71–2). Because the young child comes to know the missing father primarily in a fantasy-relation, the child tends to idealize him, associating him with the virtues of freedom and autonomy. The mother, who regularly attends the child in the home, does not come to inhabit as affirmative or opulent a place in the child's psychic life. Chodorow's position is a valuable alternative to biological theories that feature the mother's castrated or castrating body as the source of her rejection.
10 This eroticism supposedly manifests itself in the satisfied humor of the boy's upturned mouth. But the boy's mouth is not satisfied, or mischievous (if that is lust's attendant impulse). Scarcely upturned, it is solemn, staid, unflinching, even dissatisfied and disappointed. I, too, see both unresolved loss and ambivalence in Gorky's boy, but not mainly, or even necessarily, with reference to the father.
11 The photo was taken at a studio in Van, during the father's absence (Jordan and Goldwater 51; Spender 28-9).
12 See 'Infantile Sexuality: The Period of Sexual Latency in Childhood' *Three Essays*, in *Works* 7.
13 Perhaps we should qualify the boy's 'love' here. Irving Crain has effectively argued that Freud consistently conflates love and sex, so that 'incest' is imputed to the child who simply wants personal intimacy with a parent. Crain points out that this conflation functions to sexualize women. Indeed, we might ask Freud why the son's identification with the mother is defined as 'incestuous,' but his identification with the father not. (On this score, Sophocles' play bears remarking in that Oedipus never knew his mother as mother. Jocasta was neither comfort-giver, nor nutritive body for the child Oedipus. We might ask whether this is the play's way of sublimating content that its audience would have found even more scandalous or repulsive. Perhaps Oedipus' self-inflicted 'castration' would have been the more cathartic had Oedipus known Jocasta as mother.) The mother may be an object of attachment for the young boy simply because she is his source of comfort and pleasure. Freud had theorized the affection in a literally sexual way, arguing that the boy actually wants to give his mother a baby; and that he comes to fear her body because her vagina is too large for his tiny penis. But Freud does not consider whether, instead, the boy only wants to possess her intimately, to have her nurturing attentions all to himself, without the interference or competition of the father. In that reading, the mother need not be a site of copulative cathexis. My reading of Gorky is not a recall of the incest taboo; instead, it is a story of thwarted desire for the feminine.
14 Freud devalues the girl's resolution: since, for her, castration is not a threat, but an accomplished fact, she does not develop a strong sense of justice, but is destined, instead, to a life of low self-esteem, and envy of the male. See especially, 'Some Psychic Consequences of the Anatomical Distinction Between the Sexes,' and 'Femininity,' in *New Introductory*

Lectures on Psychoanalysis (*Works* 22.112–35). I do not critique this misogynist reading here, not only because much effort in this direction has already been expended by other feminists (see especially Miller, Chodorow), but also because it is the boy's resolution that is my primary interest here.

15 The girl has no such contradiction to negotiate. Her object of desire has no negative qualities associated with his identity. The father is wholly *good*, and wanted by all members of the Oedipal family.

16 In 'Mourning and Melancholia' (*Works* 14.237–60), and *The Ego and the Id*, Freud argues that the 'lost object' is always introjected back into the ego, and, in a sense then, rediscovered within the system.

17 With my critique of the male-male bond, I do not mean to suggest that male homosexual practice is misogynist. Freud proposes this, arguing in 'Some Psychical Consequences of the Anatomical Distinction Between the Sexes' for example, that the woman's castrated body makes her an objectionable sex partner for some men, and thus prompts them to homosexuality (157). Freud's ridiculous theory that the homosexual man seeks other men with whom to copulate that remind him of *women with penises* follows from his inability to imagine a sexuality that was not founded on dichotomously gendered sex roles, and corresponding body parts. The homoeroticism that I critique here is specifically that directed by an immature male toward an empowered father figure.

18 Spender offers the most recent complete account of Gorky's early experience in Armenia.

Bibliography

Abject Art: Desire and Repulsion in American Art. New York: Whitney Museum, 1993.
Ben-Levi, Jack. 'A Sadomasochistic Drama in an Age of Traditional Family Values.' *Abject Art: Desire and Repulsion in American Art*. New York: Whitney Museum, 1993. 16–31.
Butler, Judith. *Gender Trouble: Feminism and the Subversion of Identity*. New York: Routledge, 1990.
Chicago, Judy. *Menstruation Bathroom*. Whitney Museum, New York.
Chodorow, Nancy J. *Feminism and Psychoanalytic Theory*. New Haven: Yale UP, 1989.
Cixous, Helene. 'The Laugh of the Medusa. *Signs I* (Summer 1976). Rpt. *Critical Theory Since 1965*. Ed. Hazard Adams and Leroy Searle. Tallahassee: Florida State UP, 1986. 309–21.
Crain, Irving J., M.D. 'The Origin of Love.' *Women and Psychoanalysis: Contributions to New Theory and Therapy*. Ed. Jean Baker Miller, M.D. New York: Brunner/Mazel, 1973. 301–10.
Deleuze, Gilles and Felix Guattari. *Anti-Oedipus: Capitalism and Schizophrenia*. Trans. Robert Hurley, Mark Seem, and Helen R. Lane. Minneapolis: U of Minnesota P, 1983.
Freud, Sigmund. *The Standard Edition of the Complete Works of Sigmund Freud*. Vols. 1–23. Trans. James Strachey. London: Hogarth, 1981.
Gorky, Arshile. *The Artist and His Mother*. Whitney Museum, New York.
Grosz, Elizabeth. *Sexual Subversions*. Boston: Allen and Unwin, 1989.
Haraway, Donna. *Simians, Cyborgs, and Women: The Reinvention of Nature*. New York: Routledge, 1991.
Horney, Karen. *New Ways in Psychoanalysis*. New York: Norton, 1939.
Houser, Craig. 'I, Abject.' *Abject Art: Desire and Repulsion in American Art*. New York: Whitney Museum, 1993. 85–101.
Irigaray, Luce. *Speculum of the Other Woman*. New York: Cornell UP, 1985.

Jordan, Jim M. and Robert Goldwater. *The Paintings of Arshile Gorky: A Critical Catalogue*. New York: New York UP, 1982.

Kristeva, Julia. *Powers of Horror: An Essay on Abjection*. Trans. Leon Roudiez. New York: Columbia UP, 1982.

Lacan, Jacques. *Ecrits*. Trans. Alan Sheridan. New York: Norton, 1977.

—— *The Four Fundamental Concepts of Psychoanalysis*. Ed. Jacques-Alain Miller. Trans. Alan Sheridan. New York: Norton, 1981.

Lader, Melvin P. 'Arshile Gorky's *The Artist and His Mother*: Further Study of its Evolution, Sources, and Meaning.' *Arts Magazine* 58 (January 1984): 96–104.

—— *Arshile Gorky*. New York: Abbeville Press, 1985.

Laqueur, Thomas. 'Orgasm, Generation, and the Politics of Reproductive Biology.' *The Making of the Modern Body: Sexuality and Society in the Nineteenth Century*. Catherine Gallagher and Thomas Laqueur, eds. Berkeley: U of California P, 1987: 1–41.

Miller, Jean Baker, M.D. *Women and Psychoanalysis: Contributions to New Theory and Therapy*. New York: Brunner/Mazel, 1973.

Mooradian, Karlen. *Arshile Gorky Adoian*. Chicago: Gilgamesh, 1978.

Spender, Matthew. *From A High Place: A Life of Arshile Gorky*. New York: Knopf, 1999.

Zilboorg, Gregory, M.D. 'Masculine and Feminine: Some Biological and Cultural Aspects.' *Psychoanalysis and Women: Contributions to New Theory and Therapy*. Ed. Jean Baker Miller, M.D. New York: Brunner/Mazel, 1973. 83–114.

Chapter 6

The Gaze and its Specular Perversions: Marcel Duchamp's *Étant donnés**

Ernestine Daubner

> [Fetishism] is the most semiotic of perversions. It does not want its forms to be overlooked but to be gloried in. This is, of course, a ruse to distract the eye and the mind from something that needs to be covered up. And this is also its weakness.
> (Laura Mulvey, *Fetishism and Curiosity* xiv)

Commonly called *Étant donnés*,[1] Marcel Duchamp's last artwork is a complex mixed-media installation constructed in total secrecy during the last twenty years of his life.[2] Prior to his death in 1968, this avant-garde artist left strict directives for what would be the posthumous reconstruction of his clandestine work in the Philadelphia Museum of Art. He stipulated that the installation of *Étant donnés* in this permanent venue receive no press and that no photograph be permitted of the interior tableau for a period of fifteen years. Because of this strange demand, Duchamp's last *magnum opus* remained enveloped in an aura of invisibility for nearly two decades, presenting viewers with the possibility of inadvertently stumbling upon it. Such a surprise encounter with *Étant donnés*, I have come to realize, serves an express purpose: to entrap viewers within its boundaries, and so engaging them in its specular games.

Having myself fallen into Duchamp's trap,[3] I have come to recognize that the games played out in *Étant donnés* are, in effect, specular perversions, which are subversive and transgressive, as well as resolutely regressive. Now with the advantage of a certain rational distance, I comprehend how the regressive specular perversions provide the greatest challenge, and the most significant insights. But I am getting ahead of myself here. Let me backtrack for a moment.

Walking, for the first time, through the Duchamp room in the Philadelphia Museum of Art[4] and accidentally coming across *Étant donnés*, without the prior benefit (or drawback) of a descriptive text and photographic documentation is an unsettling experience. Now, standing here, again, at the entrance of the small chamber where this enigmatic work is housed, I gaze at another viewer looking at it, and I think back and recollect my own first impressions . . .

I note that this is quite an unremarkable room, empty except for a stuccoed wall at the far end not immediately seen from the entrance. In the center of this wall, there is a wooden door, weathered by time, like a dilapidated old barn door. It is set in an arched frame of recycled bricks. Such a quaint object strikes me as totally out of place here. It does not conform to my idea of the Duchampian oeuvre.[5] Curious, I read the label on the outside wall of the gallery, noting the odd cryptic title: *Étant donnés: No. 1 la chute d'eau, No. 2 le gaz d'éclairage (Given: 1. The Waterfall, 2. The Illuminating Gas).*

Approaching the door, I notice that it is sealed shut. Then, observing a patina around two apertures in the wooden planks, at eye level, I realize that I am meant to look through these openings – and so I do. Instantly, in reflex action, I look away. Quickly glancing behind me, I am relieved to see that no one else is present in the room. No one has seen me staring through these peepholes.[6] It is at this exact moment that I begin to sense Duchamp's presence here. He appears to be quietly laughing, amused that someone, once again, has been caught and entrapped by the *look*.[7]

Despite my discomfort, I am, nonetheless, drawn again to the scene behind this sealed door. Verifying that I am indeed alone within this hidden space, I take another longer look through the peepholes. In this way, for a few moments, I comply with the artist's game as I gaze at the near-pornographic scene before me. I stare down upon the naked female figure who is lying there, altogether motionless, on a bed of dried twigs. I become increasingly disconcerted since I cannot help but acknowledge, in astonishment, that she has spread her legs wide exclusively for my eyes, exposing her genitalia for my voyeuristic gaze.

Regaining my composure, I notice other curious elements. I remark that the reclining naked figure is holding high a phallic-shaped gas lamp. It is as much the focal point of the scene as the female vulva. I also note that the restricted perspective of the peepholes deprives me of a view of her face. Only a few blond locks of hair are apparent. This headless figure, I further note, is not situated directly behind the door. Rather a dark space creates a distinct gulf between the door and the brightly lit chamber which houses her. Only an asymmetrical puncture in the brick facade of her enclosure permits one a view of this enigmatic figure. Behind the immobile, corpse-like figure, there is a pastoral scene, a rather lush landscape with a waterfall. The waterfall appears to be flowing.

The title of this work now comes back to mind. I recall that Duchamp inscribed a waterfall and an illuminating gas (light) as the 'givens.' I muse about possible meanings and begin to recognize that, here, there is definitely much more than meets the eye. I begin to suspect that Duchamp has set me up as a voyeur and that my initial self-conscious reaction to the scene behind the door is somehow a trick, a means to lure me into his game, into his trap.

I become uneasy again, troubled that this illuminated female figure, lying in a pastoral setting with a waterfall, is hidden away in this manner. I find it disturbing that she must forever remain contained in this enclosure, as if imprisoned in a cage. It is as if something vital has been held in check, restrained, suppressed. Gazing down at the enigmatic figure, I have the presentiment that something quite significant has been covered up, hidden, and that this peepshow is but a deceptive ruse to distract me.

Indeed, if I think about this peepshow, about this overtly fetishized figure,[8] indeed this whole spectacle, I realize that, like the door itself, it is so evidently out of place here. Then I recall Duchamp's other objects, those outrageous readymades he presented to us as art. Indeed, Duchamp was a master of decontextualization. He loved to displace objects, to move them out of their usual context into new foreign ones.[9] One can thus ask: is this naked female figure simply one more decontextualized object? Is she merely a representation of the female fetish, that female object of male sexual fantasy and desire, transposed from the popular to a *high* art setting? But surely this naked figure is not placed in this strange enclosure for the sole purpose of bringing a common peepshow into the context of a museum. There are too many other puzzling, and more compelling, elements here.

I keep wondering how this female figure is associated with the illuminating gas, the waterfall and the natural setting. Even the old wooden door appears to announce something very different than a simple parody of the fetish and of voyeurism – something quite significant, I feel. Indeed, does not this weatherworn door introduce something ancient, like an old readymade idea? Yes, it is as if it discloses the fact that an age-old *given* lies beyond.

I begin to see that this figure represents the generic *woman* as she has been inscribed into our cultural constructs. If this is so, then can her enclosure, the hermetic chamber which houses her, represent the framing device that contains the category, *woman*, the frame which defines, by a restrictive name or concept, heterogeneous female identities? Despite this realization, other questions continue to persist. Why did Duchamp orchestrate such a peepshow? Why must he entrap the viewer in this way? Why must he transform me, however briefly, into an unwilling voyeur? Why did he set out all these classic signs of perversion?

If this installation, *Étant donnés*, is about givens, about inscriptions of the fetishized woman, it is then most evidently also about looking and about perverting *normative* vision. I think about the manner in which I have been framed, how I have been set up as a voyeur in front of this spread-eagled nude, how I have come to participate in a quasi-deviant act. As I look down at this exhibitionist, at this fetishized figure, I understand how Duchamp has ingeniously orchestrated my voyeuristic gaze with a parodic display of perversive signs, how he has dramatically subverted my expectations as an innocent viewer.

Quite ostensibly, then, a first encounter with this provocative work readily reveals its subversive quality as it undermines, and with a vengeance, the *normal* aesthetic experience. It does so in too conspicuous a way, however. In effect, it is impossible for the fetish displayed here, that supreme perversive sign, to 'be overlooked.' Rather it quite overtly begs to be 'be gloried in' (Mulvey, *Fetishism and Curiosity* xiv).

And I realize that it is precisely because of my uneasy stare, because of my consciously voyeuristic gaze, that Duchamp prevents me from reading this work with rational detachment. Any cerebral activity on the part of this viewer is subverted by the power of this fetishized female figure. And here lies the crux of the matter – at least, this is the way I presently see it, now that I am released from its initial impact.

I have come to realize that one cannot approach this work by means of vision alone. From a more distanced vantage point, I can see how the perversions lying within this enclosure are not what they first appear to be. I begin to discern their twofold quality: how they appear to be one thing and their contrary at the same time. In fact, the more I think about it, the more I am able to see the reclining female figure as an inversion of that other *given*, the quintessential *rational* man. The generic man!

Now, if I distance myself even more, I can imagine myself standing behind Duchamp himself as *he* looks through the peepholes. From this perspective, I see him gazing at his own specular inversion, as if he were looking at his own inverted reflection in a mirror. In fact, from my vantage point as the second viewer standing behind the artist, and with a certain rational distance, I recognize that the female figure in *Étant donnés* is actually a representation of Duchamp himself. Disguised, travestied as his radical *other*, she is 'the masculine sex *encore* (and *en corps*) parading in the mode of otherness.'[10]

Duchamp was, in fact, fascinated with mirrors, with specularity. In his notes, he wrote about the manner in which the plane surface of a mirror creates a virtual reality (98). He also wrote about a 'mirrorical return' where a particular image seen from the left is perceived as one thing and from the right as another (65). This is much like the mirror itself which reflects a particular given at the same time as it inverts it. Even *The Large Glass*,[11] situated right outside this chamber, is conceived very much like a mirror or 'hinge picture' as Duchamp called it (27). Here numerous ideas or concepts can be viewed as specular inversions – as specular inversions that are, moreover, gendered.[12]

There is little doubt that in *Étant donnés* such mirroring also comes into play. Visualizing Duchamp looking through the peepholes at his own inverted self-reflection, it becomes apparent that *Étant donnés* is part of a much larger specular game played with readymade ideas, with epistemological constructs that have attained the status of normative givens. Looking at *Étant donnés* in this way, I begin to envisage two players participating in this game: a male figure and a female one. I see these two players positioned as mirror images, as inverted reflections of each other. The male player is Marcel Duchamp himself, and the female one is Rrose Sélavy, his alter ego.

Duchamp first adopted the female persona of Rose Sélavy (one 'r') around 1920, and thereafter she even came to own the copyright, so to speak, of various works such as *Fresh Widow,* 1920.[13] It was shortly after this date that Rose added another 'r' to her name, calling herself Rrose Sélavy: pronounced, *éros c'est la vie* (Eros is life). The most well-known work under the name of Rrose is her *Anémic Cinéma*, a seven-minute film shot in 1926, with a camera that carries her name. In this film, discs bearing spirals are rotated rapidly, creating suggestive erotic movements.[14]

Judging from this *sensual* film as well as from her name, Rrose, it is evident that, in contrast to the celebrated *cerebral* Marcel Duchamp, designer of the rationally-built enclosure, *Étant donnés*,[15] the persona Rrose Sélavy is cast as his *other*, the erotic female body. Further extrapolating from such gendered works, it becomes clear that the specular games operating in *Étant donnés* are played out by two protagonists: Duchamp as rational man and Rrose as female body.

Now the problems of such essentialist categories have been pointed out by authors like Judith Butler, problems which, as we shall see, become most apparent in the specular games of Duchamp/Rrose. Indeed, although these two players have made some truly transgressive moves in *Étant donnés*, I believe that their *mirroring* also contains a major blind spot, a weakness and regression. So taking to heart Paul de Man's observations that it is precisely in a writer's blindness that one encounters the greatest insights, I would like to reflect upon the specular games played out by Marcel Duchamp and Rrose Sélavy. To begin, let us see how they operate as transgressions, perverting readymade essentialist ideas.

Given this artist's notions of specularity, I would propose that the object of the game between Rrose and Duchamp is for each player to reflect *and* invert, and so pervert, a particular concept or construct: the mind-body dualism, for example. It is precisely by means of their specular perversions that these players transgress the gendered categories of mind and body. Let us then visualize *Étant donnés* in our *mind's eye* and begin to watch the specular game of Rrose and Duchamp.

Such mental visioning is more than appropriate here because the game that one can see being played is one that takes as its givens certain principles of Cartesianism. René Descartes was, of course, the initiator of a rationally-based vision and father of the mind-body dualism. For Descartes, clear mental vision and certainty of truth could only be attained by evacuating the uncertainties and confusion engendered by the body: that is, by recognizing and combating shortcomings such as optical illusions or afterimages. The Cartesian mind must counter the failings and vagaries of the body; it must categorically avert all that is carnal. Once cleansed from the body, that is, once the mind has censored all that denies rational clarity, it can attain knowledge of objective truth.

Martin Jay maintains that such decarnalized vision eradicates what St. Augustine described as 'ocular desire.' [16] He further argues that, in failing 'to recognize its corporeality, its intersubjectivity, its embeddedness in the flesh of the world,' Cartesian perspectivalism establishes itself as a resolutely ocularcentric epistemology (128). Richard Rorty has described the Cartesian mind as a great mirror capable of reflecting truth: 'For Descartes, it was a matter of turning the Eye of the Mind from the confused inner representations to the clear and distinct ones . . . Without the notion of the mind as mirror, the notion of knowledge as accuracy of representation would not have suggested itself' (159, 12).

If Martin Jay and Richard Rorty have effectively demonstrated the ocularcentrism and specularity implicit in Cartesianism, then feminists such as Susan Bordo and Luce Irigaray (to name just two) have interpreted Cartesian philosophy as being decidedly phallocentric precisely because it censors and denies the body: the body that has been inscribed into culture as a female principle. Bordo, for example, argues that Descartes' rational objectivism and yearning for certainty was a 'flight from the feminine,' a paradigmatic shift 'from the organic female universe of the Middle Ages and the Renaissance' to what she calls the 'masculinization of thought.'[17]

Irigaray maintains that the Cartesian *cogito* sublimates, in effect, the maternal body:

> The 'I' thinks, therefore, this thing, this body that is also nature, that is still the *mother*, becomes an extension at the 'I''s disposal for analytical investigation, scientific projections, the regulated exercise of the imaginary, the utilitarian practice of technique (186).

Furthermore, Irigaray deconstructs the Cartesian 'Mind as Mirror,' for such a mirror continuously frustrates the desire to see one's own female experience in it. 'I am seeking,' she says, 'in simplest terms, to be united with *an image in a mirror*' (189). For Luce Irigaray, it is only through the speculum that this can be done. This concave mirror distorts the rational, linear Cartesian kind of vision at the same time as it reveals the curves, complexities and incongruities that a boundless vision entails – vision that includes the body, the senses.

Now whether one accepts such essentialist categories or not, I think that, with our own mind's eye, we can already begin to see the kind of specular game the two players, Marcel Duchamp and Rrose Sélavy, are playing: how they have positioned themselves respectively as mind and body. Rrose most definitely represents the inscription of *woman* as the body capable of subverting clear mental vision. And importantly, Duchamp, as the male player, represents the radical *other* of this female principle, for he represents the rational mind which not only censors the body but which displaces it, reifies it, sublimates it into a rational object. By keeping these gendered personae in mind, let us look especially at the way that they reflect *and* invert these essentialist categories, the way their specular perversions transgress these gendered givens.

As we know, the viewer's first encounter with the installation is by means of the old wooden door. Compelled to approach it, the viewer, safely situated in the hallowed halls of a rather palatial museum, feels no qualms about looking through the two peepholes. It is, after all, the viewer's role, in a museum, to look. But, as we have seen, it is precisely by the look, by the gaze, that Rrose entraps the viewer. As if in a cheap peepshow, the viewer is caught in the deviant-like act of gazing at this spread-eagled nude.

In no way is this a representation of the female nude aesthetically contained by the controlling device of a frame. Rather, enclosed in this cage, and so exposing herself only to *his* eyes (for Rrose addresses an expressly male viewer in this game), the female nude becomes a disruptive force, acting upon the viewer, catching him as if in an illicit act. The viewer, so framed, becomes the self-conscious viewer, suddenly aware of his role as a voyeur. Deprived of a secret gaze, in this context of a museum, the voyeur becomes very alert to his location in a very public setting, fearing that someone is gazing at him from behind. Rosalind Krauss has compared the viewer's experience of this work to that of the voyeur in Jean-Paul Sartre's *Being and Nothingness* who, while in the act of spying through a keyhole, suddenly finds himself being spied upon from behind (435–6)

This second viewer, this second location behind the male voyeur gazing at the female nude in *Étant donnés*, is, as I see it, a crucial one. For it is precisely here, in the realm of the second viewer, that one can see the blind spot in the specular game, the regressive perversion and, therefore, the greatest insight. But this second location and this second viewer will come into play (and into our sightline) during the endgame.

A first encounter with this work certainly tends to invalidate the view that it reflects Cartesianism in any way. However, to be taken in by Rrose Sélavy's indecent exhibitionism is to be taken in by what is so evidently a pastiche, what is so explicitly a parody of the male gaze cast upon the reified woman. Showing herself here, as faceless, as only body, is Rrose not presenting herself as the generic woman, that unitary category *woman*? Is Rrose not also presenting herself here as both the earthly and the celestial Venus as she has been presented in Western art?[18] Assuming the role of the disruptive female body, that enticing object of desire, she also parodies the idealized woman, the *aesthetically-contained* reclining nude. And do these inscriptions not position her as that quintessential female fetish objectified by the penetrating eyes of the gaze?

By personifying the *body* in this way, is Rrose not exposing herself as the radical *other* of the Cartesian *mind*? And furthermore, by so entrapping the male viewer's gaze, is she not transforming that Cartesian objective mental image into a resolutely subjective and carnal one? The self-consciousness of the viewer's bodily location in front of this female figure inverts and perverts the objective distance required by the Cartesian mind-eye. Rrose, thus, transposes the Cartesian mind into a body, into a body which itself has become the spectacle. At the very moment that the viewer gazes upon Rrose's naked figure, he himself is transformed into a self-conscious body. Further, it is as body that he himself is gazed upon by that putative second viewer behind him. Rrose, importantly, undermines the mind as mirror of an extended world. On the one hand, she parodies the separation between a distinct subject-viewer and object-viewed; on the other, she melts away this separation between subject-object by means of a carnalized vision that reinstates ocular desire.

So if Rrose Sélavy, by means of her perversive act, converts the Cartesian mind into a body, the male player of this specular game, Marcel Duchamp, reflects and inverts this carnal experience by censoring the gaze and by subjecting it to a rational order: that is to say, by means of the mind, the radical *other* of the body. For Descartes, it was, of course, only by purging the mind of the defects of the senses, by denying the physical body, that absolute certainty of truth could be attained. And this is exactly what that other male player, Duchamp, does here. He hides the body, sublimating it into a fetishized object.

As one can see from a cardboard model of the interior of *Étant donnés*, Duchamp has hidden the woman's body, the female fetish, in a rationally constructed cage.[19] Indeed, the whole hermetic construction and the location of the naked figure in it were designed through precise mathematical calculations. Duchamp here emulates Descartes, the inventor of analytic geometry, who believed mathematics to be the sole key to objective truth. Furthermore, Duchamp even based the viewer's sightline on Descartes' studies of optics, of binocular and monocular vision. Descartes deduced that the two images reflected on each retinal surface merge into a single image in the material substance of the pineal gland or the 'mind-eye.' This is the physical site of monocular transformation.[20] Duchamp designed this cage or enclosure as a trope for the actual lieu of vision. It is like the *res cogitans*, the material substance of the Eye of the Mind, or single inner eye. It is here where the view from the binocular peepholes merges into one.

Significantly, it is also here where the vagaries of the body are regulated. In Cartesian fashion, Duchamp, by means of this rational construction, censors vision and restricts and contains the subversive power of Rrose's body. There is no doubt that his rationally-constructed enclosure considerably reduces the female power to subvert the mind. Kept securely distinct and separate from the viewer (by means of the sealed door, as well as by a measured distance between the viewer space and the nude), the body can only disrupt for a short period.

Hence, Duchamp constructs both a structure for the subversive female principle and a cage that effectively disposes of the body, the mother, nature, even controlling the flow of the natural waterfall.[21] By these rational means, Duchamp signals the displacement of the female principle by a male one. And it is clearly the illuminating light (enlightened reason?) that makes this all possible. Embodied here by the (male) phallic lamp, the illuminating light/reason permits one to observe and inspect a reified mother nature. And as Duchamp, the male player, shows us, it is only by the illuminating gas, by this *enlightenment*, that one can reify knowledge and construct an object of vision. He shows us how such an object fixes, freezes and stops the flow of bodily vision, how it sublimates and hides.

Duchamp, the male player of this specular game, has then constructed *Étant donnés* as a rational structure, not only as a means to contain ocular desire and the subversive power of the female body but also to reify it into a male principle. As such, he has effectively displaced the female principle, sublimated it into a reified object, and into a fetish. In contrast, the female player plays the opposite role. Rrose Sélavy's strong bodily presence is resolutely uncanny. She has the capacity to bring back to the surface all that lies hidden, sublimated; she has the power to disrupt and throw into confusion the clear mental vision of that rational, disembodied eye. Hence, Marcel Duchamp and Rrose Sélavy have here inscribed male-female principles as mind and body, and as principles that are distinct and oppositional.

Significantly, by means of their specular games, both players have transgressed their opponent's position: Duchamp displaces and sublimates the body; Rrose Sélavy transposes the mind into a body, reclaiming what the mind has hidden away. Looking at their gendered games in this way, one can recognize how they operate as specular perversions, as transgressions of essentialist epistemologies. Though quite insightful moves, Rrose/Duchamp do not end their specular game here. On the contrary. It is, in fact, in their *regressive* endgame that these two players play out their most perverse, and enlightening, specular game.

From my vantage point as the second viewer at the entrance of the chamber, I watch Duchamp looking through the peepholes at his own inverted reflection. Looking at him in this way, I see how Rrose/Duchamp also play at dissolving essentialist categories by means of androgyny – androgyny here meaning the (con)fusion of genders. And it is in their specular endgame as androgyne, that a blind spot comes into view; it is here where transgression turns into regression.

Already in 1919, Duchamp's infamous rectified readymade, *L.H.O.O.Q.* introduced the notion of androgyny. Here, he transformed Leonardo da Vinci's famous female bride, the *Mona Lisa*, into a female/male representation by adding a moustache and a goatee, a convergence of genders. Conversely, in the 1920s, Duchamp was photographed in drag by Man Ray as Rrose Sélavy a number of times. Here the male artist not only poses as his female persona, but effectively merges the two genders. In 1938, a half-clad female mannequin, posing as Rrose Sélavy, masqueraded in male garb at the Exposition Internationale du Surréalisme in Paris.[22] As I see it, this kind of androgynous convergence of male-female genders also comes into play in *Étant donnés*.[23]

Observing Duchamp positioned as the viewer looking through the peepholes, I see him staring, as if in a mirror, at his own inverted self-reflection, at his alter ego, Rrose Sélavy. It is interesting, here, to recall that Rrose Sélavy (alias Marcel Duchamp) signed a short essay called *Men before a Mirror*.[24] In it, Rrose explains how man can only see his face and body through the eyes of a woman and how this self-representation is objectified and imprisoned in the mirror. Now, in *Étant donnés*, it is Rrose, as object of the gaze, who is imprisoned in Duchamp's mirror. The androgynous reflection that ensues is much like Duchamp's notion of the 'mirrorical return' (65). When one looks one way, one sees one image, Duchamp; when one looks the other way, one sees another, Rrose. Seen from one side, she is male; seen from the other, he is female. This is his/her body; this is his representation and/or hers. Marcel Duchamp/Rrose Sélavy, one and the same: he/she, the androgyne. From my location as the second viewer, I watch their specular endgame as androgyne. I see Rrose/Duchamp situated on either side of the mirror-peepholes, and I note how their male-female identities merge on the plane surface of the mirror, how they become one. Now considering androgyny in this way, certain problematic issues begin to surface, issues that have been addressed by Judith Butler.[25]

As Butler reminds us, the normative character of an original identity is but an illusion, 'an *effect* of discursive practices' (1990a 18). For this reason, gender parody, like drag (or androgyny) *can* sometimes operate as a transgression of normative gender givens. She explains:

> In imitating gender, drag implicitly reveals the imitative structure of gender itself – as well as its contingency [. . .] As imitations that effectively displace the meaning of the original, they imitate the myth of originality itself. In the place of an original identification which serves as a determining cause, gender identity might be reconceived as a personal/cultural history of received meanings subject to a set of imitative practices which refer laterally to other imitations, and which, jointly, construct the illusion of a primary and interior gendered self or which parody the mechanism of that construction. (1990a 338)

For Butler, gender parody thus represents a perpetual displacement of the notion of an original identity, constituting 'a fluidity of identities that suggests an openness to resignification and recontextualization, and [depriving] hegemonic culture and its critics of the claim to essentialist accounts of gender identity' (1990a 338). Even though gender parodies can indeed be transgressive, as Judith Butler also acknowledges, this is *not* always the case. 'I want to underscore,' she writes, 'that there is no necessary relation between drag and subversion, and that drag may well be used in the service of both the denaturalization and the reidealization of hyperbolic heterosexual gender norms' (1990a 338).

Inspecting the specular games of Duchamp/Rrose more closely, it becomes quite evident that the androgynous (con)fusions as well as inversions of male-female genres are not transgressive gender parodies at all. Despite the spectacular display of a female body, Duchamp has not given Rrose any real corporeality. As Rachel Blau-Duplessis has so eloquently noted, Rrose

> has her bottom put on wrong... What you see, head on, ahead of you, is cunt. Estranged cunt, the cant or can't of cunt. Duchamp has made a twisted, asymmetrical gash – richly labial but curved and wayward – where a vulva 'is' (70).

Fixed as a transhistorical construct, as a *sign* of *woman*, Rrose's exhibitionist body is thus ultimately incorporeal.[26] Though positioning her as the female player in this game, Duchamp has not given Rrose any real identity, and certainly no genuine subject position. Neither does Rrose's prototypical female body in any way fuse genders into a single *human* identity. Indeed, rather than displacing the notion of an original gender identity, her fetishized body perversely reaffirms it.

If, as Laura Mulvey has noted, 'the fetish is a metaphor for the displacement of meaning behind representation' (*Fetishism and Curiosity* xiv), one can also understand how Duchamp/Rrose's specular endgame as androgyne also surreptitiously displaces an important meaning. Recognizing the androgynous representation in the plane surface of the mirror as an imaginary *woman*, it soon becomes quite clear that these players' specular games are really specular illusions that reflect back only *Duchamp's* fantasy of an original identity: the female body representing the unitary, monolithic category *woman*.

Looking at the endgame from this perspective, one can, thus, note a blind spot in Duchamp's specular games. Like all mirrors, this one reveals that there is really *no one else* on the other side of the mirror's tain. Like all mirrors, this one reflects only he who looks into it – here, the artist Marcel Duchamp. And so, even in their specular endgame, Rrose the fetish, that supreme perversive sign, serves to 'distract the eye and the mind' from the real object – Duchamp. Furthermore, the artist's specular perversions serve to obscure the intimate relation between voyeur and fetish: between Duchamp and Rrose.

In front of the mirror/peepholes gazing at his fetishized *other*, Duchamp can only remain blind to the perspective of the second viewer watching him from behind. Situated beyond the range of the reflecting surface, the second viewer is not subject to the framing device of Duchamp's mirror and, thus, can more clearly see how *Étant donnés* exposes the narcissistic premise inherent in specularity and in the voyeur-fetish relationship. Importantly, from this location, the viewer not only escapes Duchamp's blind spot but is also able to gain an important insight.

The blindness and insight inherent in *Étant donnés*, I venture to say, is more readily visible to a *female viewer*. Realizing the pitfalls of assuming such a seemingly unitary figure as a *female viewer*, I would argue that *she* can come to represent a diversity of women (and men for that matter) who recognize both the commonalities and differences in women's experiences, men and women who question the illusory nature of fixed gender identities and who explore the mechanisms in discursive and representational practices which construct and perpetuate gender hierarchies that construct false mirrors.

Though inevitably struck by the provocative pose of Rrose, the *female viewer* cannot remain fixed in front of this particular mirror for long. Unable to see how Rrose can come to represent women's diverse experiences, the *female viewer* is not mesmerized by the specular and narcissistic image likely to look back at a male spectator. Indeed, *Étant donnés* is not a mirror providing women with a self-reflection. Here Luce Irigaray's phrase comes back to mind: 'I am seeking, in simplest terms, to be united with *an image in a mirror*' (189).

Effectively placed outside the mirror's frame, the *female viewer* is decidedly positioned as the second viewer. Yet, in so situating the *female viewer* on the outside of the reflecting surface, Duchamp has, in fact, given her a privileged location. Since she is not cast as a subject looking at her own reflection through the peepholes, the *female viewer* can more easily see there only a discursive construction of femininity – Rrose as a universalized fetish, Rrose as the great fantasy, *woman*. Recognizing her as a narcissistic self-image engendered from *his* imaginary, the *female viewer* can identify Rrose as a repetition of an ancient male inscription of man's *other*.

Situated on the outside of the framing device, the *female viewer* has effectively escaped being *framed* and blinded by the specular games and is thus more apt to recognize Duchamp's Rrose as a mirage or illusion, as an empty signifier, as a *spectral image*. Not so easily duped into believing that Rrose represents a genuine feminine identity, a subject, woman, women, the *female viewer* is better able to see the regressive nature of the specular games played out in *Étant donnés*: how they subvert only to divert; how these seemingly transgressive specular games revert back to normative readymade givens. This is not, however, where the greatest insight lies. This greater, more significant insight can only come into view once the *female viewer* overcomes her own particular blind spot. Indeed, even from her privileged location outside the mirror's frame, she is still subject to the blindness caused by specularity and objectification.

Standing as the Sartrean intruder at the entrance of the chamber that houses *Étant donnés*, I watch Duchamp gazing through the peepholes. From my position as the second viewer, I am compelled to cast this artist as *my* object of vision, and to reify *him* in a further specular enterprise. Indeed, it is so tempting to yield to similar specular perversions and to view Duchamp as the generic man and his oeuvre as a readymade male discourse.

Then I think back to Duchamp's elaborate gendered construction. I reflect upon the regressive nature of his specular games, and particularly the blind spot. Recognizing how my impulse to objectify him would displace my own self-reflective image in my mirror and how it would construct Duchamp as my fetishized *other*, I refocus. Slowly, and with some effort, I try to re-vision the manner in which one objectifies one's *other* in one's mental mirror. Contemplating ways and strategies that would permit me to escape the subjecting-object stronghold, I envisage a position where a subject no longer faces a reified *other*: a fetishized object that is inevitably one's own specular reflection. I try to adopt a perspective that permits me to recognize and acknowledge another subject, another subjectivity, another subjective discourse.

At the entrance of *Étant donnés*, I now gaze at that other viewer looking through the peepholes, and I discern the distinctive positions of Marcel Duchamp: I see him as avant-garde artist, as iconoclast, as writer, as player of specular games, as Rrose Sélavy, as . . . Looking at him from these diverse perspectives, I begin to lose sight of the age-old given, the male artist, the generic man, the universal subject. Instead I see Duchamp's multiple personae, his fluid identities; I see his oeuvre as unique, singular, evoking a network of ever-changing discourses. Refocusing in this way, I am able to watch the objectifying mirror slowly shatter and the specular perversions quietly dissipate.

With the insights acquired from Duchamp's specular perversions and from the shattering of my own objectifying mirror, I re-vision *Étant donnés*. Situating myself in the role of the voyeur once again, I look through the peepholes in the old wooden door and gaze at Rrose's fetishized figure. I recognize how much her blatant exhibitionism provoked me, impelling me to take a stand and to formulate my position vis-à-vis Duchamp's readymade *woman*. I also realize how the signs inhabiting *Étant donnés* prompted me to reflect upon gendered discourses that construct false mirrors and spectral images of *woman*. Such reflections, I see, do not prevent shattering the objectifying mirror.

Endnotes

*   This is a revised version of my essay, '*Étant donnés*: Rrose/Duchamp in a Mirror' published in *Revue d'art canadien/Canadian Art Review (RACAR)* XXII, 1–2 (1995): 87–97.
1   The full title of this work is *Étant donnés: No. 1 la chute d'eau, No. 2 le gaz d'éclairage*, 1946–66, translated as *Given: 1. The Waterfall, 2. The Illuminating Gas.* Approximately 242.5 cm. in height x 177.8 cm. in width x 124.5 cm. in length, this assemblage consists of an old wooden door, bricks, velvet, wood, leather stretched over an armature of metal, as well as such other diverse material as twigs, aluminum, iron, glass, plexiglass, linoleum,

cotton, electric lamps, a gas lamp (Bec Auer type), motor, etc. A description of this installation will follow.
2. Duchamp sporadically worked on this installation, in two different studios in New York, during the period 1946 to 1966, when all believed that he had given up art to play chess.
3. The notion of entrapment is a recurring motif in Duchamp's oeuvre. One example is his readymade *Trébuchet (Trap)*, 1917. Here the title alludes to a chess move with a pawn that 'traps' the opponent's piece. It is also a French term for a cage that entraps small birds.
4. This museum contains the largest display of Duchamp's works, the Arensberg Collection, and includes this artist's other major work, *The Bride Stripped Bare by her Bachelors, Even (The Large Glass)*, 1915#23.
5. Duchamp is most well-known for iconoclastic readymades such as the snow shovel entitled, *In Advance of the Broken Arm*, 1915; the urinal entitled *Fountain*, 1917, and signed R. Mutt; the reproduction of Leonardo's *Mona Lisa*, upon which the artist drew a moustache and a goatee, entitling this readymade *L.H.O.O.Q.*, 1919, which reads phonetically as: '*elle a chaud au cul*' (She has a hot ass). This artist is also renowned for paintings such as *The Nude Descending the Staircase*, 1912, and his major work, *The Large Glass*, 1915–23, which stands as a cryptic and highly conceptualized work.
6. This self-conscious reaction to *Étant donnés* has been noted by a number of authors. See, for example, Rosalind Krauss, 'Where's Poppa?' and Amelia Jones, 'Re-placing Duchamp's Eroticism: "Seeing" *Étant donnés* from a Feminist Perspective,' in her *Postmodernism and the En-gendering of Marcel*.
7. As a self-acclaimed anti-retinal artist, Duchamp produced a number of artworks that deal with the 'look' in an ironic way. For example his glass work entitled, *To be Looked At (From the Other Side of the Glass) With One Eye, Close To, For Almost an Hour*, 1918, elicits (and frustrates as the title itself indicates) the 'look' of the viewer. Rosalind Krauss provides the most comprehensive study of Duchamp's 'retinal' works. See her 'Where's Poppa?' 454. In *Étant donnés*, the notion of the 'look' takes on a whole new dimension as the viewer is transposed into a voyeur.
8. The fetishized female figure, as object of the gaze, was theorized by Laura Mulvey, in her influential essay, 'Visual Pleasure and Narrative Cinema', *Visual and Other Pleasures* 14–28. 'Where the male viewer finds scopophilic pleasure in looking,' the female position, according to Mulvey, is one of 'to be looked-at-ness.' Although this monolithic dichotomy between male and female positions has been problematicized (even by Mulvey herself in subsequent writings), *Étant donnés* can stand as a quintessential example of Mulvey's model. See also her 'Afterthoughts on 'Visual Pleasure and Narrative Cinema' Inspired by *Duel in the Sun*', *Framework* 12–15.
9. I think of his readymades, the snow shovel and the urinal, for example. See Endnote 5.
10. She is 'the masculine sex *again* (and in *body*) parading in the mode of otherness.' Judith Butler, *Gender Trouble: Feminism and the Subversion of Identity* 12. Butler here discusses Luce Irigaray's critique of the discursive construction of the body as a female principle.
11. Also entitled, *The Bride Stripped Bare by her Bachelors, Even*, 1915–23. Philadelphia Museum of Art. Oil, varnish, lead foil, lead wire, and dust on two glass panels (cracked), each mounted between two glass panels, with five glass strips, aluminum foil, and a wood and steel frame, 227.5 x 175.8 cm. Inscribed on reverse of lower panel (on the Chocolate Grinder) in black paint: La Mariée mise à nu par/ses célibataires, même/Marcel Duchamp/ 1915–1923/ -inachevé/ – cassé 1931/ – réparé 1936.
12. For example, in the lower portion of *The Large Glass*, there is the subterranean world of the rational Bachelor Machine; in contrast, in the upper half, there is the ethereal world of the Bride's Domain. These are male and female principles inscribed as separate and distinct,

reflecting back their *other*. In his notes for *The Large Glass* collected in 'The Green Box', Duchamp makes further allusions to oppositional forces. He writes, for example, about the 'Principle of subsidized symmetries,' and how '... a point [in the lower part of the glass is] sent back mirrorically to the higher part of the glass ...' See Duchamp 30, 65.

13 Another 'window' work. The Museum of Modern Art, New York, Katherine S. Dreier Bequest, 1953. This is a miniature French window, 7.5 cm. X 45 cm., with eight panes of glass covered with squares of polished leather. It is set on a wooden sill, 1.9 cm. x 53.3 cm. x 10.2 cm. Black paper tape letters applied across the window sill read, 'FRESH WIDOW COPYRIGHT ROSE S ... LAVY 1920.'

14 On these observations, see Lawrence D. Steefel, Jr., 'The Position of *La Mariée Mise à Nu par Ses Célibataires, Même*' 312; and Rosalind Krauss, 'Where's Poppa?' 454.

15 *Étant donnés* was constructed, as we shall see, according to precise calculations.

16 Ocular desire or the 'erotic projection in vision' was, as Jay points out, condemned by St. Augustine. Martin Jay, 'Scopic Regimes of Modernity', in *Force Fields* 117.

17 Susan Bordo, 'The Cartesian Masculinization of Thought': 441. For a more comprehensive study, see her *The Flight to Objectivity: Essays on Cartesianism and Culture*.

18 For an enlightening discussion of the female nude as both the earthly and celestial Venus, see Lynda Nead, *Female Nude: Art, Obscenity and Sexuality*.

19 Duchamp inserted a folded cardboard scale model into his manual of instruction for the assembly of *Étant donnés*, contained in a loose-leaf binder, and numbered it page 1. It illustrates the artist's precise calculations for the two chambers: the dark empty space that separates the viewer at the peepholes from the tableau as well as the asymmetric room that houses the female figure.

20 In my view, Duchamp cites Cartesian studies of monocular and binocular vision in *Étant donnés* by basing the viewer's sightline, apparent in the irregular ground plan and perspective schema on the drawings of Sebastien Le Clerc, evidently a Cartesian disciple. My observations are based on Jean Clair's study of Le Clerc's perspectival drawings, particularly those that reflect the visual distortions occasioned by the transformation from a binocular to a monocular view. Clair claims Duchamp would have seen Le Clerc's illustrations at the Bibliothèque Ste-Geneviève while studying the perspectivalists. See Jean Clair, 'Marcel Duchamp et la tradition des perspecteurs': 124–59.

21 The waterfall appears to 'flow' because of a motorized disc (perforated around its circumference) that rotates in front of a light, placed behind the transparent image of the waterfall. The play of light and shadow gives the illusion of movement, of flowing water.

22 For a description of Rrose Sélavy's presence at this exhibition, see Jones, *Postmodernism and the En-gendering of Marcel Duchamp* 78–9. Jones offers a very insightful view of Rrose-Duchamp as an indeterminately gendered artist. In this regard, see particularly Chapter 5, 'The Ambivalence of Rrose Sélavy and (Male) Artist as "Only the Mother of the Work"'.

23 I have already argued that there is both a male and a female principle present in *Étant donnés*: that the naked female figure is countered by the phallic lamp and the *male* rationally constructed cage. Jean-François Lyotard has also noted that the nude figure itself is, in fact, half man (left side) and half woman (right side). See his *Les transformateurs* 18. However, I see the actual '(con)fusion' of gender from a different 'specular' vantage point here.

24 This text is a kind of literary readymade, composed by an unidentified German friend of Man Ray as *Mann vor dem Spiegel* subsequently translated into English and signed by Marcel Duchamp (Rrose Sélavy). English text originally in Man Ray, *Photographies 1920–1934*; rpt. in Marcel Duchamp, *The Writings of Marcel Duchamp* 188–9.

25 See Judith Butler, 'Gender Trouble, Feminist Theory, and Psychoanalytic Discourse', *Feminism/Postmodernism* and her *Gender Trouble: Feminism and the Subversion of Identity*.

26 On this subject of woman as an empty signifier, see Elizabeth Cowie, 'Woman as Sign' in *The Woman in Question*.

Bibliography

Blau-Duplessis, Rachel. 'Sub Rrosa: Marcel Duchamp and the Female Spectator.' *The Pink Guitar: Writing as Feminist Practice*. New York & London: Routledge, 1990. 68–82.

Bordo, Susan. 'The Cartesian Masculinization of Thought.' *Signs: Journal of Women in Culture and Society* vol. 11. no. 3 (Spring 1986): 439–53.

—— *The Flight to Objectivity: Essays on Cartesianism and Culture*. New York: State University of New York Press, 1987.

Butler, Judith. *Gender Trouble: Feminism and the Subversion of Identity*. New York and London: Routledge, 1990a.

—— 'Gender Trouble, Feminist Theory, and Psychoanalytic Discourse.'. *Feminism/Postmodernism*. Ed. Linda J. Nicholson. New York and London: Routledge, 1990b. 324–40.

Clair, Jean. 'Marcel Duchamp et la tradition des perspecteurs'. *Marcel Duchamp: Abécédaire: Approches critiques*. Ed. Jean Clair. Paris, 1977. 124–59.

Cowie, Elizabeth. 'Woman as Sign.' *The Woman in Question*. Ed. by Parveen Adams and Elizabeth Cowie. Cambridge, Mass.: The MIT Press, 1990. 117–33.

Daubner, Ernestine. '*Étant donnés*: Rrose/Duchamp in a Mirror'. *Revue d'art canadien/Canadian Art Review (RACAR)* XXII, 1–2 (1995): 87–97.

Duchamp, Marcel. *The Writings of Marcel Duchamp*. Ed. Michel Sanouillet and Elmer Peterson. New York: Da Capo Paperback, 1973.

Irigaray, Luce. *Speculum of the Other Woman*. Trans. Gillian C. Gill. Ithaca: Cornell University Press, 1985.

Jay, Martin. 'Scopic Regimes of Modernity.' *Force Fields*. New York and London: Routledge, 1993. 114–33.

Jones, Amelia. *Postmodernism and the En-gendering of Marcel Duchamp*. Cambridge: Cambridge University Press, 1994.

Krauss, Rosalind . 'Where's Poppa?' *The Definitively Unfinished Marcel Duchamp*. Ed. Thierry de Duve. Cambridge, Mass. and London, England: The MIT Press, 1991. 433–62.

Lyotard, Jean-François. *Les transformateurs Duchamp*. Paris: Editions Galilée, 1977.

Mulvey, Laura. 'Afterthoughts on "Visual Pleasure and Narrative Cinema" Inspired by *Duel in the Sun*'. *Framework* 15/16/17 (1981): 12–15.

—— *Fetishism and Curiosity*. Bloomington and Indianapolis: Indiana University Press, 1996.

—— 'Visual Pleasure and Narrative Cinema'. *Visual and Other Pleasures*. Bloomington and Indianapolis: Indiana University Press, 1989. 14–28.

Nead, Lynda. *Female Nude: Art, Obscenity and Sexuality*. London and New York: Routledge, 1992.

Ray, Man. *Photographies 1920–1934*. Paris: Cahiers d'art, 1934.

Rorty, Richard. *Philosophy and the Mirror of Nature*. Princeton: Princeton University Press, 1979.

Steefel, Lawrence D. Jr. 'The Position of *La Mariée Mise à Nu par Ses Célibataires, Même* (1915–23) in the Stylistic and Iconographic Development of the Art of Marcel Duchamp.' Ph.D. diss., Princeton University, 1960.

Chapter 7

Sade's Woman: Essential Pornogony and Virtual Embodiment

Robert L. Mazzola

Daughter in the Circle: The Case of Sade's 'Eugénie de Franval'[1]

When a man places a young woman in a moated circle, on a pedestal for the delectation of another man, his gesture is both homoerotic (whose arousal will he observe?) and venerative. In either case, he creates or produces the woman in question in a non-reproductive, erotic and submissive text over which he has, he believes, complete control. My remarks reflect thinking along homoerotic lines which may be homosexual in Leo Bersani's terms – or even Foucault's[2] – but which do *not* necessarily limit their scope to what might be called that of a homosexual aesthetic, however that may be defined. And while defining such an aesthetic, as Bersani has argued, is important from more than a simply aesthetic perspective, such an enterprise exceeds the limits of my research and very probably of my competence.

When a father places his daughter (and accomplice) in a ring or circle that as a symbol always suggests wholeness and perfection, he recreates the family circle, remakes its myth, recolors and retextures its modus operandi – in a word, *defiles* it. Defilement, I am going to argue, is distortion of the traditional belief system that operates the family, and concomitantly a resetting of its codes.[3] Redefining 'father,' 'mother,' 'daughter'; recasting our conventional notions of family ties in order to include an interpretation of the Sadian version of incest understood differently somehow, should not be misconstrued as a process in revalidation of the unthinkable. The French theorists whose work informed my early analytical training in reading use the term *impensé*, literally the *unthought* or the *unthought of*. In considering 'Eugénie de Franval' as a refashioning of the familial mythos, I want to incorporate these two related but not identical modes of thinking the *impensé* in Sade's text.

When third-party sex involves the nascent female in a theatricality of her sexual persona, placing her in the central and, at least momentarily empowered position in which we find Eugénie, an obvious triangularity of evential (i.e., of the event) and psychic distortion and displacement is at work. This triangular modus is inscribed within the circumvallation Sade describes as the centerpiece of his theater. My interest here is in the formulation of some of the *mechanisms* involved in that inscription and their relevance to a rethinking of the *unthought* and the *unthought of* in the matter of sex and the family. I want to avoid sociological commentary in this regard, however. Such commentary clearly lies outside the scope of my argument, though in light of much of what Foucault has taught us about sexual power plays, any extension of that argument beyond the perimeters I have set for it could not fail to embroil itself in the individual's concerns within the larger societal framework.

When Franval's friend, Valmont, reaches sexual climax in the circumvallation scene, the event of his coming places him necessarily close to the image Franval has made of Eugénie; he has turned her into an object beyond Valmont's reach in all but imagistic and masturbatory terms. She is 'his' only in the sense that the thought we think is ours. I contend that Sade very seriously undermines precisely that notion of the individual's possession of his or her own thoughts. *The product of desire is a bending of the other to one's own will. Sade's 'evil' character exercises this sway over nearly all who come into contact with him: his wife, his daughter, Valmont.*

Franval's contests with others are all contests of will; and Sade tells us that he is endowed in abundance with the two principal charms that serve that will: intelligence and physical beauty. As an object lesson, the story that unfolds is putatively a moral tale, that is, one specifically devised to provide a corrective to immoral actions, resulting from capitulation to the dictates of will, by showing their unfortunate consequences. As always in Sade, however, this moral lesson is an excuse to explore the limits of lubricity, and to contemplate the decline of normative behavior as an escalating fulfillment of proscribed desire. Everyone, then and now, reads through the veneer, past the patina of feigned social consciousness, to the dark heart of desire rendered even more desirous when two ancillary conditions to its enactment are met: the debasement of the Virtuous Other, and the flouting of societal conventions, i.e., by replacing those encoded conventions with others of Sade's devising.

The substitution of a theatrical device for a 'real life' situation is as old as theater itself. When Eugénie is old enough, she accompanies her father to the theater no fewer than three times a week. During her early upbringing, while she is kept, on her father's orders, completely isolated from her mother, Eugénie is taught relatively little by her tutors: she learns to read and to comport herself. Sade does not explain what is meant by Franval's notion of comportment, but we learn later that both the isolation from maternal influence and from what we today would call a more general education, has a single goal, that of making the daughter into a new kind of daughter for the father who never activates his role *as* father.

The 'new daughter,' we will discover, is one schooled in the theater of cruelty and desire; she will have become, with careful tutelage, a consummate actress of desire. For the new daughter – soon to be lover – there is no paternal presence even though she spends a great deal of her time with Franval. He is her 'friend,' her 'brother,' and with these manipulations of the names of family members, with the distorting substitutions Franval makes at so fundamental a level, he effectively calls into question the very validity of those relations. Mother is negated entirely; father is denied that name as well and becomes an ersatz or criminal brother (Sade's words); daughter is encircled by an educated desire for the only loving other she has been allowed to know; child, finally, is transmuted into other self for the pleasure of the primary self, the libertine in whose existence the reader is compelled to take a prurient interest. Well, if that is the case, shouldn't we stop right here? Our analysis of a work of literature threatens, doesn't it, to implicate us in this debasement of family values, the remaking of the family, a distortion of its history and its *purpose* in society – and *that's* the point! That's the framework of the argument I am making: that we can't divorce the Sadian project, its fundamental subversiveness, from the personal psychology of those involved directly or indirectly in his enterprise which aims to undercut and ultimately expose the hypocritical purposes to which the normative society holds its citizens prisoner. We are among those who contribute to that enterprise by reactivating the project of subversion through our recuperation of Sade the *littérateur*. We don't validate the project itself, of course, but we do lend value to his reordering of certain essential priorities that both psychology and sociology guard, in a sense, as inviolable, or at least violable only at considerable risk to personal and social well-being. In this regard, his tampering with something as basic as the *names* of familial relations is dangerous in the extreme. Nothing, we generally concede, is more disquieting (to use too bland a word) than the unnaming of the familiar. We recall Freud's penetrating essay on the uncanny, and since reading it, remain prisoners of the sensation which that writing so painstakingly evokes. Within the familiar lies the uncanny, that sense that could not in fact persist without the canny, a clever contrivance and accomplice, to frame and thus define it. The norm and the normal are therefore necessary to the full delectation of the so-called aberrational. But it isn't simply a matter of the commonplace that says that contrast, or binary opposition, is indispensable to difference and thus to the ability to *tell* that difference; Sade's uncanny sees the norm as the foundational medium for the message of the perverse. Unnaming the norm is the essential modus operandi of his project. And all *un*naming concomitantly *names*. By altering and eliminating the name 'father,' literally expunging it from the vocabulary Eugénie is taught in her isolation, that nomination takes on the full weight of the horror it is normally supposed to dispel. Freud's castrating father figure is Sade's deflowering father *manqué*. Incest is the unnaming of the family.

The father *manqué* is the unnamed father figure who disfigures that role; he is Sade's alterego, the other self alluded to earlier which reconstitutes and recodifies two identities: that of the primary self and that of the family unit as societal microcosm. What is interesting in Sade's approach in this 'moral tale' that he subtitles *Nouvelle tragique*, is the lip service paid to the conditions of society as they impact on family life, and the much deeper psychological significance he imparts to the interpersonal relations his so-called tragedy explores. [As a pertinent aside, let me note that the English version of the story, translated by Seaver and Wainhouse, omits the subtitle altogether.] Of course, *nouvelle tragique* means 'tragic novella,' but could also be construed to signify 'new tragic,' i.e., a new and other mode of constructing the tragic. *This* is the Sadian *impensé*: nowhere does he make this explicit in the text, yet his reordering of the tragic here authorizes such a reading of the unthought mutation of that genre. In that Franval is full of hubris and that this overweening pride brings about his decline, the tale is indeed a classic tragedy. That it undertakes, as Sade tells us at the start, to 'instruct man and correct his morals' (*Justine* 375) indicates that, as with Œdipus, a moral and its warning are truly being proffered to the viewer/reader. Franval finishes badly, thus giving that reader to believe that vice is punished while virtue triumphs, except, of course, that virtue in Sade's story does *not* triumph: the innocent mother, Madame Farneille de Franval, pictured throughout as virtue incarnate, dies miserably at the end of the piece; Eugénie, while certainly portrayed as cognizantly participating in the incest and its attendant crimes, is nonetheless shown as Franval's complete and utter dupe, in her way just as innocent as the mother she is taught from infancy to scorn; finally, the grandmother, Madame Farneille, is the long-suffering pious woman whom Franval berates and secretly fears; she survives only to contemplate the loss of both daughter and grandchild. This distorted, or *defiled*, tragedy exceeds the Sophoclean and Racinian models Sade would necessarily have been influenced by. Their tragic code opened the individual house, the family construct, *out* toward society and the larger world, Sade's deformation of that tragic heritage, his *nouvelle tragique*, looks stubbornly inward through a pre-Freudian analysis of moral criminality and the ways in which it misshapes (but also *re*shapes) those moral codes that, in his view, shackle the creative and sensual imagination of man. That inward view is exclusionary; it encloses in order to refacet experience, remaking God-given categories in service to proscribed pleasure.

The enclosure Sade creates is a circumvallation, a theater of desire and perversion in which the undaughtered Eugénie stars in order to prepay the accomplice Valmont, who has been enlisted by Franval in a plot to seduce Madame de Franval so as to keep her from interfering in his plans. Valmont exacts this payment despite Franval's objections. Obviously, the latter does not want to share, even at a 'safe' distance, the delectable Eugénie with another man. But he needs

Valmont's services as his wife's seducer and therefore accedes to his friend's wishes. The literal stage is set: a moat full of water separates the voyeur from the object of his desire; Eugénie is arranged on a pedestal in a *tableau vivant*, thus excluding any participation on her part in scenes that follow, leading to Valmont's climax. [Another curious omission on the part of the English translators: they write: 'There in the ornate room, Eugénie on a pedestal...' (*Justine* 419), while the original has: 'Là, dans une salle décorée, Eugénie *nue* sur un piédestal...' (*Crimes* 267, emphasis added) Her nudity is clearly important to the scene.] The succession of 'scenes' is effected by means of a cord that reaches from the rotatable pedestal to the chair where Valmont sits, watches and masturbates. In its rather simple theatricality, this circular arrangement mimes and mocks the family circle Franval is at pains (and pleasures) to defile.

As Franval looks on from his hidden position – does he masturbate as well? – Valmont watches Eugénie from 'an endless succession of angles and beauties.' (420) Inscribed within this circle, the triangle Franval/Eugénie/Valmont proposes a special scene for the viewer/reader in which the unthought of other – *we* who stand behind Franval as he watches the others without allowing himself to be seen – takes on the role of secondary self to his primary status. Our reaction to this censored scene censures *us* and may make us question prurience as a legitimate driving force in the literary text. Sade's compulsion is to cause in the reader, the free citizen, the sort of doubt (Isn't it really *self*-doubt?) that gives impetus to a revolutionary rethinking of both sexuality and the nexus we call 'family.' At the conclusion of the piece, a veil drops, obscuring from view the object of delectation. In French this veil is a *gaze*, a gauze of sorts that inevitably suggests the word 'gaze' to the English speaker. And this theatrical staging is in effect the instigation and result of a perversion of the sense of sight. The story as a whole is reflected in this scene (one of two which Sade himself suppressed[4]) and its object is the distortion of a view: the family is under attack, its power structure corrupted from the top in a curious illustration of what Foucault saw as the unsexing of certain relations, in private and in society, as part of the manipulation of power. By separating Valmont from physical contact with Eugénie, Franval creates a new structure of desire itself. Masturbation replaces sexual contact, not as a Rousseauvian 'evil supplement,' but as reactivated means to power in which sex serves as instrument and not as final aim. In fact, all the sexual situations in the novella serve as means to some other greater, that is, baser, end. Franval is attacking more than conventional morality, a pleasure inducing activity no doubt; he is debasing convention's underpinnings in the values that the family was, and *is*, purported to embody. Incest is, for him, not an end but a means. Just as he insists that Eugénie call him anything but 'father,' and calls her 'friend,' French *ami(e)* which always suggests more than the English anyway, so he would rename all familial relations and thus de-file naming itself. The word 'defile' derives, fittingly enough, from the French *défiler*, to unravel. This unraveling of a value system aims at nothing less than a contravention of divine Word as represented in the Bible – a book Franval claims to admire because it presents models like Lot who was in love with his own daughter. Speaking to Clervil, the priest Madame Franval and her mother have persuaded to intercede with Franval in the name of decency, the libertine enlists 'Holy Scriptures [which he holds in "highest esteem"] . . . as I have always been persuaded that one accedes to Heaven by emulating its heroes.' Thus Franval goes far beyond ordinary sacrilege; he replaces the extant belief system, which Clervil rightly contends obtains through consensus of the nation – a nation whose rule under God through the divine right of kings was about to be severely tested (the novella was written in 1788).

In the end, we know, Franval repents in order to save the immortal soul whose presence he has denied through his acts. The credulous Clervil is taken in and finally Franval gets his way once again: he is buried in the same coffin that contains the body of his wife, poisoned by Eugénie at his instigation. Perhaps we can believe in the daughter's repentance – she appears from Clervil's account to have died spontaneously and contritely once she realized the full horror of what she had done. Franval's death at his own hands is another matter. At the last his tone – and Sade's – is ironic. He beseeches the gullible cleric to grant his dying wish and cajoles the man into becoming the unwitting accomplice to this final defilement. Sade demonstrates the ultimate success of treachery even at the moment of the deceiver's own death. Beseeching God's forgiveness in a Catholic country while in the very act of condemnable suicide ends the family myth on the highest possible note for the consummate libertine. *In extremis*, he must once and for all persuade God's emissary of a sincerity he has never possessed – that is his triumph. To believe in Franval's confession would be the final *coup de grâce* dealt to that value system which the family is purported to symbolize.

The obvious impasse brought about by this revision of morality as a code in flux reveals the circle, the family circle, as both travesty and ineluctable desire. This circle is the site of both misfortune *and* virtue and the paradox engendered by what society calls the pornographic (relation and word). Franval's fate is much commented on because it is the crux of the moral lesson Sade puts forward in an ironic mode. He has 'produced' a woman to play a role. Eugénie is born into a non-reproductive existence – following Franval's wishes, though he appears to give her the choice – she refuses marriage. The role she is taught to play is essentially erotic – no individual self as Eugénie can emerge from the eroticism Franval has created for her. Finally, the role is one of total submission – she freely, enthusiastically acquiesces to all of Franval's suggestions, requests and demands. As daughter – he only ever refers to her as such toward the end when the consequences of his acts begin to overtake him – her relationship to father and mother is eclipsed, circumscribed (literally 'written around' or surrounded by the scenario Franval [Sade] is writing). He (and here I mean both Franval and Sade) is 'father' only in the sense of *producer*. He produces the scenes (tableaux) that constitute the narrative. He produces the theater in which he alternates between the roles of central actor and stage director, watching from the wings. Ultimately the burnt offering to the Goddess Venus, reified in Valmont's ejaculate as the result of a sterile gesture, is the liquid that makes the writing, i.e., producing, possible in the Sadian mode: the lubricity he exposes exudes bodily fluids and productivities and embraces the phallic pen in the solitude of language (for Sade, a true prison-house ... but also a theater in which desire and empowerment – the myth of total control – are enacted).

In commenting on Foucault's treatment of sex and power, Jean Baudrillard in *Forget Foucault* pits the tenets of productivity against those of seduction. His comments are germane to Sade's exegesis of the family myth:

> The original sense of 'production' is not in fact that of material manufacture; rather, it means to render visible, to cause to appear and be made to appear: *pro-ducere*. Sex is produced as one produces a document, or as an actor is said to appear (*se produire*) on stage. To produce is to force what belongs to another order (that of secrecy and seduction) to materialize. *Seduction* is that which is everywhere and always opposed to *production*; seduction withdraws something from the visible order and so runs counter to production, whose project is to set everything up in clear view, whether it be an object, a number, or a concept. (21)

Baudrillard identifies pornography with production and thereby aligns it against seduction. Franval is thus correct (within his *nouvelle tragique*, his newly founded, yet ancient, code) when he tells Clervil at their first meeting that he has *not* seduced Eugénie. He is in Sade's and Baudrillard's sense a producer rather than a seducer. His voyeuristic pleasures as he surveys the scene in the circumvallation enact a productivity of the ejaculate, a masturbatory and auto-(homo-)eroticism that is, to use Baudrillard's terms, 'a frenzied activation of pleasure' (22). The scene Sade has Franval concoct can be described perfectly as one in which

> we find no seduction in those bodies penetrated by a gaze literally absorbed by the suction of the transparent void. Not a shadow of seduction can be detected in the universe of production, ruled by the transparency principle governing all forces in the order of visible and calculable phenomena: objects, machines, sexual acts, or gross national product.

Sade's productivity reminds us that virtue can participate in this 'transparent void,' and that norms of behavior and their transgressive counterparts are in constant need of revaluation, revision, and, possibly renaming. Perhaps Baudrillardian hyperspace conceals within its hyperbola the *impensé* that underlies the exposure of production, pornographic or other, and effects there the erasure of the *impensé* in the guise of sexual seduction.

Essential Pornogony and Virtual Embodiment

This is a reading of a particular scene in Sade's *Eugénie de Franval* that suggests that the *incest motif* illustrates Jean Baudrillard's dichotomous reading of what he sees as the fundamental and fatal opposition of production and seduction in a world of hyperreality in which reality *itself* has become a sort of null set. It exists to occupy a space, much as the zero does, but it has lost what might loosely be called its content-value. In hyperreality like hyper*space*, virtual embodiment of, say, images and other information*s*, displaces (rather than *re*places) conventional reality, that is, what we take for reality in the workings of our everyday lives. This displacement – a shunting aside of the modern, in one view – holds that convention in reserve so that hyper- and 'actual' reality coexist. For Baudrillard seduction both displaces production and is in its turn displaced by it. My example of the Sadian circumvallation in the novella typifies this dual and agonistic displacement by viewing seduction in both its hot and cold manifestations, to use Baudrillard's language.

This encapsulation serves to illustrate the hyperreal quality of the novella: *In the Franval story, a father enters into an incestuous relationship with his daughter; corrupts and ruptures her relationship with her mother; seduces a friend, Valmont, into seducing Madame de Franval in order to compromise her and thus short circuit her efforts to curtail his, Franval's, activities vis-à-vis Eugénie. He finally induces Eugénie to murder her mother, an act that momentarily brings the girl to her senses, at which point she dies, putatively because she cannot live with the horror she has helped cause. At this moment in the narrative Franval uses his own suicide to debase further the church and its moral teachings, an effort that has underlain his entire enterprise from the start.*

In an effort to circumscribe Baudrillard's notions of hot and cold seduction and apply them to a view of what constitutes the Sadian woman, I want to place this 'view' within the concept of hyperreality as a displacement of the scene of the Sadian brand of seduction. Whether what Sade enacts there is more *pro*ductive than *se*ductive is a question that may lead to an initial limning of Sade's woman as more than the puppet she is often portrayed to be. In order to talk about one Eugénie in this light, it is necessary to invoke another, the sexual initiate of Sade's *Philosophy in the Boudoir*. Though the two young women are willing acolytes in Sade's theater, one remains unregenerately Sadian throughout the text (*Boudoir*) while the other appears to die of shame, or guilt, or perhaps a particularly Gallic form of *chagrin*. The two characters overlay one another, partake of vice in a similar fashion as part of their initiation into the libertine lifestyle, and both exhibit a tenacious loyalty to their initiators. Yet I would contend that they also differ significantly and that it is that difference *coupled* to the similarity which authorizes a reading of the Sadian woman as a kind of composite of both.

I've already used the terms hot and cold by which Baudrillard often distinguishes between early historical simulations (seduction operates through simulations) and what he more recently labels a fourth-order simulation called the 'viral.' 'Viral' because it spreads by a sort of contagion and notably by proximity, on the analogy of the spread of technologies. That is, it is part of a metonymic process in language and economy more interested in syntax than in semantics. In some significant ways, the two Eugénies in Sade's two texts represent respectively the hot contractual rhetoric of a more primitive level of simulation (Eugénie de Mistival in *Boudoir*), and the distancing cool simulation that operates by placing the subject in proximity to the contagious element (Eugénie de Franval). Of course, this latter contagion is one promulgated at one remove by Franval himself – from behind the scenes. In seducing his own daughter and using her as an agent of his sexual and social iconoclasm, Franval is the chief artificer of the virus which will destroy Madame de Franval, Eugénie and himself.

The composite view of Sade's woman relies on a reading of the contractual in the two stories. The contract for Baudrillard is the realm of production in which he would place Sadian pornography, *the pragmatics of a linguistic and economic use-value* predicated on exchange. The two women named Eugénie make the respective contracts possible and thus represent simulacra of two different but related orders. The element that distinguishes them is the contriteness – if it is that – which releases Eugénie de Franval from her part in the contract thus expiating the sin of murder through the advent of her own death. Her homologue goes from willing acolyte to even more willing libertine, rivaling the cruelty and sexual aggression of her masters.

In *Philosophy in the Boudoir* the contract is established between Eugénie's absent father and the libertines who introduce his daughter to the world view of vice, a *Weltanschauung* that requires the practice of extremities in order fully to enact the terms of the contract. Angela Carter has pointed out that the contract in *Boudoir* aims at canceling motherhood to further the libertine's view of woman as subservient to him so long as she holds to those tenets of womanliness he sees as embodied in woman's role as mother. The contract with Monsieur de Mistival, like Franval's with his surrogate seducer Valmont, devalues the mother so that the libertine woman, Sade's woman, may be released to take her place as a surrogate man. Only as a sexual aggressor herself can she aspire to that state. Thus, the two contracts involve seduction as a means, while neither seduces as an end. In both cases violence replaces the sort of seduction which aims ultimately at seducing the seducer him- or herself. According to Baudrillard, without this element of what he terms reversibility, seduction degenerates into production, and what is produced is anathema to seduction and to *seductiveness*, that is, the potential for seduction inherent in things, people, events. There is nothing less seductive than the production line of sexual permutations, it would seem.

When Baudrillard contends that '[seduction] always annuls [production],' he is not saying that the former is always triumphant over the latter. In fact, *productivity* as a 'duellistic' element vis-à-vis seductiveness, thrives on the antagonistic relation engendered by the scene in which the 'duel' is enacted. In Sade this scene is a series of sexual and political tableaux which push to the limit the manipulative, i.e., productive, mechanisms of representation. What is represented in these tableaux vivants – living gestural exercises that seem to mime death in their 'still-lifeness' – is woman as revised archetype, her power lying in her femininity, which, to quote Baudrillard again, inverts the power of production that is a 'masculine power' (15). She is archetypal in that she must emerge as a new woman by destroying the 'old' woman, her mother. So, in both the polemical *Boudoir* and the moralistic *Eugénie de Franval*, the mothers are the object of loathing and attack: one is brutally assaulted, her vagina sewed up by her daughter after she has been raped by a syphilitic; the other is poisoned to death. What emerges as new in woman here is the dual stance erected on what I see as the composite of these two homologous characters. By juxtaposing the unregenerate libertine in the boudoir with the assumedly contrite or at least mortally chagrined seductress of Franval's circular display case, the circumvallation, we see that the new woman, *Sade*'s 'new woman,' forges a sexual archetype that will survive as the repentant whore, the working girl, the harlot with a heart of gold. While these images would certainly be repugnant to Sade, they can bring us closer to an understanding of at least one essentializing function of the Marquis' *pornogony*, or production of the pornographic as means to an end.

That function is the derailment of the so-called norms of socio-sexual behavior. While Sade continually claims through such mouthpieces as Dolmancé in the boudoir that woman's function is to provide man's pleasure – thus appearing to cast her once again in an essentially subservient role – he sees that function as one among near or nearer equals, a notion that extends the Enlightenment view of equality to something approaching more recent ideas of equality between the sexes, or among the various orientations that sexuality has always already taken.

'Pornogony,' as I use this neologism, participates in a cold seduction/simulation in Sade's *Eugénie de Franval*; whereas in *Philosophy in the Boudoir* a hotter contractual seduction is in operation. If an equal partner to sexual *libertinage* is to result from a composite view of these two forms of seduction-as-production, we need to understand them in some detail. For the sake of this essay I shall limit my examples of two kinds of seduction to the already mentioned circumvallation or display in *Franval* and the motif of cruelty as liberatory in *Boudoir*. Both texts are traditionally viewed as pornographic in that both elicit a degree of sexual excitation in the reader. However, where the pornographic text usually stops once its onanistic purpose has been served, the 'pornogonic' text produces a pornographic reading that could also stop at that point – the writerly text allows for the reader's choice here – or continue on toward other goals. These other goals in Sade are also deviant since they aim at derailing the socio-sexual contract. In *Boudoir*, of course, this strategy is deliberately transparent: interspersed with the sexual tableaux are exhortations to throw off the civilized mantle of sexual repression and become open to the true nature of man as dominant and cruel. Since nature knows neither cruelty nor kindness, our vocabulary, the very productivity of our language, will have to be altered to accommodate this new liberalizing worldview. However, it is not in the political/theoretical harangue but rather in the application of these liberating precepts that the libertine ideal is finally actualized in the tableaux themselves. Eugénie must cross over and thereby obliterate the social and moral contract that ties her to her mother in a repressive gesture toward both the sexual and the political in order to partake fully in the libertinage of her tutors in their world of closeted spaces, *salons privés*, and most particularly that uniquely French invention for seclusion and seduction, the boudoir. This notion of apartness is crucial to an understanding of just how Sade's idea of woman emerges. The closet, the alcove, the *petit salon* with its literary connotation, serve to expand the sexual experience into a more generalized view of the self as willful and purposive. *The power to will what one wants* is for Sade the Will to Power, as, significantly, this power is available equally, or nearly equally, to women as well as to men. That man, so far, is the dominant one does not preclude the possibility of woman's accession to dominance through desire. And here the critical division of meaning for Sade between desire and love must be recalled. Sade almost never mentions love, whereas appetite dominates his pedantry. The distinction I am drawing between hot and cold seduction necessitates a clear understanding of Sade's aversion to the sentimental in all but its ironic mode. In this sense cold and hot seduction lose much of their separate values of exchange and take on Baudrillard's symbolic value. I would argue that the boudoir functions as the place where hot and cold seduction coalesce into an amalgam no longer identifiable as to its constituent parts. The hot seduction of romantic and pre-romantic literature may set the stage for seduction in terms of the decor of Sade's spaces; what happens within the confines of those spaces defies the spontaneity necessary to accomplishing that romantic hot variety of seduction, replacing it with the cool calculations of theatricality and sexual precision which obviate that spontaneous response, bringing down the temperature of the scene and thereby transforming the commonly held definition of romantic seduction into a new vocabulary of formalized cruelty and liberation. For it is only through cruelty, according to Sade, that liberation can be accomplished, including liberation from the traditional definition of cruelty itself. It should be remembered in this regard that Sade's cruel lessons are never only gestures in themselves; they are always also productive of a stated end, what Baudrillard might style a fatal strategy, i.e., one that moves toward its own annihilation in death. Both Sade stories considered here (as well as most others) ape the life cycle with its ultimate sepulchral gesture. It may be an empty gesture or one suffused with spiritual and philosophical import.

I have suggested that a composite of woman based on the two Eugénie characters aids our understanding of the Sadian woman her author forges. While Baudrillard's cold and hot versions of seduction can now be seen to commingle in Sade's text, to become identified with a symbolic order of value rather than one of exchange, the element that unites these versions of seduction is incest. In *Philosophy in the Boudoir* incest is introduced at the end of the story where Eugénie violates her mother. In a real sense, for Sade, this intimacy is the sign of rupture and thus of liberation. He is equating, as elsewhere in his *úuvre*, vice with virtue. That this confusion or displacement is intended can be seen in his subtitle for *Eugénie de Franval: The Misfortunes of Incest*. Of course Sade is presenting the novella as a moral lesson, but we know that he has also used the framework of this title to celebrate the triumph of vice over virtue in *Les Infortunes de la vertue* (*The Misfortunes of Virtue*). The unencoded equation thus becomes 'incest equals virtue,' and brings us to the Sadian formula that makes vice and virtue, evil and good, inseparable, a formula that aims at the total disruption of the socio-sexual contract. As Susan Sontag has noted, one of the chief aims of the pornographic imagination is to create disruption. Of course, and a bit facilely perhaps, in Sade's case this penchant or drive to disrupt is usually attributed to the workings of a disordered mind.

I want to conclude with a return to a reading of the circumvallation scene in *Franval* as a case in point in this argument on the coalescence of Baudrillardian modes or manners of seduction. Remembering that Sade puts the full productive use of his pornogony in the service of what might be called a psychic disruption of libidinal economy, we can see that a by-product of that rupture might be the emergence of a liberatory function for woman. If she is free to choose sexually in full recognition from Sade's point of view that cruelty will necessarily be the result of her choice, then she may step out of the decor, shed the role of puppet, and decide what other choices she can make. Obviously both Eugénies or daughter characters are *bound entities* in the Sadian texts, texts that resemble the closeted spaces they describe. To assert the contrary would be to misread Sade to no purpose. But the scene in which Franval offers his daughter to Valmont in order to purchase another seduction, that of *Madame* de Franval, does in fact bring about the liberation – albeit a temporary one – of Eugénie and places her on a par with her libertine father. Earlier in the story we learn that upon seducing Eugénie Franval has 'fallen hopelessly in love' and that this fact has led inevitably to his cruel abandonment of his wife. This rather rare instance of love as a topic for Sade's discourse must arouse the reader's suspicion. In a moralizing piece in which the lesson is that vice actually does triumph over virtue even when the cruel perish of their own deeds, the very concept of love thus contextualized becomes equated with the cruel lesson of incest. Love's hot seduction (Franval's hopeless love, a romantic conceit) must be re-produced in the Sadian theater – here a circular display with Eugénie nude on a revolving pedestal controlled by Valmont and subject to his lust but outside his reach – as a cold masturbatory contagion that epitomizes Baudrillard's fourth order simulacrum, the viral. As Franval had fallen victim to a love perverted by its very circumstances and condition, so Valmont is infected. The difference is that in the first, hot instance of incestuous seduction, love in whatever guise sprang unbidden and flooded Franval with hopelessness, whereas in the second, all such spontaneous response is submerged in calculation and deceit. No love, no matter how tainted, results from the circumvallation. It is a seduction calculated to lead to and make possible the perfidious blackmail of Madame de Franval in order to circumvent the working of virtue she embodies. It is a technological seduction, one that uses a device – the circumvallation 'mechanism' itself – to achieve an end that can never involve reversibility, that necessary component of a reciprocal seduction according to Baudrillard. Since Franval and Eugénie as co-seducers of Valmont are never in 'danger' of being seduced themselves, what results from the scene is a veritable instance of cold seduction.

Virtual embodiment, or the embodiment of virtue is, of course, a play on Baudrillard's sense of the perils and temptations of various forms – and new *norms* – of virtual reality, what he calls hyperreality with its simulation of seduction, its displacement of desire, its *commodification of wanting* that parallels Sade's productivity of desire. Real embodiment, white slavery for example, has true exchange value. And while this particular commodification still continues, a lesser embodiment of desire has become more usual. Since desire and virtue, the trammeling of virtue, are coextensive elements of Sade's pornogony; the fates of both concepts in his closed world cannot be considered separately where the image of woman he projects is concerned. The cruel gesture, the proscribed word, both become tools of the woman who flouts societal expectations and takes her place alongside her male counterpart. Libertinage is the necessary debasement and voiding of virtue; and where virtue and desire coalesce in the Sadian plan for power, hot or romantic seduction and cold viral seduction play to one another within a reality of language that is a language game and an interiority of will. That is the power Sade desires and which he offers to woman as co-conspirator.

Endnotes

1   'Eugénie de Franval,' *Les crimes de l'amour*, Union Générale d'Editions, Paris, 1971: 202–302; 'Eugénie de Franval,' Marquis de Sade, *Justine, Philosophy in the Bedroom, and Other*

Writings, trans. Richard Seaver, Austryn Wainhouse, Grove Weidenfeld, New York, 1965 (1990): 373–445. (The two texts are cited parenthetically in this essay as *Crimes* and *Justine* respectively.)

2   Bersani follows Foucault's social structuration of desire, the notion that classification determines socially constructed gender categories. '... [T]he social project inherent in the nineteenth-century invention of 'the homosexual' can perhaps now be realized: visibility is a precondition of surveillance, disciplinary intervention, and, at the limit, gender-cleansing. The classification into character types of how people imagine and pursue their bodies' pleasures greatly reduced the heterogeneity of erotic behavior. A psychology of desire, as Foucault forcefully argued, drew those readable psychic maps on which human beings had to be assigned their places before territory could be occupied. Psychology in this argument *discovered* nothing; the questions it asked created the answers necessary to the social strategies that produced the questionnaire. Confession is a form of ventriloquism.' Obviously, for the present argument, the view of an erotics of the homosexual or the 'auto-sexual' relates to the visualization of desire that takes place in the circumvallation scene in 'Eugénie de Franval.' All of Foucault's prerequisites as Bersani outlines them (surveillance, disciplinary intervention, gender-cleansing [in the case of Sade, I would reconstruct the latter as 'gender-reordering' where Franval's theatricality controls the situation in which gender priorities are arranged in the circumvallation: primary self (Franval 'in the wings'); his stand-in Valmont (whose order is reduced – or promoted – to that of masturbator); Eugénie as gender quasi-indeterminant (in that no sexual self is ever activated *for/by* her in the scene)]) are satisfied in the novella where the scopticism of Franval/Sade's erotics is clearly in evidence. Following Bersani's tracing of Foucault's trajectory here, we could say that just as the classification 'homosexual' had to be named in order to be seen and then seen in order to be watched, i.e., surveyed, disciplined, and then even placed under erasure, i.e., cleansed (or re-ordered), so the extant term libertine needed to be outed, a process Sade accomplishes by throwing open the situation called libertinage (in his art if not in his life), in order for us to survey its content and potential *for woman*, in order to intervene in the disciplinary mode Sade always favors, and in order finally to place both ~~woman~~ and ~~libertine~~ under erasure. In this context, erasure aids in enacting a Sadian liberation of woman by allowing for the possibility that her old and new voices may coexist.

3   The family code, as I refer to it here, requires the stability of terms (language) associated with naming family members, for example, as well as with maintaining the reliability of other terms such as virtue. Since Franval declares his intention 'to bring about the downfall of virtue' (*Justine* 393), we observe this intentionality at work not only in his dealings with the cleric Clervil and Valmont, but especially in those with his wife whom he accuses of adultery knowing full well she is innocent. Her response to his goading assertions illustrates that he is using the reversal of codes, or accepted norms, in order to carry out his plans with Eugénie: 'It takes all your cunning, all your wickedness, Monsieur, *to accuse innocence the while excusing crime with such audacity.*' (*Crimes* 403, emphasis added) Once the code innocence-crime is reversed, the defilement of virtue becomes the ally of a concomitant violation of significance-reliability.

4   Serge Leclaire, *A Child Is Being Killed* 32–3. Leclaire, for example, identifies the need to forget the phallus with the Freudian death drive, the analysand's 'un-thought-of.' He recognizes and labels the impossibility of this separation from the phallus-as-signifier while reiterating the necessity of the separation. That which we cannot 'erase' in ourselves leaves a residue, or what Jacques Derrida has called a *restance* (remainder), at once 'unthought,' i.e., not (re)called to consciousness, and 'unthought-of,' i.e., neglected or, at best, *left aside* as a remainder or remains. '*What we must bring about so as to exist is our separation from the*

phallus. At the same time, however, what we cannot erase in ourselves is the figure of that phallus: circumcisions, baptisms, and initiations are only its intensified seal, be it taken as redemptive, propitiatory, or preventive. It sticks to us blindly but we must rid ourselves of it in order to recognize it. A passion for living moves us like a forever powerless yet victorious effort to free ourselves nonetheless from what is hooked to each of our words and glued to each of our cells: this devil of a phallus, from which we have to separate and 'dissex' ourselves if we want to have any reason for living and hope for *jouissance*. This is the *unthinkable object*, the ongoing work, the always focused-on goal of the death drive' (emphasis in original with the exception of *'unthinkable object'*). The 'unthinkable object,' the recognition of the symbolic power of the phallus, becomes the 'unthought' and the 'unthought-*of*' in the Sadian discourse.

5   The two passages are: 1. The 'seduction' of Eugénie (*Crimes* 215–18; *Justine* 383–5); 2. The circumvallation scene, or the 'seduction' of Valmont (*Crimes* 267–8; *Justine* 419–20). Maurice Heine restored them based on ms. 4010, Bibliothèque nationale (*Crimes* 214n, 266n; *Justine* 374).

6   'Stereo-Porno' in *Seduction* 28: 'The *trompe-l'œil* removes a dimension from real space, and this accounts for its seduction. Pornography by contrast adds a dimension to the space of sex, it makes the latter more real than the real – and this accounts for its absence of seduction.' Here the contrasting of the *trompe l'œil* effect as one of seduction with the three-dimensionality of the pornographic scene solidifies the opposition between Sade's *productive* theater (a hyperreal space in Baudrillard's terms, that is, a space where an overinvested or superadded reality overdetermines what poses as seduction and thereby turns it into its antithesis) and the truly *seductive* sleight-of-hand (the *trompe l'œil*) which works by virtue of an *under*investing of reality.

7   In commenting on the role of mother in Justine's and Juliette's experiences in their respective Sadian texts, Carter in *The Sadeian Woman and the Ideology of Pornography* attempts a reconstruction of motherhood as she sees it in Sade's writing. In writing of the character Durand, who plays instructress and mother substitute to Juliette, Carter describes what she sees in Sade as 'an anti-myth of mothering. In place of a reproductive function, she has acquired an absolute mastery of the physical world. She has exchanged motherhood for domination.' (113) Carter suggests that for the Marquis 'misanthropy bred a hatred of the mothering function that led him to demystify the most sanctified aspects of women and if he invented women who suffered, he also invented women who caused suffering. The hole the pornographer Sade leaves in his text is just sufficient for a flaying; for a castration. It is a hole large enough for women to see themselves as if the fringed hole of graffiti were a spyhole into territory that had been forbidden them.' (36) The female libertine thus can aspire to that status on a par nearly equal to that of man *only* by liberating herself from the mother function embodied in her own mother. This is especially true for the Eugénies in Sade's two texts under discussion in the present essay. Both follow their libertine masters' decree that the mother must be trammeled (and *not* merely symbolically, since as we see in the two stories the mother is physically tortured or murdered). In *Boudoir*, [Eugénie de Mistival] savages her mother in order to achieve sexual autonomy, according to the rules of the academy [of libertinage]; to attack Father or his substitutes [the other libertines] in order to achieve existential autonomy is against the rules.' (133)

8   For Jean Baudrillard (*Seduction* 37–49), production (what we may here call staging in the context of the Sadian tableaux and specifically in that of the circumvallation scene) is antithetical to seduction: 'Seduction's entanglement with production and power, the irruption of a minimal reversibility within every irreversible process, such that the latter are secretly undermined, while simultaneously ensured of that minimal continuum of pleasure without

which they would be nothing – this is what must be analyzed. At the same time knowing that production constantly seeks to eliminate seduction in order to establish itself on an economy of relations of force alone; and that sex, the production of sex, seeks to eliminate seduction in order to establish itself on an economy of relations of desire alone.' (47) The imperative to analyze the dynamic between production and seduction gives impetus to the present work. Sade's theater creates a mechanical mode of sexuality which partakes of the fruits (actually, sterility) of production and productivity with their necessary elements of irreversibility (as an ideal) and what Baudrillard styles immortality. He concludes that while seduction is not invincible – it is in fact losing ground to its inimical other in our time – it is 'stronger that power because it is reversible and mortal, while power, like value, seeks to be irreversible, cumulative and immortal. Power partakes of all the illusions of production, and of the real; it wants to be real, and so tends to become its own imaginary, its own superstition (with the help of the theories that analyze it, be they to contest it). Seduction, on the other hand, is not of the order of the real – and is never of the order of force, nor relations of force. But precisely for this reason, it enmeshes all power's *real* actions, as well as the entire reality of production, in this unremitting reversibility and disaccumulation – *without which there would be neither power nor accumulation.* (46, emphasis in original) I would add that seduction *always* colludes with production and therefore, even when the latter 'wins out' over the former, the former envelops ('enmeshes') the very immortality of productivity and thus disallows any ultimate sovereignty of the power base. It is this enveloping of the victor by the vanquished that permits Sade to frame his morality play in the trappings of romantic hot seduction while promoting a cold (i.e., in his case, a calculated and cumulative) brand of seduction which serves only to mask the production that underlies it.

9   From the book *Fatal Strategies* to the interview with Guy Bellavance that centered on that text (both 1983, the latter collected in Gane) Baudrillard mapped a movement toward death, or toward that movement's own extinction, which he labeled 'fatal': 'For me it is . . . a fatal strategy: something responds of its own accord, something from which it is impossible to escape, but which you cannot decipher either, an immanent type of fatality . . . It is there at the heart of the *system*, at a strategic point in the *system*, at its point of inertia, at its blind spot. That is my definition (there isn't any other) of the fatal.' (50, emphasis added) While 'stated end,' as I have here qualified what amounts to Sade's fatal strategy in his pedagogy of sex/cruelty, implies a conscious intent (one I believe he freely exhibits), the unconscious element in the Baudrillardian fatal strategy cannot be overlooked in the organization of sexual patterns Sade's tableaux (his 'system') enact. In every instance of his writing, the movement toward annihilation and death implicitly permeates the quest for pleasure/power.

10 My word 'disruption' as used here is intended to subsume Sontag's disorientation and dislocation: 'Pornography is one of the branches of literature – science fiction is another – aiming at disorientation, at psychic dislocation.' (47) As Sontag points out, '[pornography's] celebrated intention of sexually stimulating readers is really a species of proselytizing. Pornography that is serious literature aims to 'excite' in the same way that books which render an extreme form of religious experience aim to 'convert.' (47–8) Sade's open pedantry is an ample illustration of this: he claims to 'instruct' and implicitly to convert to the ways of libertinage through his challenge (*défi*) launched at what society calls the natural order. In this, his motto might be '[N]othing exists naturally, *things exist because challenged, and because summoned to respond to that challenge.*' (Baudrillard, *Seduction*, 91)

Bibliography

Baudrillard, Jean. *Fatal Strategies*. Trans. Phillip Beitchman, W. G. J. Niesluchowski. New York: Semiotext(e)/Pluto, 1990 (1983).
—— *Forget Foucault*. New York: Semiotext(e), 1987 (1977).
—— *Seduction*. Trans. Brian Singer. New York: St. Martin's Press, 1990 (1979).
Bersani, Leo. *Homos*. Cambridge: Harvard University Press, 1995.
Carter, Angela. *The Sadeian Woman and the Ideology of Pornography*. New York: Pantheon, 1978.
Derrida, Jacques. *Resistances of Psychoanalysis*. Trans. Peggy Kamuf, Pascale-Anne Brault, Michael Naas. Sanford: Stanford University Press, 1998 (1996).
Gane, Mike, ed. *Baudrillard Live: Selected Interviews*. London: Routledge, 1993.
Leclaire, Serge. *A Child Is Being Killed: On Primary Narcissism and the Death Drive*. Trans. Marie-Claude Hays. Standford: Stanford University Press, 1998 (1975).
—— *Psychoanalyzing: On the Order of the Unconscious and the Practice of the Letter*. Trans. Peggy Kamuf. Stanford: Stanford University Press, 1998 (1968).
Sade, Marquis de. *Justine, Philosophy in the Bedroom, and Other Writings*. Trans. Richard Seaver and Austryn Wainhouse. New York: Grove Weidenfeld, 1965.
—— *Les Crimes de l'amour*. Paris: Union Générale d'Editions, 1971.
—— *La Philosophie dans le boudoir*. Paris: Gallimard, 1976.
Sontag, Susan. *Styles of Radical Will*. New York: Delta, 1966.

Chapter 8

'On the Beach of Elsewhere': Angela Carter's Moral Pornography and the Critique of Gender Archetypes

Gregory J. Rubinson

'Moral Pornography' and the Anti-Pornography Movement

The burgeoning women's liberation movement in the 1960s and 70s recognized and sought to correct the myths associated with femininity which have accrued through depictions of women in various influential discourses: myths, for example, that linked virtue to virginity (as in the Christian archetype of the Virgin Mary), charm and attractiveness to suffering (as in the Marilyn Monroe-style Hollywood icon), femaleness to 'lack' (as in psychoanalysis' Oedipus Complex), and sexual agency to whorishness (as in pornography). Whereas the women's movement was able to unite behind the project of demythologizing the majority of such representations, pornography has proved an ongoing source of division among feminists.[1]

Since the late seventies, the most publicly visible forms of feminist action in both the US and Britain have centered on pornography.[2] More than just a convenient focus for all the injustices that women suffer, pornography is a political rallying point that can be identified as vivid evidence of those injustices. Andrea Dworkin and Catherine MacKinnon – the most prominent feminist anti-pornography campaigners – argue that pornography is the primary cause and manifestation of male dominance, misogyny, and women's victimization and objectification.[3] Ann Snitow, however, argues that the focus on anti-pornography campaigning has re-directed the feminist movement away from the struggle for sexual and economic equality and child-care reform and towards 'an emphasis on how women are victimized, how all heterosexual sex is, to some degree, forced sex, how rape and assault are the central facts of women's sexual life and central metaphors for women's situation in general' (Ellis 11).[4] In her essay 'Feminist Fundamentalism: The Shifting Politics of Sex and Censorship,' Elizabeth Wilson goes a step further, suggesting that the antiporn movement is a new manifestation of fundamentalism: 'To have made pornography both the main cause of women's oppression and its main form of expression is to have wiped out almost the whole of the feminist agenda, and to have created a new moral purity movement for our new (authoritarian) times' (Segal and McIntosh 15–28: 28).

At roughly the same historical moment as the antiporn campaign was beginning to dominate the feminist agenda, British novelist Angela Carter published *The Sadeian Woman* (1978), her cultural study of pornographic depictions, especially those written by the Marquis de Sade. In it, Carter proposed the radical theory of the 'moral pornographer': an artist who 'might use pornography as a critique of current relations between the sexes' (19).[5] Today, despite the wide-ranging critiques of the anti-pornography dominance of feminist agendas, the false equation of feminism, antiporn agendas, and 'male-bashing' is so common that Carter's early proposal of pornography's potential to be critical of gender relations seems even more radical than when it was first published.

Carter derived her idea of the 'moral pornographer' from her reading of Sade. She values his unrestricted disclosure of sexual power dynamics and reads him as a satirist who 'describes sexual relations in the context of an unfree society as the expression of pure tyranny, usually by men upon women' (*SW* 24). In contrast to Sade's pornography, Carter critiques quotidian pornographic writing as a genre which depicts and perpetuates 'mythic' versions of femininity (and masculinity):

> Since all pornography derives directly from myth, it follows that its heroes and heroines ... are mythic abstractions ... Any glimpse of a real man or a real woman is absent from these representations of the archetypal male and female ... [P]ornography reinforces the archetype of [women's] negativity and ... it does so simply because most pornography remains in the service of the status quo. (6, 16–17)

For Carter, Sade certainly portrays mythic notions of femininity, but he does so in large part to satirize the assumptions underlying them. She argues that Sade's Justine – the archetypical suffering woman – suffers principally because of her 'virtuous' insistence on the preservation of her virginity despite her multiple brutal rapes. Obviously, Carter's reading is problematic in that it at times seems to suggest that Justine should enjoy the abuse she suffers,[6] but what she reads as important in Sade's representation of Justine is his satire of the male-authored myth which insists that a woman's value is dependent on her virginity.

Even more importantly for Carter, Sade challenges archetypical models of femaleness by creating antithetically mythic models, that is, 'Sadeian Women,' or 'women as beings of power' (*SW* 36) like Juliette and Durand. Such transgressive women, Carter interprets, wield power by actively 'fucking' and thereby overturning the 'normal' dynamic of sexual relations:

> Women do not normally fuck in the active sense. They are fucked in the passive tense and hence automatically fucked-up, done over, undone. Whatever else he says or does

not say, Sade declares himself unequivocally for the right of women to fuck ... [Sade] urges women to fuck as actively as they are able, so that powered by their enormous and hitherto untapped sexual energy they will then be able to fuck their way into history and, in doing so, change it. (27)

These are provocative claims, but Carter admires Sade for his uncompromised flouting of so many of the institutions, virtues, ideals, and taboos of a theistic, androcentric world. She reads Sade's libertines as desacralizing crusaders who 'turn the Blessed Virgin over on her belly and sodomise her' and debunk the notion that 'sex is sanctified only in the service of reproduction' (76). Carter celebrates their desacralization of the bourgeois sexual ideals of chastity and purity. Similarly, the libertines defy the ideal of feminine physical beauty by taking pleasure in its opposite – excessive ugliness. '[N]onsense! cry the libertines' (76) and this might be considered Carter's rallying cry as well.[7]

The language, also, of the above passage emphasizes Carter's irreverence towards androcentric social conventions. 'Fuck,' she implies, is a masculine word about masculine activity – sexual or otherwise. It functions as a pervasive social metaphor for action and in an androcentric world it is inevitably women who are the implied recipients of the word and all of its connotations. With her aggressive appropriation of this masculine discourse, Carter upsets the bourgeois ideal of women as demure drawing-room objects and asserts their right to be part of the culture of 'fucking' – the society of activity – and shape history in the active sense.

As might be expected, Carter's interpretation of Sade has been a major source of contention for antiporn feminists such as Susanne Kappeler, Susan Brownmiller, Susan Griffin, and Andrea Dworkin – their writings on pornography are implicitly, and occasionally explicitly, in dialogue with Carter. Nevertheless, Carter's relationship with them is complex, full of curiously overlapping sympathies which neither Carter nor her interlocutors would be (or would have been) likely to recognize or admit. Carter clearly abhors the predominance of the 'woman as victim' archetype which Dworkin and Catherine MacKinnon purposefully perpetuate; however, there are a few striking similarities in their ideas. For example, Andrea Dworkin, whose *Pornography: Men Possessing Women* is an implicit denunciation of Carter's *Sadeian Woman*,[8] shares her anti-mythologizing agenda and concerns about the trend among some feminists to want to replace patriarchy with matriarchy (Dworkin, *Letters* 110–16).[9] And, like Carter, Dworkin views sex in terms of a power struggle between the sexes: 'Fucking is the means by which the male colonializes [sic] the female . . . [I]t is regarded as an act of possession' (119). The important difference, however, is that Carter, as I intend to show, can imagine a reversal of this dynamic, a perversion and consequent subversion of the social order on which such a sexual power dynamic relies.

What I find hypocritical, however, is that Dworkin, like Carter, uses language, scenarios, and themes in her own fiction that could be (and have been[10]) construed as pornographic. Her novel *Mercy*, for example, which describes a woman's physical/sexual suffering in explicit detail, might easily be classified as Carter's brand of 'moral pornography,' but Dworkin would no doubt consider it as belonging to a genre of realism rather than pornography. For Dworkin, the label 'pornography' automatically implies an exploitative, misogynistic authorship, whereas Carter treats the genre as historically dominated by misogyny but not essentially tied to it. Dworkin argues that pornography inevitably represents women as sexual objects in subservient or subordinate positions to men and so is inherently degrading towards women. The points of contention for the antiporn camp, then, are Carter's propositions that pornography, even in its most violent and misogynistic forms, always has something to teach us about sexual power relations and the cultural construction of gender; and that pornography can be used to present alternative images of sexual empowerment for women.

Despite some similarities between Carter and the antiporn feminists, then, one ought not to underestimate their differences. Catherine MacKinnon, who views pornography as 'constructing and performative rather than merely referential or connotative' (*Only Words* 21), takes it as a given that the use of pornography leads directly to the forceful re-enactment of the scenarios it presents. Carter too views pornography as 'constructing and performative,' but sees in that the potential to revise the traditional message of male dominance which pornographic scenarios often convey. Carter doesn't want a simplistic inversion of the current power disparity between men and women. Rather, she wants to protest the naturalization – through genres like pornography – of sexual inequalities. If women can achieve autonomy with their sexuality and their sexual relations, Carter suggests, then equality can be achieved in economic and other spheres of society.

To understand Carter's concept of a moral pornographer, then, one has to be willing to see pornography as having the potential to criticize as well as reinforce sexist ideals. It is this view that Susanne Kappeler, for example, cannot tolerate, arguing that pornography informs actual sexual practices in the most causally direct manner (1–4).[11] Kappeler, MacKinnon, and Dworkin do not consider that pornography can be (and in most cases is) non-violent; they seem unwilling to consider pornography as anything other than mimetic and prescriptive.[12] My purpose in these comparisons is not to dismiss the concerns of the antiporn feminists.[13] Their goal to prevent the exploitation of women is certainly no different from that of other subgroups of feminism. However, their focus on pornography as the principal cause and manifestation of women's oppression is misguided (see Strossen, Ellis, Williams, and Segal and McIntosh). There are many genres, including pornography, that subordinate and demean women through their representations. But since gender roles are naturalized in artistic, literary, and other representational genres, critical readings and rewritings of genre present the opportunity to challenge those roles – to show their androcentrism. According to Linda Hutcheon, postmodern writers such as Carter seek to 'point out that those entities that we unthinkingly experience as "natural" ... are in fact "cultural"; made by us, not given to us' (2). A 'moral pornographer,' then, would use pornographic forms, language, and other conventions to 'de-naturalize' (3) commonly held values about sex and gender.

Perversion and Gender Archetypes

I have already raised the concept of perversion with regard to Carter's proposed strategy for moral pornography. In this section, I demonstrate how perversion is especially relevant to the project of critiquing naturalized gender roles.

Historically, the term 'perverse' has been used by a variety of authoritative discourses – e.g. legal, psychoanalytic, theological – to define and contain behavior (usually sexual, but not necessarily so) that deviates from prescribed social norms. One early use of the term, by Francis Bacon, describes an inversion of 'naturalized' hierarchies: 'Women to govern men ... slaves freemen ... being total violations and perversions of the laws of nature and nations' (*OED*). Continuing in this tradition of conceiving the perverse as a deviation from dominant social norms, nineteenth and twentieth-century legal and psychological discourses defined perversion in terms of criminality and pathology. For example, in *Psychopathia Sexualis*, Richard von Krafft-Ebing asserts that any sexual act 'that does not correspond with the purpose of nature, i.e., propagation' (52) is perverse and therefore pathological. A little later, Freud defined perversion as simply any erotic fixation on part(s) of the body not designed for heterosexual penetration or fetishized objects which substitute for the 'natural' object of sexual focus – the phallus (150). Implicit in this use of the term, obviously, is the naturalization of heterosexuality and heterosexual intercourse. Other sexual behaviors are pathological. This bias (of non-heterosexual behavior as pathologically perverse) has remained dominant in much of modern Western psychiatry. Robert Stoller, for example, defines perversion as 'the erotic form of hatred ... the reliving of actual historical sexual trauma aimed precisely at one's sex ... or gender identity. ... [I]n the perverse act the past is rubbed out ... trauma is turned into pleasure, orgasm, victory' (Stoller 4, 6).

Implicit in these and many other usages of the term 'perverse' is a perceived link between perversion and social subversion. One definition of the perverse, which Mandy Merck calls attention to, is 'the opposition to what is "right, reasonable or accepted"' (6). Kaja Silverman argues, in fact, that perversions have the potential to subvert social hierarchies by negating the 'binarisms that reinforce each other' and uphold 'the principle of hierarchy' (185). Foucault, of course, asserts that perversions fed the workings of power by opening up new avenues for the exercise of power – regulation, intervention, etc. The authority of legal and medical discourses was predicated on the extent to which they intervened on 'perverse' sexual practices in order to regulate them (Foucault 47–9). Nevertheless, the historical fact of prescriptive sexual legislation indicates a fear of non-normative sexuality on the part of institutions of power. Like Silverman, then, it seems to me that Foucault's dismissal of the subversive potential of perversions is inadequate (see Silverman 186–7). Certainly, repressive attitudes towards sex and legislation prohibiting non-reproductive, non-marital sexuality only served to increase the proliferation of sexual discourses. But this does not disprove the subversive potential of such sexual discourses.

One place where I see the potential for perversions to be socially subversive is in the production of the social values that have supported gender inequalities. Gender norms are constructed and disseminated through sources such as myth, religion, psychoanalysis, and Hollywood cinema. These sources proffer a common cultural base of archetypical figures which provide authoritative models for gendered behavior. For Luce Irigaray, there are three central female archetypes which define and limit women's social behavior:

> *Mother, virgin, prostitute: these are the social roles imposed on women.* The characteristics of (so-called) feminine sexuality derive from them: the valorization of reproduction and nursing; faithfulness; modesty, ignorance of and even lack of interest in sexual pleasure; a passive acceptance of man's 'activity'; seductiveness. (186–7)

Scholars contributing to *Feminist Archetypal Theory* (Lauter and Rupprecht) argue that such archetypes are cultural constructs which *prescribe* and reinforce stereotypical gender roles and behavior rather than 'innate' human categories which *describe* some putatively universal reality (as in Jungian archetypal theory). In *The Sadeian Woman*, Carter forcefully announces that archetypal depictions of femininity are the target of her critique as well: 'All the mythic versions of women, from the myth of the redeeming purity of the virgin to that of the healing, reconciling mother, are consolatory nonsenses' (5).

In Sade's Justine, Carter sees a re-manifestation of the 'holy virgin,' while Juliette is the 'profane whore' (101). The antiporn feminists perceive women represented in pornography as Justine-figures – women for whom suffering is made (in the pornographic context) to seem 'natural.'[14] It is this Justine archetype that Carter is most critical of in her analysis of Sade, suggesting that women must not give in to the idea of themselves as victims. While Justine embodies victimhood – the archetype which the antiporn feminists actively encourage – Juliette, in Carter's opinion, does not simply act out the role of the archetypical prostitute; rather, she is a 'blasphemous guerilla of demystification' (105). Defying objectification, Juliette becomes an autonomous sexual being. In doing so, 'she rids herself of some of the more crippling aspects of femininity' (79). Juliette achieves her autonomy because she is able to become sexually and economically exploitative: like men, she 'fucks.' True, she participates in many horrifying acts of sexual violence and economic crime, but Carter is not suggesting that women literally adopt Juliette's methods. Carter characterizes Juliette as empowered but also as another source of tyranny. 'I do not think I want Juliette to renew my world,' Carter writes, 'but, her work of destruction complete, she will . . . have removed a repressive and authoritarian superstructure that has prevented a good deal of the work of renewal' (111).

Perversion, as we have seen, has long been associated with women taking power. Juliette's 'perverse' sexual activity, then, not only enables her to break the mold of Justine's victimhood, but by taking power she perverts and, consequently, subverts gender hierarchy. If dominant gender roles are made 'natural' in representations and archetypes such as the ones I have been discussing, then *representations* of the perverse can aid the process of debunking the myths that uphold gender inequality. Carter's theory of the 'moral pornographer' hinges on this idea. She seeks to turn our perception of the perverse upside down. To set constraints on womens' bodies in representation – whether the impulse originates with the moral majority or the antiporn feminists – is, in effect, setting limits on women's agency. Perversion in Carter's theory, then, is seen as liberatory rather than confining, immoral, or pathological. In the following analysis of Carter's novel *The Passion of New Eve*, I will suggest how Carter puts this theory into practice.

The Perversions of Eve

Although the Marquis de Sade is Carter's historical model for the writer who comes closest to her paradigm of the 'moral pornographer,' her own fiction evolved from this concept. *The Passion of New Eve* (1977), written around the same time as *The Sadeian Woman*, is an explicit attempt to write 'moral pornography.' In *The Passion of New Eve*, Carter uses pornographic conventions to rewrite archetypical representations of Woman as Mother, Nature, Biblical Eve, sex symbol or screen icon, profane whore, and sacred virgin, as well as the sources of these archetypes (e.g. psychoanalysis, religion, Hollywood). As Nicole Ward Jouve remarks, Carter perceived these incarnations of womanhood as mere stage machinery: 'She finds ropes and pulleys, props, make-up, dye, sequins, where others saw gods, virgin mothers, stars, and angels' (158).[15] Jouve's reference to theatricality is an important one, for if these paradigmatic figures of femininity are revealed to be performances or artifice, then those performances can be changed.[16]

An early scene in *New Eve* imports narrative elements from a clichéd pornographic pursuit scene.[17] Leilah, an exotic dancer dressed in fetishistic heels and crotchless panties, leads Evelyn, a young English misogynist newly arrived in America, on an erotic chase through a near-future New York immersed in dystopian chaos. In a graphic sexual depiction, Carter parodies pornographic language, critiquing the essentialism of pornography which symbolically reduces people to genitalia. When Evelyn and Leilah are at the climax of their pursuit, Evelyn comments:

> All my existence was now gone away into my tumescence; I was nothing but cock and I dropped down upon her like, I suppose, a bird of prey, although my prey, throughout the pursuit, had played the hunter. My full-fleshed and voracious beak tore open the poisoned wound of love between her thighs. (25)[18]

There is a heightened quality to the language here that imitates (albeit at a more sophisticated level than most) pornographic literature. Perhaps the most recognizable language convention of pornographic literature, whether of the 'lowbrow' or 'highbrow' variety, is to substitute a variety of metaphors for parts of the body. Here Carter does the same, but with metaphors that draw attention to the dehumanizing facets of a sexual act in which the participants are playing out a violent sexist fantasy. The aggressiveness of the language Evelyn employs to narrate the event reveals a mind dominated by an association of sex and violence: thus, he *tears* into her *voraciously*. Evelyn's violent desire deforms both of them so that, for that moment, they *become* the metaphors used to describe them. They have become grotesque, inhuman: he is a 'bird of prey' whose human body is gone, leaving only his penis depicted as a vicious animal – a 'cock' in two senses; and she is reduced to a 'poisoned wound,' echoing the myth of God's blood vengeance on Eve.[19]

The fact that Leilah initiates this pursuit and encourages it by dropping her dress and then her underwear for Evelyn to pick up at first seems problematic for reading this scene as critical of rather than complicit with sexist representations. On the one hand, her initiation of sex in this instance and others indicates a strong sexual autonomy. On the other hand, she seems trapped in a view of herself as a sexual object – a view perpetuated by the sex work she performs.

Her status as an object is evident in her nightly ritualistic cosmetic preparations. Standing before a mirror, she creates the 'edifice' (29) of her femininity from a vast 'assemblage of... paraphernalia that only emphasized the black plush flanks and crimson slit beneath' (30). Leilah paints both her face and body, reifying a male libidinal fantasy – the archetypical porn model who exists solely for a man's pleasure and is cosmetically enhanced and posed to draw attention to her genitalia. She conforms to the conventional portrayal of women in heterosexual, androcentric pornography and becomes, in Luce Irigaray's comparable terms, an 'obliging prop for the enactment of man's fantasies' (25). Irigaray elaborates on this by arguing, as Carter might, that women's bodies are commodities which must conform to social expectations: 'Participation in society requires that the [female] body submit itself to a specularization... that transforms it into... a 'likeness' with reference to an authoritative model' (179–80). In this case, Leilah imitates the 'authoritative model' of the porn icon. Thus, when Evelyn comments that he 'never knew a girl more a slave to style' (*PNE* 31), he may mean to be hyperbolic, but he is in fact merely stating it as it is. Leilah is literally enslaved to style: she is meticulous about embodying male pornographic fantasies, and the image of herself as an object in the mirror holds her captive. The fact that she is black further emphasizes her position as an exotic, enthralled woman.

Despite this, Leilah cannot be viewed solely as a victim of pornography and prostitution. She is not entirely the 'born victim' that Evelyn perceives her to be (28). By leading the chase, Leilah presents herself as a sexual subject. Similarly, Leilah later exhibits aggressive sexual agency: 'she would clamber on top of me ... and *thrust* my limp cock inside herself... Waking just before she *tore* the orgasm from me, I would ... remember the myth of the succubus' (27, my emphases). Here Carter, like Sade, affirms women's right to 'fuck' – that is, to be sexual agents and consequently to exercise power. But Carter goes on to suggest that in a male-dominated world there is inevitably a price that women have to pay for the 'perversion' of exercising sexual autonomy: the climax of the pursuit scene is described as a brutal domination of Leilah by Evelyn and, subsequently, Evelyn punishes Leilah regularly by tying her to the bed and beating her with a belt. Evelyn and Leilah play out a sadomasochistic cycle of power reversals in which Leilah exhibits sexual desire and initiative and Evelyn punishes her for this perversion.

Thus, although Leilah exhibits some sexual agency, she is not a 'Sadeian Woman' such as Juliette. Her 'perversions' – her acts as a sexual aggressor – meet with violent, misogynist retaliation in which Evelyn re-establishes his dominance by beating and penetrating her. Ultimately, Leilah remains trapped in the role of sexual object – 'the woman watching herself being watched' (30) – prescribed by the pornographic archetype of womanhood. At this stage of the story, Leilah is more Justine than Juliette, though later she reappears radically transformed and empowered.

It would be naïve to read this portrayal of Leilah as somehow merely replicating the power inequities represented in the bulk of pornography.[20] Carter's writing is highly self-conscious and ironic in such a way that it is perpetually commenting on the nature of the sexual relations being depicted. And if there is any doubt as to the critical thrust of Carter's writing, it quickly becomes evident that Evelyn's mistreatment of Leilah is to be severely paid for: he himself becomes the subject of all the abuses (and more) of which he previously had been the instigator.

This reversal begins in 'Beulah,' a womb-like underground city housing a women's resistance group, where Evelyn is forcefully castrated, surgically sex-changed, and subsequently re-programmed as a woman complete with a 'maternal impulse.' On the run from Leilah after she has a nearly fatal encounter with a back-alley abortionist, he is captured in the desert and presented to 'Mother,' the matriarch of the women's group. Mother is one of Carter's most brilliant grotesque figures. She has surgically altered herself to incarnate a mythic and *deformed* notion of motherhood. Described in gargantuan terms, Mother is 'a sacred monster ... personified and self-fulfilling fertility ... [B]reasted like a sow – she possessed two tiers of nipples . . . Her ponderous feet were heavy enough to serve as illustrations for gravity' (59). Carter emphasizes the grotesqueness and artificiality of Mother in part to draw attention to the artificiality of the figure she replaces – the traditional white male, patriarchal, bearded, and vengeful god of Judaism and Christianity. Mother perverts the 'natural' order which Francis Bacon defined. Of course, Carter is not actually trying to write a new theology. Mother is an ironic figure who represents a warning against the dangers of merely inverting patriarchal myths, a point Carter makes explicit in *The Sadeian Woman* when she declares that 'Mother goddesses are just as silly a notion as father gods' (5).

Mother, then, is a manifest perversion of the maternal archetype. She parodies how warped the *concept* of motherhood has become, not only in androcentric discourses like psychoanalysis, but in some feminist circles. Reclaiming the maternal archetype as the primary emblem for women's political emancipation, Carter believes, is a particularly seductive impulse for it does represent the major biological function that men can never perform but have sought to regulate throughout history. But, warns Carter,

> The theory of maternal superiority is one of the most damaging of all consolatory fictions and women themselves cannot leave it alone, although it springs from the timeless, placeless, fantasy land of archetypes where all the embodiments of biological supremacy live. It puts those women who wholeheartedly subscribe to it in voluntary exile from the historic world, this world . . . where actions achieve effects and my fertility is governed by my diet, the age at which I reached puberty, my bodily juices, my decisions – not by benevolent magics. (*SW* 106–7)

Carter's comments here are aimed at sacralized fantasies of a protective, conciliatory, 'all-affirming' mother such as those offered by Cixous and Kristeva.[21] Mother in *New Eve* is more akin to Carter's description of Sade's Durand: 'she is the omnipotent mother of early childhood who gave and withheld love and nourishment at whim . . . The cruel mother, huge as a giantess, the punishment giver, the one who makes you cry' (*SW* 114). Mother, like Durand, represents an 'anti-myth of mothering' (113), a 'phallic mother.' In one scene which showcases Carter at her most jubilantly parodic, Mother declares 'I am the Great Parricide, I am the Castratrix of the Phallocentric Universe' (*PNE* 67).

Hyperbolic pronouncements like this one, coupled with the grotesque presentation of Mother, make it apparent that Carter is also targeting Freud, who promoted many of the most problematic myths regarding sexuality, gender roles, and perversity. Freud's notion of the Oedipal Complex, especially, has been perhaps the most influential narrative of sexual 'normality' and 'perversity' in modern history. Carter, then, rewrites the archetypical tale of incestual perversion in a highly stylized fashion to parody some of the more androcentric facets of psychoanalysis and undermine its authority. Against a background of women chanting the names of female deities and mythic figures, Evelyn is raped by Mother and so forced to re-enact the Oedipal transgression. Sophia, one of his captors, adjures him:

> 'Kill your father! Sleep with your mother! Burst through all the interdictions!' ...
> 'Reintegrate the primal form!' she urged me.
> 'Reintegrate the primal form!' shrieked Mother ...
> I caught one glimpse of her gaping vagina as I went down; it looked like the crater of a volcano on the point of eruption ... Then her Virginia-smoked ham of a fist grasped my shrinking sex; when it went all the way in, Mother howled and so did I.
> So I was unceremoniously raped. (64)

The massive irony of the last line (with a chorus chanting in the background, what could be more 'ceremonious'?) calls attention to the ritualistic elements in this passage, highlighting the fact that the inhabitants of Beulah have incorporated motifs from psychoanalytic theory into their theology. The voguish uses of psychoanalysis by many feminist theorists is clearly something Carter is suspicious of and so the aggressively hyperbolic language of the passage (such as the entreaties to 'Reintegrate the primal form!') ridicules this trend. Mother inverts psychoanalytic themes to put the power in womens' hands: Evelyn's 'shrinking' penis is divested of all the symbolic power attributed to it in psychoanalysis while Mother's 'gaping' vagina – yet another perverse image – is 'erupting' with power. But the sexual inequalities which are evident throughout Freudian theory remain. That patriarchy should be replaced by matriarchy is, as Carter suggests, a 'consolatory nonsense.' So Carter desacralizes the mother-goddess fantasy by dramatizing its consequences as an extended joke in which the maternal figure is grotesquely misshapen and merely attempts to rewrite psychoanalytic motifs to her own advantage.

Mother also falls prey to inverting androcentric ideals when she attempts to rewrite Old Testament mythology by 'trimming' Evelyn to Eve. Evelyn's body becomes the text on which Mother will inscribe a new story. He is in part to be reconstructed as a new Virgin Mary archetype; that is, he is to be impregnated with his own sperm to produce the 'Messiah' of a new matriarchal world order to overthrow the old patriarchal one. Mother's mistake, however, is that by constructing a 'New Eve' she is doing nothing more than re-creating the original archetype of the patriarchal Old Testament myth. She does not 'subvert' the dominant paradigm; she merely attempts to invert it. As an alternative to Mother's inversion of patriarchy, Carter is steering us towards imagining a deconstruction of gender hierarchies.

To do so, the rest of the novel follows New Eve as she undergoes a series of experiences and picaresque adventures which produce her female subjectivity. Carter's strategy here is closely related to Irigaray's idea of 'mimicry' – that is, she writes from the subject position of an incipient woman caught in a male-dominated world in order to uncover the mechanisms of androcentric exploitation and the formation of gender roles (Irigaray 76).

The first of these experiences occurs subsequent to Evelyn's sex change during Mother's attempt to 'program' Eve with a new feminine, maternal subjectivity. Eve is exposed to Hollywood movies featuring Tristessa – a female screen icon reminiscent of Marilyn Monroe, Western European portraits of the Virgin and Child, slides of suckling mammals and 'non-phallic imagery such as sea-anemones opening and closing,' and audio tapes of gurgling babies and contented mothers (*PNE* 72).[22] It is also critically important that Eve's body is constructed to fit 'the physical nature of an ideal woman drawn from a protracted study of the media' (78). Eve assesses her new self in the mirror: 'They had turned me into the *Playboy* centerfold. I was the object of all the unfocused desires that had ever existed in my own head' (75). Like Leilah, she has become a pornographic archetype – a 'woman watching herself being watched' (30). Ironically, however, she still possesses a man's libidinal mindset, causing the 'cock in [her] head' to '[twitch] at the sight of' herself (75). This ironic play on the narcissistic perversion heightens our awareness of the artificiality of pornographic icons: Eve's new archetypical physique is as much an artifice as that of the porn centerfold – a theatricality whose effect and coherence depend on lighting, make-up, set, positioning, air-brushing, and other illusionary techniques. And it produces the expected, programmed effect: arousal for the male viewer.

It might seem that Mother's strategy is akin to that of a postmodern writer. Eve is the product of a bricolage of myths derived from psychoanalysis, Old and New Testament scripture, pornography, and Hollywood film. Mother takes motifs from these sources and attempts to rewrite them from a feminist perspective to give women the power. But she fails because she is still drawing on and therefore validating androcentric source material. She creates a fundamentalist religion out of her version of feminism, but this is hardly a victory for sexual equality. Her failure is deliberate, however, for it is Mother and her fanatical attempt to rewrite patriarchy as matriarchy that is the target of Carter's ridicule in this section of the novel. Carter's parody desacralizes systems of social organization based on sexual inequality whether they are androcentric or gynocentric.

Carter shifts her focus to critique a masculine archetype when, after an escape from Beulah, Eve is captured by the mad 'poet' Zero, initiated into her womanhood by being raped, and made one of his harem of wives. A foil for Mother, Zero is a one-eyed, one-legged desert patriarch – in essence, a personified penis – who has convinced his harem that his sexual attentions are necessary for their continued health. His wives are reduced to unindividuated combatants for equal access to his 'elixium vitae' (92) – i.e., his semen. Sex with Zero, then, is literally the means of their subordination. Again, the scenario draws on and refers to the tropes of pornography: Carter depicts Zero's wives as masochistic sex objects – willing, submissive, 'wanting it,' even 'needing it'; they are archetypical figures of heterosexual, androcentric pornography. They accept Zero unquestioningly as a godhead, and, as with Mother's Beulah, their community is a kind of fundamentalist cult – in this case structured as an androcentric pornotopia. And Carter does not shy away from critiquing the link between some pornographic ideas and physical violence: Zero's wives are the object of much physical abuse, including having had their front teeth knocked out to prevent nicks to Zero's penis while performing oral sex. This pornotopia, then, is inherently sadomasochistic and Carter's emphasis on this highlights the link between sexual/ physical cruelty and male social dominance.

Zero not only physically abuses his wives but he deprives them of the capacity to communicate. Describing the linguistic order of this micro-patriarchy, Eve tells us that Zero:

> would bark, or grunt, or squeak, or mew at us because he only used the language of the animals towards his wives . . . [H]e would savage . . . offender[s] unmercifully with his bullwhip. So our first words every morning were spoken in a language we ourselves could not understand; but he could. Or so he claimed, and, because he ruled the roost and his word was law, it came to the same thing. (96–7)

Zero speaks a different language, a language that imitates the sounds of animals and so automatically degrades those to whom it is directed – his wives. By forcing them to use it despite their incapacity to understand it or express meaning in it, Zero reinforces their status as animals rather than people. Zero's wives (including Eve) produce meaning by uttering signifying noises but they have no access to that meaning themselves and so must resort to whispering to each other in secret, afraid of being detected and punished for transgressing Zero's law. Here again Carter's fictional society makes explicit the radically unequal distribution of power among men and women. Luce Irigaray suggests that access (or lack thereof) to language – the means of signification – is a key factor in the gender power imbalance: 'Women, animals endowed with speech like men, assure the possibility of the use and circulation of the symbolic without being recipients of it. Their nonaccess to the symbolic is what has established the social order' (189).[23]

Irigaray's comments suggest that Zero's power is predicated on his ability to exclude his harem from speech. Without language, there can be no autonomy of thought or action: they remain enslaved and utterly dependent on him. In her essay 'Notes From the Front Line,' Carter suggests that language itself is androcentric and leads women, including herself, unconsciously to 'posit a male point of view as a general one' (71). Language, she writes, 'is power, life and the instrument of culture, the instrument of domination and liberation' (77). It is for this reason, she asserts, that 'it is so enormously important for women to write fiction *as* women – it is part of the slow process of decolonialising our language and our basic habits of thought' (75).

Just as Zero denies his wives the capacity to communicate anything that might express individuality, he denies them individuality in appearance: their behavior, their hair, and their dress – either naked except for dungarees or, for ritual poetry recitations, 'dressed up, or undressed, in the style of high pornography' (*PNE* 103) – are all identical, all designed to meet Zero's desire. Similarly, their backgrounds are expeditiously summarized as that of archetypically abused women: 'All the girls had the same dreary biographies; broken homes, remand homes, parole officers, maternal deprivation, inadequate father figures, drugs, pimps, bad news. They were case histories, rather than women' (99). Eve mimics the experience of these women by fabricating an autobiography that conforms to the conventions of such 'case histories': 'a cruel mother who kept me locked in the coal-shed, a lustful step-father' (87). Through mimicry, then, Eve becomes a kind of undercover chronicler of their experience which is denied articulation in Zero's regime.

Similarly, Eve's sexual interactions with Zero put her on the receiving end of the violence she (as Evelyn) enacted on Leilah. Sex with Zero is brutal, described in metaphors allusive of Sade: 'I was in no way prepared for the pain; his body was an anonymous instrument of torture, mine my own rack . . . He entered me like the vandals attacking Rome' (88, 91). After raping her a second time, Zero announces that she is now his eighth wife, forcing Eve into a situation tantamount to Sade's Justine – the virgin archetype made unwilling whore.[24] The sexual abuse Eve suffers at Zero's hands completes her programming as a 'woman': 'Zero turned me into a woman. More. His peremptory prick turned me into a savage woman' (107–8). The implication here is that to be a woman is to be the object of male sexual violence. Thus, Carter draws attention to the problem of sexual violence – either in the 'real' world or in representations of women such as those of pornography – as a factor often contributing to the development of women's personhood. In Zero's community, it becomes apparent, sadomasochism is integral to the establishment of gender roles.

With an exuberant lack of subtlety, Carter mocks the patriarchal archetype by naming its embodiment 'Zero,' drawing attention to his infertility and symbolic impotence. Zero attributes his infertility to Carter's fictional screen icon, Tristessa. Carter portrays Tristessa – who is famous for her masochistic depictions of Madeline Usher, Desdemona, and Catherine Earnshaw – as a descendent of Sade's Justine, the 'mythically suffering blonde' (*SW* 102). Combining the appeal of sex symbol and female masochist, she is another incarnation of male sexual fantasies. In Tristessa, Carter finds a potent image for the problematic link between male desire and female suffering – a link perpetuated in pornography and Hollywood cinema. For Evelyn especially, Tristessa was yet another pornographic archetype, the object of his sadistic sexual fantasies: as a youth he 'dreamed of meeting Tristessa, she stark naked, tied, perhaps to a tree in a midnight forest under the wheeling stars' (7); and even the night before he arrives in New York he goes to see an old film of *Wuthering Heights* and, moved by the spectacle of Tristessa's suffering as Catherine Earnshaw, pays her 'a little tribute of spermatazoa' (5). In Zero's monomaniacal imagination, however, this archetypal object of the 'male gaze' bites back: Tristessa transcends the cinema screen and 'her eyes [consume] him in a ghastly epiphany' (104). The 'male gaze' which, in Laura Mulvey's discussion of cinema, tends to view women as passive sexual objects (19) is turned with searing effect back at the gazer. Ironically, the archetypal sadist believes himself unmanned by the archetype of female masochism.

Given new insight by her trans-gendered status, Eve notes that, like the porn model whose personhood or self 'is reduced to its formal [sexual/genital] elements' (*SW* 4), Tristessa has 'no ontological status; only an iconographic one' (*PNE* 129). A 'high-class' version of Leilah, Tristessa employs the theatrical tools of artifice (i.e., cosmetics and costumery) in conjunction with her characteristic display of masochism to simulate a masculine ideal of femininity. This artifice is literally torn away when Zero cuts through her g-string to reveal that Tristessa is a man in drag. It is one of the more dramatic, humorous, and critically incisive moments in Carter's fiction. Tristessa's artifice perverts heterosexual, androcentric gender norms: this idealized incarnation of 'femininity' is a theatrical illusion, one which fools heterosexual men into betraying the sexual orientation that is so critical to their self-identity. It is this 'perversion' of 'nature' that has the emasculating effect on Zero, the parodic figurehead of patriarchy.

The revelation of Tristessa's transvestitism again highlights the performative/ simulacral nature of gender: alterations to the surface of the body produce what is assumed to be a universal essence – femininity or masculinity. The presentation of Tristessa, of course, asks us to question the relation between appearance and essence. As Judith Butler argues, 'Just as bodily surfaces are enacted *as* the natural, so these surfaces can become the site of a dissonant and denaturalized performance that reveals the performative status of the natural itself' (146). The revelation of Tristessa's perversion results in exactly the kind of 'denaturalizing' effect that Butler imagines: the 'loss of gender norms ... depriv[es] the naturalizing narratives of compulsory heterosexuality of their central protagonists: "man" and "woman"' (146). In other words, Carter purposefully departs from narrative conventions which clearly delineate and maintain masculinity and femininity as discrete concepts defined in opposition to each other. With the explicit examples of Leilah, Tristessa, and Eve *performing* gender, Carter, pre-dating Butler's idea that gender performances are a compulsory facet of human behavior, demonstrates that gender is an 'act.'[25]

Butler emphasizes the compulsory nature of such performances: as I have already discussed, in legal, medical, religious, and moral discourses about sexuality and gender roles, behavior or presentations of self that do not fit with heterosexuality, procreative/marital sexuality, and the clear-cut separation of gender roles very often remain classified as perverse and are treated as a pathological deviancy. Although the gender transgressions of Carter's characters challenge traditional concepts of 'masculinity' and 'femininity,' the effects of androcentric norms are still evident: Eve, Leilah, and Tristessa are all compelled to mimic the role of 'Woman' according to a set of dominant cultural expectations, and the common defining feature of their experience as women is suffering. Through mimicry, Eve comes to the realization that 'femininity' is an amalgamation of male-authored conventions to which women feel compelled to conform throughout their lives: 'although I was a woman, I was now also passing for a woman, but, then, many women born spend their whole lives in just such imitations' (*PNE* 101).

At the same time, however, perversion calls into question the naturalized status of such constraining narratives and presents the possibility of departing from them. Linda Williams, in her excellent analysis of the conventions of pornographic film, proposes a model of 'perverse' sexuality free from the androcentric heterosexual norm: 'as discourses of sexuality name, identify, and ultimately produce a bewildering array of pleasures and perversions, the very multiplicity of these pleasures and perversions inevitably works against the older idea of a single norm . . . against which all else is measured' (114–15). Carter's fiction occasionally presents a sexual scenario that transcends the aggression endemic to a world where desire is determined by androcentrism and gender archetypes. In *New Eve*, the one scene that gives a glimpse of what such a positive sexuality might look like is structured in such a way that Carter, like Williams, suggests the need for 'perversion' in constructing alternate sexualities, for its two protagonists have transcended the limits of polar sexuality. Having escaped from Zero, Tristessa and Eve form a transgressive figure which defies the norms and categories of heterosexist society. Up until this point, Carter has evoked 'perversions' like masochism, narcissism, sadism, and transvestitism for a variety of deconstructive purposes. In this scene, Carter represents a perverse union as having the potential to transcend pre-determined norms. Carter is not, of course, literally offering a paradigm for sexual fulfillment; she is merely speculating on a sexuality fantastically separate from patriarchal social reality. 'I know who we are,' says Eve, 'we are Tiresias . . . [O]ut of these fathomless kisses and our interpenetrating, undifferentiated sex, we had made the great Platonic hermaphrodite together, the whole and perfect being' (*PNE* 146, 148).

As Tiresias – the blind, gender-transgressing prophet of Greek myth who illicitly obtained knowledge of male *and* female sexuality – Eve and Tristessa represent a synthesis of polar modes of being: 'masculine' (phallic) and 'feminine' or aggressive and submissive. Carter is not literally proposing that hermaphroditism is a prerequisite for liberated sexuality; she is presenting a fantasy image of a sexual union in which the participants have transcended the limiting gender values that pervade our theistic, androcentric world. The transcendence of this moment gestures towards hope, a hope that Carter finds lacking in Sade's (*SW* 129). But the legend of Tiresias' blinding (whether by Athena because he saw her bathing or by Hera because he sided with Zeus on the question of whether men or women derive more pleasure from love) foreshadows a necessary fall from their utopian union. Like Tiresias, they must be punished for having obtained a forbidden knowledge of sexuality and pleasure. The transcendental moment is checked by a starker social reality when an ad hoc militia of fundamentalist Christian boys tear them apart and execute Tristessa. The fact that these boys are Christian fundamentalists further implicates religion as a damaging source of intolerance with regards to human diversity.

While Eve and Tristessa are together, however, another important critique of gender takes place. They both abandon the performance of masculinity and femininity and Eve's experience of sexual pleasure precipitates an epiphany regarding the arbitrariness of gender: 'Masculine and feminine are correlatives which involve one another. I am sure of that – the quality and its negation are locked in necessity. But what the nature of the masculine and the nature of feminine might be, whether they involve male and female . . . that I do not know' (*PNE* 149–50). This is the end to which Carter has evoked the perverse gender-transgressing figure of Tiresias: to express skepticism about the presumed link between biology and gender. Seventies' feminism, like feminism today, was in part divided by the debate over whether gender is the product of 'nature' or 'nurture.' Carter is careful in the above passage not to dismiss completely a possible connection between gender and innate, biological factors, but it is clear that she repudiates the notion that biology is entirely responsible for how gender is expressed in human society. This matter requires further investigation on a number of disciplinary fronts, but one of Carter's main objectives with her 'moral pornography' is to promote the idea that a variety of social and cultural factors contribute significantly, and perhaps entirely, to the determination of gender traits: gender is a learned behavior and an artifice. To understand this point of view creates the possibility for change in received gender roles and relations between men and women, and it has the potential to benefit humanity as a whole by enabling both women and men to participate in society in ways that were previously deemed taboo.

The finale of the novel reunites Eve with Leilah, who is now part of the women's resistance and (significantly) calling herself Lilith.[26] She gives Eve the news that 'Mother has voluntarily resigned from the god-head' and 'retired to a cave by the sea for the duration of the hostilities' (174). With a masterstroke of comic irony, Carter confines Mother to a 'cave beyond consciousness' (184) – the mystical womb central to Freudian psychoanalysis and its later feminist revisions. The goddess, if not dead, as Carter wishes in *The Sadeian Woman*, is at least in hibernation. Desacralizing myths of deities, heaven, and eternity is fundamental to Carter's objectives:

> with the imaginary construct of the goddess, dies the notion of eternity, whose place on this earth was her womb ... There is no way out of time. We must learn to live in this world ... because it is the only world we will ever know ... I think this is why so many people find the idea of the emancipation of women frightening. It represents the final secularisation of mankind. (*SW* 110)

To give up entirely our religious myths, Carter suggests, would mean giving up once and for all the institutions that uphold male social dominance. It is for this reason that Carter relentlessly attacks religious and pseudo-religious figures. Nicole Ward Jouve writes that in *New Eve* Carter 'hunted the [maternal] archetype down to extinction' (157). It is a dramatic assessment which gets at the root of what Carter is attempting in all of her writings: to eradicate myths and archetypes which define social roles and limit human potential by attributing essential qualities to people based on their gender.[27] Like Sade's libertines, Carter cries 'nonsense!' in the face of received social and religious values.

Along with Mother, the rest of the archetypes have become redundant, as Lilith/Leilah notes: 'when there was a consensus agreement on the nature of the symbolic manifestations of the spirit, no doubt Divine Virgins, Sacred Harlots and Virgin Mothers served a useful function; but the gods are all dead, there's a good deal of redundancy in the spirit world' (*PNE* 175). Nowhere is the desacralizing thrust of Carter's fiction more explicit. Carter speculates that dispensing with this pantheon of deified archetypes would result in a liberatory social destabilization: Eve and Lilith arrive at an apocalyptic California riven by a civil war that has destroyed Hollywood, the most influential source of American myths. The old society is being torn down, presenting revolutionary opportunities not just for women but for Blacks and other disempowered freedom-fighting groups as well.

By the seacoast they encounter a mad old woman sitting in a wicker chair. Her face is 'magnificently painted' (177) and she is burlesquely costumed in a two-piece bathing suit, stole, and high-heeled sandals. The burlesque aspects of her appearance again suggest a pornographic and performative embodiment of femininity. With her theatrically heavy make-up and costume, Carter depicts her as an old performance artist – the quintessential performer of femininity – in her twilight. The artifice of femininity remains, but the overall effect is eroded as the decaying underside shows through: her face is dirty, 'her flesh . . . wrinkled and ravaged and sagged from her bones,' and the polish on her six-inch fingernails is 'badly chipped and scratched' (177). The garishness of her appearance augurs the dying days of this constraining version of femininity.

Looking at this decaying archetypical figure, Eve asks herself, 'how would the old ones fare, in the post-apocalyptic world?' (178). In Carter's scenario, the apocalypse constitutes the end of one iconography or set of expectations for the performance of gender and the birth of another, formerly repressed one: Lilith and Tiresias – irreverent, disobedient, and marginal figures in myth – will ascend to central positions in the new order. Having found both sexes so constricted by archetypal expectations, Carter's protagonist transcends the limits of gender and is reborn, expelled from Mother's womb-like cave by the seashore as the 'apotheosis of Tiresias' (186). Carter is hostile to myth as we know it but ironically delights in scripting new mythologies by salvaging marginal mythic figures like Tiresias. As an incarnation of Tiresias, *New* Eve manifests a new kind of liberated personhood or subjectivity which combines the knowledge of what it is to be male and female. The narrative ends ambiguously but with an optimistic note. The old woman tells Eve that they 'are on the beach of elsewhere' (190) and Eve sets sail in a small boat with her unborn child (conceived in the desert with Tristessa) to begin a new world. Though formed from a melting pot of female archetypes, Eve emerges as an icon of social perversity – a deviant from what is widely considered to be 'natural' – and heralds a 'new' era.

The Uses of Pornography

Linda Williams, who defines genre as a problem-solving technique,[28] asserts that male-authored heterosexual

> pornography is a speculation about pleasure that begins, as does Tiresias, from a phallic perspective, journeys to the unseen world of the sexual other, and returns to tell the story. An ideal of bisexuality drives the quest for the knowledge of the pleasure of the other: that one sex can journey to the unknown other and return, satiated with knowledge and pleasure, to the security of the 'self.' (279)

The Passion of New Eve follows this path but not with the purpose of uncovering the 'secrets' of female pleasure for the male reader. It begins from Evelyn's 'phallic'/male perspective and journeys to a female perspective to tell a story not principally of pleasure (though there is an important moment of this with Tristessa) but of pain. 'Moral pornography' represents a conceptual change in pornography as a genre. It is not a fantasy depiction of women performing sex for the titillation of male viewers or readers; instead, it is aimed at demonstrating the real problems of life as a woman in a male-dominated society and culture. And for Eve/lyn, importantly, there is no return to the 'security' of masculinity.

Williams also notes that 'Pornography as a genre wants to be about sex. On close inspections, however, it always proves to be more about gender' (267). This is the assumption that underlies Carter's concept of moral pornography. Her fiction purposefully employs the conventions of pornographic literature to critique traditional ideas about gender. One by one, Carter evokes, rewrites, and so dispenses with the old gender archetypes: 'Mother' retires to a 'cave beyond consciousness' and expels New Eve from that haven, Leilah is reborn as Lilith, and Zero is nullified. *The Passion of New Eve* dramatizes an apocalyptic end for many of the myths related to gender which have historically limited human, especially women's, potential. Carter's ultimate destination is, like New Eve's, beyond the social construction of gender, beyond outmoded archetypes, beyond myth, to an 'elsewhere' place where these concepts have lost their authority.

Endnotes

1. In 'The Popularity of Pornography,' Andrew Ross chronicles the split between antiporn feminists and what he terms the 'anti-antiporn feminists.'
2. See Elizabeth Wilson, 'Feminist Fundamentalism: The Shifting Politics of Sex and Censorship' (Segal and McIntosh 15–28: 16).
3. See, for example: Dworkin's *Pornography: Men Possessing Women* and *Letters from a War Zone*; MacKinnon's *Only Words*. See also Kappeler, Griffin, and Brownmiller.
4. Snitow's essay is 'Retrenchment vs. Transformation: The Politics of the Antipornography Movement' (Ellis 10–17).
5. Future references to Carter's *The Sadeian Woman* are marked in the text as *SW*.
6. Carter, as Elaine Jordan implies (27), was frequently contentious for the sake of unsettling our assumptions.
7. In '(Male) Desire and (Female) Disgust: Reading *Hustler*,' Laura Kipnis appreciates similarly iconoclastic strategies at the heart of one of today's most infamous products of pornography: *Hustler* magazine. Though an intensely misogynistic publication, Kipnis, similar to Carter's appraisal of Sade, notes that *Hustler* presents irreverent images that attack the ideologies of a reactionary, theistic, and morally hypocritical society.
8. See especially pages 84–5. Carter, in turn, has confided to Elaine Jordan that 'if I can get up ... the Dworkin proboscis, then my living has not been in vain' (Sage 332, n5).
9. Also in that essay – 'Biological Superiority: The World's Most Dangerous and Deadly Idea' – Dworkin criticizes some feminists who believe in the biological superiority of women.
10. Naomi Morgenstern discusses *Mercy* as a text whose foremost generic traits are derived from pornographic and gothic fiction – two of the genres most used by Carter. Harriet Gilbert,

in 'So Long as It's not Sex and Violence: Andrea Dworkin's *Mercy*' (Segal and McIntosh 216–29), finds numerous parallels in *Mercy*'s story line to that of Sade's *Justine*. While not wanting to establish that the novel is 'pornographic,' Gilbert makes it clear that it would be very easy for a legal authority to do so. Gilbert's argument was prophetic as, ironically, one of the censorship laws inspired by MacKinnon and Dworkin's antipornography ordinance resulted in the seizure of Dworkin's books *Woman Hating* and *Pornography: Men Possessing Women* by Canadian customs officials (see Strossen 158, 205–6).

11 There have been many arguments that there is no evidence for such a causal relationship (see, for example, Goldstein and Kant; McNair 60–71). By the same token, a view of fantasy as utterly divorced from reality is naive. Certainly, pornographic depictions can be a part of the construction of real-life sexuality, though Goldstein has suggested that, if anything, it is the withholding of pornographic materials and other sources of information about sex in adolescence that can contribute to the development of criminal sexual behavior. But what Carter wants to convince us of is that pornography can also be scripted and/or perceived in such a way as to critique the power relations between the sexes.

12 Mackinnon, like Kappeler, makes an over-simplistic equation between pornographic representations and sexual reality: 'Pornography is not imagery in some relation to a reality elsewhere constructed. It is not a distortion, reflection, projection, expression, fantasy, representation, or symbol either. It is sexual reality' (*Feminism Unmodified* 149).

13 Nor do I mean to endorse uncritically all of Carter's ideas on the subject. I find some of the details of Carter's analysis of Sade unconvincing and misguided. For all of her glorification of Juliette's transgressions of taboo, Carter does, as Kappeler points out, relish the representation of woman as inflictor of suffering – a role that has historically been exercised exclusively by men. While this does represent an upheaval of gender power dynamics, it is not, to say the least, the most humanitarian attitude towards gender role reformation. Fortunately, Carter does qualify her celebration of this impulse (*SW* 111).

14 Linda Williams critiques Dworkin's appeal to the archetype of the 'suffering woman' to broker an alliance with the conservative, male-dominated Meese Commission on Pornography: 'only by casting her archetypal 'suffering woman' in the role of the absolute victim of history can Dworkin utter her appeal to the compassionate man who will save her' (21).

15 See Jouve's '"Mother is a figure of Speech . . ."' (Sage 136–70).

16 This is one of Judith Butler's arguments in *Gender Trouble*, but Carter had conceived and, more importantly, dramatized the idea of gender as performance years beforehand.

17 Susan Rubin Suleiman notes that Carter derives elements of this scene from the Surrealist writer Robert Desnos's *La Liberté ou l'amour!* (see Suleiman 137).

18 Future references to Carter's *The Passion of New Eve* are marked in the text as *PNE*.

19 Other sexually explicit scenes in Carter's fiction similarly demonstrate how the conventions of pornography highlight sexuality devoid of humanity, as when Desiderio, the protagonist of *The Infernal Desire Machines of Doctor Hoffman*, accompanies the Sadeian Count to the 'House of Anonymity': they don costumes which are 'unaesthetic, priapic and totally obliterated our faces and our self-respect; the garb grossly emphasized our manhoods while utterly denying our humanity' (130).

20 Robert Clark is notorious for having done so. His arguments against Carter have been more than adequately debated in Elaine Jordan's article 'Enthralment: Angela Carter's Speculative Fictions' and elsewhere.

21 Gerardine Meaney contrasts Carter's critique of the maternal archetype to Cixous and Kristeva's ideas (98–100).

22 Marianne Warner writes that the kind of 'double drag' Carter performs here – 'a woman speaking through a man disguised as a woman' – was her favored stratagem for questioning

how sexual identity is attained; see 'Angela Carter: Bottle Blonde, Double Drag' (Sage 243–56: 251).
23 Irigaray is implicitly responding to Lacan's exclusion of women from the symbolic in his model of psycho-linguistic development (see 'The Mirror Stage'). Given the numerous allusions to Lacan in this part of *New Eve*, it is reasonable to assume that Zero is intentionally a parody of Lacan.
24 In *The Sadeian Woman*, Carter suggests that Justine relocates her virginity from her hymen to her frigidity: as long as she represses all possibility of experiencing pleasure, she is still 'pure' (48–9). Similarly, each sexual encounter between Eve and Zero is 'a renewed defloration, as if his violence perpetually refreshed my virginity' (*PNE* 101).
25 Or, as Alison Lee notes, 'Both Eve and Tristessa learn to *perform* their genders, and the very act of performance suggests a liminality that would seem to argue against an original essence' (246).
26 According to Kabbalistic tradition, Lilith was the first wife of Adam who was destroyed by God for insisting on sexual equality.
27 It is also important to note that the text does warn of the persistence of archetypes: Mother has 'retired' but only 'for the duration of the hostilities' (*PNE* 174). And the text ends with Eve at sea, ironically praying to the ocean as mother: 'Ocean, ocean, mother of mysteries, bear me to the place of birth' (191).
28 Williams derives this idea from Jameson's analysis of the medieval romance in *The Political Unconscious* (Williams 129).

Bibliography

Brownmiller, Susan. *Against Our Will: Men, Women, and Rape*. New York : Simon and Schuster, 1975.
Butler, Judith. *Gender Trouble: Feminism and the Subversion of Identity*. New York: Routledge, 1990.
Carter, Angela. *The Infernal Desire Machines of Doctor Hoffman*. 1972. London: Penguin, 1982.
—— 'Notes from the Front Line.' *On Gender and Writing*. Ed. Michelene Wandor. London: Pandora, 1983. 69–77.
—— *The Passion of New Eve*. 1977. London: Virago, 1982.
—— *The Sadeian Woman*. New York: Pantheon, 1978.
Clark, Robert. 'Angela Carter's Desire Machines.' *Women's Studies* 14 (1987): 147–61.
Cixous, Helene. 'The Laugh of the Medusa.' Trans. K. and P. Cohen. *Signs* 1(1): 875–99.
Dworkin, Andrea. *Pornography: Men Possessing Women*. New York: Putnam, 1979.
—— *Letters From A War Zone*. Brooklyn, NY: Lawrence Hill, 1993.
—— *Mercy*. New York: Four Walls Eight Windows, 1991.
Ellis, Kate, et al, eds. *Caught Looking: Feminism, Pornography, and Censorship*. East Haven, CT: Long River Books, 1986.
Foucault, Michel. The History of Sexuality. Vol. 1. Trans. Robert Hurley. New York: Vintage, 1990.
Freud, Sigmund. 'Three Essays on the Theory of Sexuality.' *The Standard Edition of the Complete Psychological Works*. Trans. James Strachey. Vol. 7. London: Hogarth Press, 1953.
Goldstein, Michael J. and Harold Sanford Kant. *Pornography and Sexual Deviance*. Berkeley: University of California Press, 1973.

Griffin, Susan. *Pornography and Silence: Culture's Revenge Against Nature.* New York: Harper & Row, 1981.
Hutcheon, Linda. *The Politics of Postmodernism.* London: Routledge, 1989.
Irigaray, Luce. *This Sex Which Is Not One.* Trans. Catherine Porter. Ithaca: Cornell University Press, 1985.
Jameson, Fredric. *The Political Unconscious.* Ithaca: Cornell University Press, 1981.
Jordan, Elaine. 'Enthralment: Angela Carter's Speculative Fictions.' *Plotting Change: Contemporary Women's Fiction.* Ed. Linda Anderson. London: Edward Arnold, 1990. 19–40.
Kappeler, Susanne. *The Pornography of Representation.* Cambridge, UK: Polity Press, 1986.
Kipnis, Laura. '(Male) Desire and (Female) Disgust: Reading *Hustler.*' *Cultural Studies.* Eds. Lawrence Grossberg, Cary Nelson, Paula Treichler. New York: Routledge, 1992. 373–91.
Krafft-Ebing, Richard von. *Psychopathia Sexualis.* 1893. New York: Stein and Day, 1978.
Kristeva, Julia. 'Women's Time.' Trans. Alice Jardine and Harry Blake. *The Kristeva Reader.* Ed. Toril Moi. New York: Columbia University Press, 1986.
Lacan, Jacques. 'The Mirror Stage.' *Écrits: A Selection.* Trans. Alan Sheridan. New York: Norton, 1977. 1–7.
Lauter, Estella and Carol Schreier Rupprecht, eds. *Feminist Archetypal Theory: Interdisciplinary Re-visions of Jungian Thought.* Knoxville: University of Tennessee Press, 1985.
Lee, Alison. 'Angela Carter's New Eve(lyn): De/En-Gendering Narrative.' *Ambiguous Discourse: Feminist Narratology & British Women Writers.* Ed. Kathy Mezei. Chapel Hill: University of North Carolina Press, 1996: 238–49.
MacKinnon, Catherine. *Feminism Unmodified: Discourses on Life and Law.* Cambridge, MA: 1986.
—— *Only Words.* Cambridge, MA: Harvard University Press, 1993.
McNair, Brian. *Mediated Sex: Pornography and Postmodern Culture.* London: Arnold, 1996.
Meaney, Gerardine. *(Un)like Subjects: Women, Theory, Fiction.* London: Routledge, 1993.
Merck, Mandy. *Perversions.* New York: Routledge, 1993.
Morgenstern, Naomi. '"There is Nothing Else Like This": Sex and Citation in Pornogothic Feminism.' *Genders 25: Sex Positives? The Cultural Politics of Dissident Sexualities.* Eds. Thomas Foster, Carol Siegel, and Ellen E. Berry. New York: New York University Press. 39–67.
Mulvey, Laura. 'Visual Pleasure and Narrative Cinema.' *Visual and Other Pleasures.* Bloomington: Indiana University Press, 1989. 14–26.
Ross, Andrew. 'The Popularity of Pornography.' *No Respect: Intellectuals and Popular Culture.* New York: Routledge, 1989. 171–208.
Sage, Lorna, ed. *Flesh and the Mirror: Essays on the Art of Angela Carter.* London: Virago, 1994.
Segal, Lynn and Mary McIntosh, eds. *Sex Exposed: Sexuality and the Pornography Debate.* New Brunswick, NJ: Rutgers University Press, 1993.
Silverman, Kaja. *Male Subjectivity at the Margins.* New York: Routledge, 1992.
Stoller, Robert J. *Perversion: The Erotic Form of Hatred.* 1975. Washington: American Psychiatric Press, 1986.
Strossen, Nadine. *Defending Pornography: Free Speech, Sex, and the Fight for Women's Rights.* New York: Scribner, 1995.
Suleiman, Susan Rubin. *Subversive Intent.* Cambridge, Mass.: Harvard University Press, 1990.
Williams, Linda. *Hard Core.* Berkeley: University of California Press, 1989.

Chapter 9

Perverse Writing – Maternity and Monarchy: Fictocriticism and Exorbitant, Plural Bodies

Heather B. Kerr

Following Dollimore's call for the deployment of perversion as a cultural category (14), I want to explore the possibility that fictocritical writing in the academic context is an instance of the perverse. As objects for analysis I take theoretical and other representations of two apparently discrete models of plural embodiment, bringing together discursive constructions from early modern English culture, contemporary feminisms and children's fiction. Deploying fantasy and postmodern allegory, I undertake a feminist engagement with the essay as a potentially 'perverse space' (Burgin). I will dwell on theories of the king's two bodies (Kantorowicz; Axton; Žižek) and ask what would happen if we brought back into view that which the theory of the motherless state (Gatens) is in part designed to supersede: maternity.

Both these discourses of embodiment imagine pluralities and both can be understood as (differing) models of the perverse. In the case of kingship the so-called 'body natural' (the finite, material body) incorporates the 'body politic' (understood as a perpetual ideality). This effectively refigures the masculine body, standing for both king and state, as 'not of woman born'. The annointing that marks the plural kingly body as sublime body, effects a fantastic perpetuity. The theory of the king's two bodies strives to bi-pass the abject, that which is encountered in the corpse (the king's dead body) and in what Kristeva calls 'something maternal' (*Powers of Horror* 208). Kantorowicz and Maitland alert us to the conceptual perversity of such a 'fantastic and subtle description of the king's superbody' (Kantorowicz 4), a 'ludicrous, and in many respects awkward, concept' (5) that was at one and the same time 'an important heuristic fiction' (5). This wilful 'man-made irreality' (5), 'that curious freak of English law' (Maitland 105), is one of those perversions that 'deviate from a destiny understood as natural' (Dollimore 2) (in this case, the necessities of birth and death). The maternal and the corpse are sites of abjection, and as Kristeva remarks, 'abjection is related to perversion' (*Powers of Horror* 15). Bataille offers a model for the necessary politico-theological fiction of the king's two bodies as defense against the abject:

> Abjection . . . is merely the inability to assume with sufficient strength the imperative act of excluding abject things (and that act establishes the foundations of collective existence) . . . The act of exclusion has the same meaning as social or divine sovereignty, but is not located at the same level; it is precisely located in the domain of things and not, like sovereignty, in the domain of persons. (Qtd in Kristeva, *Powers of Horror* 56)

The fiction of the king's two bodies has sufficient strength to exclude the mother and death with respect to the king's person: sacred annointing is a rite of purification. But its acknowledged status as a legal fiction (even a fiction within a fiction) (Kantorowicz 5) marks out its perversity. As the fiction is exposed to corrosion we encounter the abject: abjection 'accompanies all religious structurings and reappears, to be worked out in a new guise, at the time of their collapse' (*Powers of Horror* 17). I will turn especially to texts of the early modern period to illustrate the culture's awareness of its vulnerable perversity, such 'art' perhaps fittingly understood as 'destined to survive the historical forms of religions' (*Powers of Horror* 17).

In the case of the maternal body in patriarchal culture, her plurality is by contrast the mark of a (doubly) inescapable materiality (as woman and as mother), birthing an unavoidable scene of grotesque abjection. I take the 'idealizing' of maternity to be a relatively weak defense against the masochism that is the mark of women's perversion (Kristeva, 'Stabat Mater' 183; Welldon), just as the pregnant body is medicalized as a perversion, 'a condition that deviates from normal health' (Young 161). As Young suggests, the pregnant subject is 'split or doubled in several ways' (160):

> She experiences her body as herself and not herself. Its inner movements belong to another being, yet they are not other, because her body boundaries shift and because her bodily self-location is focussed on her trunk in addition to her head. The split subject appears in the eroticism of pregnancy, in which the woman can experience an innocent narcissism fed by recollection of her repressed experience of her mother's body. Pregnant existence entails, finally, a unique temporality of process and growth in which the woman can experience herself as split between past and future. (160)

In Young's summary of the lived pregnant body as an implied critique of 'assumptions of a unified subject and sharp distinction between transcendence and immanence' (161) we encounter a celebratory discourse of utopian materiality 'in which the transparent unity of self dissolves and the body attends positively to itself at the same time as it enacts it projects' (161). My interests in this essay have less to do with the phenomenology or 'lived experience' of maternity and more to do with its poetics. In the maternal's doubling and splitting, in the spatializing of its metaphorics, in its religiosity founded upon an error of translation (Kristeva, 'Stabat Mater' 163), and in the mother's being 'coded as "abject"' (*Powers of Horror* 64, cf. 'Stabat Mater' 183) I want to trace the contours of a writing practice that would do justice to this investment we might make in the exorbitant, the fantastic, the grotesque literalism of plural embodiment. Rather than seek to reinstate and revalue the mother of the king, a drab enterprise, I want to deploy the maternal as a monster proper to the monarch. I will model some versions of fictocritical practice as tactical monstrosity, a cyborg writing in the spirit of Haraway's commitment to '*pleasure* in the confusion of boundaries and ... *responsibility* in their construction' (150).

> [The perverse] neither gives up nor assumes a prohibition, a rule, or a law; but turns them aside, misleads, corrupts; uses them, takes advantage of them, the better to deny them. (Kristeva, *Powers of Horror* 15)

The cyborg 'is a condensed image of both imagination and material reality' (Haraway 150), 'resolutely committed to partiality, irony, intimacy and perversity' (151). Cyborg writing is 'postmodernist' (150). As Dollimore points out, 'we can see that the concept of perversion always embodied what has now become a fundamental and crucial proposition, call it deconstructive, poststructuralist, postmodern, whatever' (12). Perverse/cyborg writing 'acknowledges the impossibility of Religion, Morality, and Law – their power play, their necessary and absurd seeming.... it takes advantage of them, gets around them, and makes sport of them' (Kristeva, *Powers of Horror* 16). Perverse writing already goes by several names: *l'écriture feminine*, fictocriticism, paraliterature, postmodern allegory, postcriticism, and experimental hypertextual writing. In the academic context, these potentially perverse writing practices have some dominant tendencies. I will confine my discussion to two of these: firstly, the aestheticizing of ethics, secondly, textual collage.

Contemporary cultural studies frequently enact politics of text and commentary that endorse poststructuralist models of partial, situated knowledges and multiple speaking positions as ethical virtues. The aesthetic surface must work to mark the presence of a principled stance characteristically assumed in the glaring light of the question 'who can speak?' (Roof and Wiegman). One answer is to 'write with the discourse of others' (Ulmer, 'The Object of Post-Criticism' 96). In more narrowly literary critical practice, commentary must negotiate between a suspect 'mastery' of the object of criticism and a dubious promise of 'liberty' for textualized voices that must now speak for themselves (cf. Hodge and McHoul).

One strategy is the double-columned essay. In Kristeva's 'Stabat Mater' the two columns spatialize different registers belonging to the same signature. Cixous's and Clément's *Newly Born Woman*, and Wittig's *Lesbian Body*, are examples of works that enact similar effects on a larger scale. The parallel textuality of Muecke's important engagement with 'textual spaces' marked out for aboriginal and settler discourses (for example 'Body, Inscription, Epistemology: Knowing Aboriginal Texts') demonstrates its ethical commitments by deploying an aesthetic of the border territory, 'the space between', literalizing a refusal to speak for the other, a refusal to settle matters in the name of an unproblematized enlightenment epistemology.

It would appear that academic fictocritical practices endorse Ulmer's assertion that

> 'post-criticism' (-modernist, -structuralist) is constituted precisely by the application of the devices of modernist art to critical representations; furthermore, that the principal device taken over by the critics and theorists is the compositional pair collage/montage. ('Object' 83)

Academic collage writing in cultural studies does depend sometimes on invigorating distinctive geometries. We should pay attention to the prevalent metaphoric of gaps and spaces on the one hand, and on the other the lines, grooves, ridges and slashes that articulate them. One example of this metaphoric fixation will suffice:

> Of course this would mean risking falling into the well-defined spaces of mastery and libertarianism. Those grooves would always be beckoning to either side of the space or spacing between them. But it remains the case that any such pair of grooves (if they are in any way distinct, and we think they are) must, as it were, throw up a ridge between them. It is this ridge that we would be wanting to try to negotiate (almost in the topographical sense). And here we are reminded of the poststructuralist 'doctrine' that any binary is always a triplet, consisting as it does of a first and second element plus the relation of difference (the slash or ridge) between them. (Hodge and McHoul 205)

For Hodge and McHoul, such geometries 'might open up the space of a positive and self-reflective politics' (206).

It must be said that we are still in need of ways of understanding the 'spaces' and 'gaps'. Might it be that the typographical space between textual fragments, a literal instance of the 'space' that 'opens' within and between discourses, has too much work to do? How can it bear the weight of our desire that it 'open' at all? In our writing with the voices of others, especially the writing that refuses to take up a mediating role, or a magisterial tone in regard to what is said, how do we signal that the typographic space stands for the blankness of contradiction or the conceptual similarity between fragments? These real and imagined spaces must sometimes promise utopian freedom and play, and must sometimes remind us of an inevitability, the burden of memory and dread. We need to consider the space/gap and its connection to differing metaphorics of movement and containers. So much depends upon these 'spaces between'.

The self-conscious aestheticizing of an ethical stance, what Hillis Miller sees as an 'act in the name of a universal justice' (54), insists that collage writing bring things into the light, works with edges and boundaries. Its commitment may be likened to a thinly disguised police-work, simultaneously displaying something of what remains hidden in the 'classic' 'objective' (normative) academic essay, and restlessly patrolling the lines of discursive demarcation. The paradigm of this not-quite-perverse-enough writing is encountered in interdisciplinary projects where differing disciplinary protocols of evidentiary status and argumentation remain untroubled, working in parallel, kept intact by 'the space between' (Kerr and Nettelbeck), or where autobiographical agency inflects the representation of the writing subject (Probyn; Rosaldo; Stanley). At best, this border-patrolling displays a productive commitment to what Barthes called 'complication' in our academic work, 'combining . . . at the same time theory, critical combat, and pleasure' (Bensmaia 99). But we could also say that to insert unproblematically the autobiographical as the familiar 'other' of objective writing is an illustration of the potential banality that might stall our interdiscursive work. De Bolla has suggested the need to be alert to

> the tendency of any cross-disciplinary or inter-textual reading practice to posit an excluded 'other' to which it makes reference, and to bring into focus the difficulties surrounding a textual reading practice which strives to continually insert the excluded domain within the interior of analysis and description. (53)

If we substitute 'writing' for 'reading' here, the rehearsal of this wholly predictable 'return of the repressed' might just as well be a pedagogical exercise. It takes us away from the deployment of perversion as a dynamic cultural category; it seems overly invested in the clean and proper.

The problem might lie in the priority given a metaphorics of planes and edges. The result is an analytic form of collage. Following Ulmer's suggestion that modernist aesthetics serve as our model, we could name this Cubist writing. To reanimate fictocritical collage writing with perversity we need to supplement Ulmer's implied Cubist paradigm with, and pay attention to, the resources of Surrealist and Dadaist collage (Waldman). If Surrealism still depends upon a frame within which to dispose apparently incompatible elements, it is nonetheless an aesthetic with wilful and risky attachments to the resources of fantasy, excess, and error. Its characteristic form is an aesthetic equivalent of the dream work. Its characteristic method is play. Thus it is possible to imagine a spectrum of academic fictocritical writing. At one extreme: analytic, self-conscious, well-behaved work; at the other: more ficto than critical, more imaginative than reasonable, less responsible about borders and taking pleasure in a writing more akin to fluid dynamics (Irigaray). A collage writing that draws on Surrealist models might give more attention to the indeterminacies of the gap and spaces between rather than self-consciously stake out the lines of dispute that constitute positive knowledges. There is always the potential for a Surrealist turn within any analytic collage work. Just as we know that the perverse is produced in 'the simultaneous acknowledgement of what's being negated and disavowed' (Dollimore 13), so we find in analytic collage writing the mark of perversion understood as 'struggle and conflict . . . between desire and the law, and between transgression and conformity' (9). Surrealist collage, if it could ever emerge fully from within the analytic geometry of well-behaved cultural studies writing would be (presumably) conflictual, desiring, transgressive, and fluid.

We can see the potential for a perverse modality in the curiously hyperbolic demand that a complex and important political work be effected by the modest labour of a tone or feeling: thus 'it's a question of tone, of keeping open the possibility of hope and the hope of possibility' (Wark 45), and 'I want to research . . . a feeling . . . The discipline name of my feeling is "justice"' (Ulmer, 'The Miranda Warnings' 346). We might recognize this as the 'ambiguity of an interpretive position that is at once untenable and pleasurable' (Kristeva, 'Psychoanalysis and the Polis' 92): is a 'tone' adequate to the task of holding 'justice' up to view? In other words, it seems a perverse demand. Importantly, it is a utopian one. If we return to Hodge's and McHoul's model for fictocriticism we can see the shadow of a potentially perverse writing practice literally bracketed off from the analytic, reasonable/rational work of a self-reflective (utopian) politics:

> This kind of strategy (writing in the spaces of differences, compounding textual enigmas and indeterminacies) might open up the space of a positive and self-reflective politics. (206)

A differing, enigmatic, indeterminate writing is made possible by its 'other', a purposive, self-conscious project. The parenthetical disclosure of the potentially perverse has been mapped more fully in an exemplary work of cultural studies, Gail Jones' 'Skulls, Fontanelles and the Spaces Between' and in a diagnostic essay on the conditions of writing for higher degree students in the so-called 'New Humanities', Bob Hodge's 'Monstrous Knowledge'. Together, these essays gather up a number of the issues I have been tracing here. We could say that Hodge offers the macro-economy, Jones the micro-economy of a potential perversity in our academic work.

On the macro level then, Hodge sketches a model for research and writing, offering it at the same moment as he disqualifies it as too risky (37). This utopian 'manifesto', its pleasures hedged about by responsibility, echoes Haraway's cyborg writing, an ironic model of tactical monstrosity, positing an interpretive position that is at once pleasurable and untenable: 'my ironic faith, my blasphemy' (149). It is a three point plan:

- Be open to the monstrous – take specially seriously those problems, beliefs and experiences that are annulled by ('quaint', 'naïve', 'outrageous', unthinkable in terms of) a dominant discipline, whether they are intractably personal or contaminated by the disreputable demotic or popular, by passion or anger or delight, by the desire to change the world or to dream a new one.
- Be transdisciplinary – follow the curves of a folded disciplinary space, seeing what disciplines are necessarily super-imposed in the common space of your problematic, what the new centre of gravity is that is formed by the intrusion of this density of layered disciplinarity, what is the emergent structure of the disciplinary formation.
- Detect the shadow – work with the old prohibitions as well as the new knowledges incorporated into the 'field of the true' and made visible by the juxtaposition of disciplines; especially the proper monster, the unspeakable, the forbidden Other of a given discipline. (37)

To work in this way is to produce monstrously open and porous, exorbitant and plural knowledges, committed to the supplementarity of 'both/and' in the face of any disapproving 'either/or'. This is grotesque writing, investing simultaneously in (sublime) utopias and abjected matter.

In Jones' micro-economy of the essay an intense attachment to ethical dilemmas is articulated through a hybrid textual field (for example, autobiography, ethnography, historiography, genre theories and rhetorical traditions, postcolonial theory). The surface of the essay is marked by italicized, parenthetical interruptions, each serving to imagine speaking differently. Jones' detailed engagement with her investments in postcolonial cultural studies practices seems to repeat precisely the model of a potentially perverse strategy parenthetically nested in the midst of 'a positive and self-reflective politics'. Again, there are three points:

(Yet our theorising suppresses the resources of melodrama. Why, I wonder? It is, after all a mode which recognises and theatricalises aspects of horror, and its currencies are uncanny return – which may be read as misrecognised resistance – and the monstrous and cruel appetites of white mythologies. It has a quality of exaggeration that, pertaining above all to the symbolic, well equips it as a heuristic device to discuss the projection mechanism of the imperial.)

(We tend to discount not only melodrama but the broad resources of the rhapsodic. In high theorising we aim for tonal equanimity, for a tone hieratic, magisterial, and remotely impersonal. So academic prose is marked, for the most part, by a repressive absence of the lyrical. By wide-awake realisms. By studious passionlessness. By loss of affirmation.)

(Where, in our theorising, is the space of the elegaic? Where is the space within which the mourning grounds beneath the Government houses might be clearly discerned and properly honoured? The spaces of political bravery. Of risk. Of loss. Post-colonial studies is a melancholy field, concerned as it is with the elucidation of barbarity. Perhaps, therefore, it needs access to a language (a tone, a poetics) to express the ethical imperatives of mourning.) (174, 178, 179: italics in the original)

Like Hodge's and McHoul's model of fictocritical work, this parenthetic opening up of academic writing to the possibility of other tones and other voices is hedged about by its ethical imperatives. Would the resources of tonal impropriety be able to open up a space proper to justice? Can abjected matter hold a utopia up to view? Jones' summary of our potential 'method' is both a version of Hodge's 'monstrous knowledge' and a model for a perverse writing:

> To put it more simply, there is a need to supplement rationalist and mimeticist explication, to veer and seek out the new surfaces of difficult subjects. To veer, perhaps wildly, into realms of melodrama, rhapsody, the intolerable elegaic. (179)

I propose that we take this supplementary (excessive), perhaps wild (exorbitant) veering as definitive signs of perverse writing.

Motility defines perversity. The perverse is necessarily a movement, at once capable of acceleration, swerving, and of straying, wandering, queering, remaining unsettled and labile, but capable of stopping just short. That this metaphorics of velocity and movement might be crucial will come as no surprise. Elspeth Probyn has asked us to 'consider queer as movement, to turn queer into a verb' (*Outside Belongings* 14): 'This problematic I am calling queer belonging is essentially about the movement between bodies and points of departure in theory' (*Sexy Bodies* 5). It is a desiring writing in which desire can be understood as a method of sorts: 'the question is how can we use desire so as to analyse it as a specific queer form of movement and mediation between individuals' (*Outside Belongings* 14).

It could also be argued that glimpses of a perverse writing can be found in many practitioners of the essay form. Kauffman's summary of Adorno's 'unmethodical method' is a case in point:

> The essay observes a 'pleasure principle' which mocks the stern 'reality principle' of official thought ... But it does not follow mere whim or fancy: 'determined by the unity of its object' ... the task of the critical essay ... is to follow 'the logic of the object's aporias' ... Since the object ... is itself contradictory, 'antagonistic', the essay is structured 'in such a way that it could always, at any point, break off. It thinks in fragments such as reality is fragmented, and gains its unity by moving through fissures, rather than smoothing them over'.
> In such expressions as 'methodically unmethodical', 'exact fantasy', and 'arrested conflict', the dialectical play of opposites works against the illusion of stasis, identity, or totality, allowing the reader to feel the motion of transgressing epistemological taboos and boundaries. (230, 231)

Similarly, Heath has suggested that 'what is at stake' in Barthes' *A Lover's Discourse: Fragments*

> is the practice of a new writing, ... neither analysis nor autobiography (which is not to exclude elements of analysis, elements of autobiography), it sets out the space of an

> imaginary, the reflections and recognitions and crystallizations of an 'I' . . . In this writing . . . the main accompanying text, the 'regular reading' is not an object of study but a reconstituted nearness. (101)

It will already be clear that a perverse writing cannot be apocalyptically new. Similarly, the objects of its inquiry will be familiar/strange on account of their having strayed, or even veered wildly from some 'elsewhere' in order to become 'a reconstituted nearness'.

There remains one important and enabling resource to point out in tracing the contours of perverse writing: postmodern allegory. Of the varieties of work that might be undertaken in its name, I will confine myself to the idea that postmodern allegory does not posit an object or concept that must speak of that which is not present. Postmodern allegory works with circumstantial evidence. It often works on the surface of difficult subjects, it models its writing on the very structure of a 'found object' (cf. Ulmer, 'Object'; Owens). For example, Derrida has 'mimed' the structure of 'theoretical objects' such as an umbrella, a pair of shoes, a fan, a matchbox, a postcard (Ulmer, 'Object' 99). Postmodern allegory is often very literal-minded at the same time as it plays imaginatively with its object of inquiry. Perhaps we can see something of this procedure in Adorno's concept of 'exact fantasy': 'Fantasy which abides strictly within the material which the sciences present to it, and reaches beyond them only in the smallest aspects of their arrangement: aspects, granted, which fantasy itself must originally generate' (Ulmer, 'Object' 98). Straying in the direction of postmodern allegory, I propose to fantasize upon the conjunction of the monarch and the mother via a structure that Kantorowicz regards as a literalizing of the King's two bodies: the late medieval double-tomb. Typically the prince is 'buried in a tomb showing the body in corruption below the effigy in glory' (435).

> For the decrepit and decaying body natural [all too human king] in the tomb, now separated from the awe-inspiring body politic [sacred and perpetual, sublime King] above it, appears like an illustration of the doctrine expounded over and over again by medieval jurists . . . – 'The incumbent of a Dignity may decay, the Dignity itself is nonetheless forever; it does not die'. (436)

These two bodies, the one sublime, the other abject, lie in repose, the necessary space between opened up by slender columns (see e.g. Kantorowicz, figures 28, 30, 31, showing fifteenth-century spiritual and secular 'princes'). These structures model the perversity of the doctrine they illustrate. The sublime body politic literally depends upon the abject body natural, figured as the cadaver, death itself. The slender columns which hold the sublime body up to view attempt to separate it from defilement by deathliness and materiality, the abject which, in Kristeva's words, is 'something maternal'. The mother is always already there in the tomb, the columns effecting an opening that simultaneously disavows and makes possible a desiring movement in the space between.

If we take this monument as a potentially allegorical structure it will be possible to stage a perverse reinscription of the monarchic within the space marked out by/for maternity. To use the metaphorics of 'fluid mechanics', my 'exact fantasy' decants two early modern literary representations of the king's two bodies into the formal container made available by Kristeva's double-columned essay, 'Stabat Mater', that essay understood as another instance of circumstantial matter. This veering towards deliberate collision, combining collage and allegory, might stage a 'queering' of the images of plural embodiment marked out by discourses of monarchy and maternity. It literalizes a return of the repressed 'other' to the discourse of monarchy, the examples chosen because they show the proper indivisibility of the body natural and the body politic under considerable pressure. As Kantorowicz notes in his important chapter on the play, '*The Tragedy of King Richard II* is the tragedy of the King's Two Bodies' (26). The same should also be said of Marlowe's earlier dramatic exploration of the metaphor, *Edward II*, in which the king parcels out powers proper to his body politic on the basis of passions that compel his body natural. Read as a presexological text, the play does not suggest that Edward 'perverts' sovereignty because he is homosexual but because he risks the coherence of the realm which depends on a 'clean and proper' unity of the body politic. By parcelling out to his friends (metaphoric) bits of his body politic's capacity, Edward divides the body politic between his person and Gaveston, and then Spencer. His perversity lies in the compulsive repetition of that which he knows to be improper. By making the body politic into a (dangerously) double thing he produces an exorbitant plural embodiment. Supplementing what is already conceptualized as a dualist structure, Edward makes the state, imaged in his body politic, a two-headed monster, producing what is described as a debilitating growth, a cancerous parasite.

Christopher Marlowe, *Edward II* (1591–3)	William Shakespeare, *Richard II* (1594–5)
Herald: You will this grief have ease and remedy, That from your princely person you [remove This Spencer, as a putrefying branch, That deads the royal vine, whose golden [leaves Empale your princely head, your diadem, Whose brightness such pernicious [upstarts dim . . . (III.ii.160–5)	Richard: Not all the water in the rough rude sea Can wash the balm off from an anointed [king; The breath of worldly men cannot depose The deputy elected by the Lord. (III.ii.54–7) Richard: I had forgot myself, am I not king? Awake thy coward majesty! thou sleepest, Is not the king's name twenty thousand [names?

Queen:
Misgoverned kings are cause of all this
[wrack,
And, Edward, thou art one among them
[all,
Whose looseness hath betrayed thy land
[to spoil . . .
(IV. iv. 9–11)

Edward:
The griefs of private men are soon allayed
But not of kings; . . .
For such outrageous passions cloy my
[soul
As with the wings of rancour and disdain
Full often am I soaring up to heaven
To plain me to the gods against them both;
But when I call to mind I am a king,
Methinks I should revenge me of the
[wrongs
That Mortimer and Isabel have done.
But what are kings when regiment is gone
But perfect shadows of a sunshine day?
My nobles rule, I bear the name of king;
I wear the crown but am controlled by
[them . . .
(V.i.8–9; 19–29)

Edward:
Here, here! [Resigns the crown] now,
[sweet God of heaven
Make me despise this transitory pomp
And sit for aye enthronised in heaven;
Come death, and with thy fingers close
[my eyes,
Or if I live, let me forget my self.
(V.i.107–11)

Edward:
My mind's distempered and my body's
[numbed,
And whether I have limbs or no I know
[not;
Oh would my blood dropped out from
[every vein
As doth the water from my tattered robes;
. . .
(V.v.63–6)

Edward:
Know that I am a king; oh, at that name

Arm, arm, my name! A puny subject
[strikes
At thy great glory. Look not to the ground,
Ye favourites of a king. Are we not high?
High be our thoughts.
(III.ii.83–8)

Richard:
. . . for within the hollow crown
That rounds the mortal temples of a king
Keeps Death his court, and there the antic
[sits
Scoffing his state and grinning at his
[pomp,
Allowing him a breath, a little scene,
To monarchize, be fear'd, and kill with
[looks;
Infusing him with self and vain conceit,
As if the flesh which walls about our life,
Were brass impregnable;
. . . For you have but mistook me all this
[while.
I live with bread like you, feel want,
Taste grief, need friends – subjected thus,
How can you say to me, I am a king?
(III.ii.160–8; 174–7)

Richard:
I'll give my jewels for a set of beads
. . .
And my large kingdom for a little grave,
A little, little grave, an obscure grave.
(III.iii.147; 153–4)

Richard:
My crown I am, but still my griefs are
[mine.
You may my glories and my state depose,
But not my griefs; still am I king of those.
(IV.i.191–3)

Richard:
Now mark me how I will undo myself.
I give this heavy weight from off my head,
And this unwieldy sceptre from my hand,
The pride of kingly sway from out my
[heart;
With mine own tears I wash away my
[balm,
With mine own hands I give away my
[crown,

I feel a hell of grief; where is my crown?
Gone, gone! and do I remain alive?
(V.v.88–90)

King:
My father's murdered through thy [treachery,
And thou shalt die and on his mournful [hears
Thy hateful and accursed head shall lie,
To witness to the world, that by thy means
His kingly body was too soon interred.
(V.vi.28–32)

With mine own tongue deny my sacred [state,
With mine own breath release all duteous [oaths;
All pomp and majesty I do forswear; ...
Long may'st thou live in Richard's seat to [sit,
And soon lie Richard in an earthy pit.
(IV.i.203–211; 218, 219)

Like the two play-texts upon which I have drawn, the tomb structure still speaks to us of a desiring movement between the sublime and the abject. If we have forgotten the sacred dimension, we nonetheless experience the tomb as a reminder of 'something maternal'. The tomb articulates a relationship between the 'clean and proper' body politic and its 'proper monster', the body natural. Even if the body politic cannot face the body natural it is necessarily kept aloft by something that connects them and by a dreadful space between, perhaps the promise of that materiality and deathliness that is borne by the mother, the cadaver an uncanny reminder of the proper monster of maternity itself, her shadow. The necessarily perfunctory double-columned collage/allegory forces a literalized contamination of discourses that would usually be kept apart. It hints at a crisis of category. The desiring movement between these knowledges requires an effective conductor. In keeping with the definitive quality of veering, perhaps wildly, in order to 'seek out the new surfaces of difficult subjects' (Jones 179), my perverse trajectory will detour and wilfully err on the side of the exorbitant and fantastic body of another king, a direction made possible by compounding an already productive error.

> After the publication of *A Lover's Discourse*, the novelist Marie Cardinal mistook an invitation from *Nouvelles Litteraires* to write on Prime Minister Raymond Barre, writing instead on Roland Barthes. Thus a critic is mistaken by/for a novelist, a Prime Minister for a critic/novelist: a crisis of category, name and identity of a kind that could signal the arrival of the fictocritical. (Muecke, King, and Miller 5, citing Heath 100)

Recalling that Barre was nicknamed 'Babar', I propose to pay homage to Cardinal's error, rerouting the conjunction of discourses of monarchy and maternity through representations of Babar, king of the elephants (De Brunhoff). What does Babar show us about the fate of the king's two bodies as it surfaces in these popular twentieth-century children's picturebooks? There is already something grotesque in the representation of an elephantine monarch, but children's literature is home to any number of exorbitant bodies. In the stories of Babar we encounter an exorbitant supplementarity attached to his authorship. In an ironic effect of doubling, Laurent De Brunhoff takes up the labour of production upon the death of his father Jean. This substitution repeats the supplementarity that characterizes motherhood in the early stories of Babar. In Laurent De Brunhoff's *Babar the Sportsman*, the king of the elephants forgets his dependence on the maternal in a scene of spectacular misrecognition. The story also might have served Kantorowicz as a literal mapping of the theory of the king's two bodies. As in *Edward II* and *Richard II* we see a potential splitting or rupturing of the ideal coherence of the monarch's two bodies.

In *Babar the Sportsman* Celeste, queen of the elephants, suggests Babar needs to enter a sports contest 'being organised to find the champion father . . . "After all you are a father as well as a king" '(np). (After all you are a body natural and a body politic, Celeste told him. The vigour of the former guarantees the perceived vitality of the latter.) He dreams of being 'carried in triumph'(np), winner of the contest. (Babar dreamed a secular apotheosis, body natural and body politic joyously coherent.) After vigorous training Babar succeeds in confirming his status as (ideal) father (of the nation): 'Babar saw himself on his own television set' (np). (The television screen effected an [imaginary] conjunction of the body natural and the body politic.)

Babar splits himself up at the very moment he is assured of ideal unity, firstly in the representation of the dream work that brings the future into view, secondly in the representation on the television screen that brings the past before our eyes. These collisions of what-might-be and what-has-been upon the body of the present seem to confirm the power and coherence of the 'speculating' king's identity. The work of the dream and the work of the television screen duplicate in different registers the sense in which Babar is in the thrall of a belated or parodic version of the mirror stage. The television is an electronic prosthesis for producing a misrecognition of the king's two bodies understood as an ideal unity. For Babar, the image on the screen must be imagined as a portrait, a copy of the Babar who 'saw himself on his own television set' (np). For the reader, Babar has failed to see that he requires that image as a necessary supplement, the image of the body natural completing and adding to the body politic, an exorbitant category, a kind of Siamese twin joined by an invisible (electrified) hinge. The smug conviction of his unitary ideality is in absolute contrast to the crisis of Richard II's 'mirror scene'. Babar's bloated narcissism is in absolute contrast to Edward II's conviction of insubstantiality and loss of self in the dreadful space that opens up between the body natural and the body politic. Babar's comfort seems to require amnesia. Babar ignores the necessary arms that hold him in triumph (in his dream and on the television screen). They are reminders of other arms that held him up: Babar has forgotten that he depends on the maternal.

Babar's mother, carrying him high (oddly for an elephant, aptly for a sacred mother), is suddenly, shockingly, the dead body from which he must veer wildly: 'One day Babar was having a lovely ride on his mother's back, when a cruel hunter, hiding behind a bush, shot at them)' (Jean De Brunhoff, *The Story of Babar the Little Elephant*, np). Precisely to the degree that she fails him (catastrophically) Babar is propelled into modernity and the arms of the (thin/ little) 'very rich old lady', a phallic mother 'who understood little elephants and knew at once that he was longing for a smart suit . . . so she gave him her purse' (np). His longing will always be for a covering over the nakedness that belongs to 'something maternal': 'the [naked] mothers went to the town to fetch [the now smartly dressed] Arthur and Celeste' (np). Naked mothers disturb the surface of modernity. Babar's fetish object will always be 'a smart suit':

> And yet Babar was not altogether happy: . . . He often gazed out of the window dreaming of his childhood, and when he thought of his dear mother he used to cry. (np)

On returning to the Great Forest, Babar insists that Celeste is a necessary supplement to his monarchy: 'If I become King, she will be your Queen' (np). The crown is in the power of his subjects to bestow: 'Let us offer him the crown. . . . Long live Queen Celeste! Long live King Babar!! the elephants shouted with one voice. And that was how Babar became King' (np).

In *Babar the Sportsman*, the king forgets that the people hold him up. The supplementary mother has been superseded by the television, an agent of specular proliferation, a technology for reproducing the king's two bodies in the field of the postmodern. Babar imagines that this technology replicates his ideal unity, forgetting, along with western philosophy and political theory, that the maternal body is the site for the reproduction of the social body (Diprose 25; Gatens; Cheah): the maternal body 'does not simply repeat itself but rather becomes itself only by becoming-other' (Patton 51). In the seventeenth century Milton diagnosed a perverse amnesia in the monarch's tendency to arrogate maternal powers to himself:

> certainly it was a Parliament that first created Kings, and not onely made Laws before a King was in being, but those Laws especially, whereby he holds his Crown. He ought then to have so thought of the Parliament, if he count it not Male, as of his Mother, which, to civil being, created both him, and the Royalty he wore. And if it hath bin anciently interpreted the presaging signe of a future Tyrant, but to dream of copulation with his Mother, which can it be less than actual Tyranny to affirme waking, that the Parliament, which is his Mother, can neither conceive or bring forth any authoritative Act without his Masculine coition . . . ('Eikonoklastes' 186)

We can say that Babar forgets his dependence on the maternal, literalized as riding on the mother's back and refigured in the acclamation of the elephantine parliament. The two parts of this structure of dependence enjoy a conflation and repetition in the dreamed apotheosis, and the plaudits of the subjects who carry him in triumph. From Milton's perspective, Charles merely extends on what was evident in his father's supercession of the feminine. Like James I, Babar imagines himself, via a misrecognition of the television image of an ideal father, the 'loving nourish [nurse]-father... simultaneously father and mother of his realm' (Goldberg 142). Babar, like James, misrecognizes himself 'as a hermaphrodite, an ideal form' (Jones and Stallybrass 100). The 'nourish-father' of the body politic can be read as a refiguring of Christ as mother/lactating Christ, available, like the theory of the king's (grotesque, perverse) two bodies, in medieval theological discourse (Bynum). Thus, 'two separate systems of metaphoricity conflate, two distinct discourses merge in Christ's dying body' (Ash 85). If we follow Milton's metaphoric, the king's plural embodiment properly depends on the maternal, what must be kept at arms' length but never forgotten; the tyrant is the proper monster of the king. In *Babar the Sportsman* the king must be thought of as momentarily on the cusp of tyranny. The extremity of Babar's reaction to a possible splitting apart of the king's two bodies effects an answering movement. In the potentially exorbitant totalitarian figure the systems of metaphoricity that attach to the sublime and the abject veer wildly into a perverse conflation. The tyrant mistakes his monstrosity for an ideal, self-generated unity. Žižek has traced the fate of 'this sublime body' and its transformation in contemporary political thought. The tyrant wants to 'flay off the animal, barbaric skin' of a 'corrupted body' in an 'astonishing transition from nothingness to existence' (262). The tyrant cannot recognize his own monstrosity even as it casts an obscuring shadow over 'something maternal'.

> Thus, fear having been bracketed, discourse will seem tenable only if it ceaselessly confront that otherness, a burden both repellent and repelled, a deep well of memory that is unapproachable and intimate: the abject. (Kristeva, *Powers of Horror* 6)

Perverse writing will not only detect the shadow, it will dwell there. If the king's two bodies have as their proper monsters an abject mother and a tyrant, what might lie in the shadow of the folds of 'something maternal'? What is hinged to maternal embodiment? Can we redeploy the tomb structure in the knowledge that all along we confuse 'real space with psychical space' (Burgin 231), that our fantasy is 'a surrealist jumble of elements' 'counterproductive to fetishism' but productive of 'a *mise-en-scène,* a staging of a fundamental incoherence' (Burgin 238)? This would be to move away from the usual deployment of the 'theoretical object' as a 'fetish object' (Ulmer, 'Object' 99). We would not fetishize the body. It would be to consider the body as a point of departure for a desiring movement in 'the spaces between', a queer allegory. But to dwell fantastically in the shadows might be dangerous. First, because 'In the space of events in which this vignette is situated nothing is fixed, everything is mobile, there is no particular aim; it is a perverse space' (Burgin 239). Secondly, because fantasy 'is not the object of desire but its setting. In fantasy the subject does not pursue the object or its sign; [she] appears caught up [her]self in the sequence of images' (Burgin 234).

Imagine the body of the mother held up to view as an ideality. Her shadow falls across another body, 'something deathly'– the monarch's shocking skeletal form. Something has strayed from 'elsewhere' to become 'a reconstituted nearness' I recognize. She is hinged to the anorexic body. The anorexic is a metaphoric tyrant: 'You make of your own body your very own kingdom where you are the tyrant, the absolute dictator' (Bordo 150). The mother and the anorexic cannot face each other. The mother is reconceptualized in this model as a poetic embodiment of fantasy and excess, a utopian play-fullness. The anorexic is the site of an intractable misrecognition of her dreadful emptiness and the desire to flay off the animal, barbaric skin, the corrupted body. The 'closed classical body', the 'clean and proper body' is her ideal, imaginary body (Russo; Stallybrass and White). She holds away from herself the open, bleeding, and grotesque, maternal body that is monstrous to her, at the same time as she stages a perverse masochism more unbearable than any maternity. But she cannot prevent a collision with 'something maternal', her abject body staging the death of which she stops short. The mother collapses into her, repeating on the surface of the anorexic body the knowledge that the mother's arms cannot always hold us up. Kristeva asks if the analyst can 'allow the most deeply buried logic of our anguish and hatred to burst out' (*Powers of Horror* 210): 'Would [she] then be capable of X-raying horror without making capital out of its power? Of displaying the abject without confusing [her]self for it? Probably not' (210). Certainly not if her writing is a perverse space of 'surrealist fantasy' in which she is caught up in 'the sequence of images' (Burgin 238; 234), momentarily, fantastically, stretched out between these two grotesque possibilities of embodiment. An exorbitant instance of the 'knowing because experiencing subject' (Stanley). Collapse is inevitable.

If we redeploy these elements to model perverse (academic) writing we must notice that what is perverse in terms of organic life is precisely that which is rewarded in academic life. Clean and proper writing, the essayist's equivalent of the (imaginary) closed, classical (in fact masculine) body, cannot face its monstrous other in the embarrassingly open, messy, and grotesque practice of 'pregnant' cyborg, fictocritical writing. Similarly, perverse fictocritical writing must not turn away from the fact of its being hinged to an anorexic other. But fictocriticism is not the therapeutic *mise-en-scène* for a repressed academic discourse. We cannot simply fill up anorexic writing with our pleasures, decanting an 'excluded domain within the interior of analysis and description' (De Bolla 53). In our writing we will trace out an exorbitant desiring movement in the spaces between the polarities of anorexic and pregnant/cyborg writing, playing in the shadows of these monstrous knowledges. In the academic context we can stage a perverse work, veer and seek out the new surfaces of difficult subjects, be open to the monstrous, follow the curves of a folded disciplinary space, detect the shadow of the proper monster, the unspeakable. Our writing can risk fantasy, excess, and error coming to the surface. Perverse writing can work in the spaces opened up by struggle and conflict between desire and the law, transgression and conformity. But in the academic context our fantasy always/already knows that, just as we want the mother to hold us up in triumph, just as she cannot tirelessly bear us, so we may have to face the possibility that a 'tone' (Wark), 'a language (a tone, a poetics)' (Jones 179) cannot labour tirelessly on behalf of 'the possibility of hope' (Wark) nor 'act in the name of a universal justice' (Hillis Miller; Ulmer). Similarly, we must not fetishize the aesthetic surface of our writing: it cannot guarantee ethical effects. Despite this, always/already knowing this, perverse writing will insist on tactical monstrosity, positing interpretive positions at once untenable and pleasurable: 'my ironic faith, my blasphemy' (Kristeva, 'Psychoanalysis and the Polis' 92; Haraway 149), making of our writing (and the writing self) not a fetish object but a 'specific queer form of movement' (Probyn, *Queer Belongings* 14).

Bibliography

Ash, Jennifer. 'The Discursive Construction of Christ's Body in the Later Middle Ages: Resistance and Autonomy'. Cranny-Francis and Threadgold. 75–105.
Axton, Marie. *The Queen's Two Bodies: Drama and the Elizabethan Succession*. London: Royal Historical Society, 1977.
Barthes, Roland. *A Lover's Discourse: Fragments*. Trans. Richard Howard. London: Jonathan Cape, 1979.
Bensmaia, Réda. *The Barthes Effect*. Minneapolis: University of Minnesota Press, 1987.
Blundell, Valda, John Shepherd, and Ian Taylor, eds. *Relocating Cultural Studies: Developments in Theory and Research*. London and New York: Routledge, 1992.
Burgin, Victor. 'Perverse Space'. Colomina. 219–40.
Butrym, Alexander, ed. *Essays on the Essay: Redefining the Genre*. Athens and London: University of Georgia Press, 1989.
Bynum, C. W. *Jesus as Mother: Studies in the Spirituality of the High Middle Ages*. Berkeley and Los Angeles: University of California Press, 1982.
Cheah, Pheng, David Fraser and Judith Grbich, eds. *Thinking Through the Body of the Law*. Sydney: Allen and Unwin, 1996.
Cixous, Hélène, and Catherine Clément. *The Newly Born Woman*. Trans. Betsy Wing. Minneapolis: University of Minnesota Press, 1986.
Colomina, Beatriz, ed. *Sexuality and Space*. New York: Princeton Architectural Press, 1992.
Cranny-Francis, Anne, and Terry Threadgold, eds. *Feminine, Masculine, and Representation*. Sydney: Allen and Unwin, 1990.
De Bolla, Peter. 'Disfiguring History'. *Diacritics* 16 (1986): 49–58.
De Brunhoff, Jean. *The Story of Babar the Little Elephant*. London: Methuen, 1955.
De Brunhoff, Laurent. *Babar the Sportsman*. London: Methuen, 1973.
Diprose, Rosalyn. *The Bodies of Women: Ethics, Embodiment and Sexual Difference*. London and New York: Routledge, 1994.

Diprose, Rosalyn, and Robyn Ferrell, eds. *Cartographies: Poststructuralism and the Mapping of Bodies and Spaces*. Sydney: Allen and Unwin, 1991.

Dollimore, Jonathan. 'The Cultural Politics of Perversion: Augustine, Shakespeare, Freud, Foucault'. *Genders* 8 (1990): 1–16.

During, Simon, ed. *The Cultural Studies Reader*. London and New York: Routledge, 1993.

Epstein, Julia, and Kristina Straub, eds. *Body Guards: The Cultural Politics of Gender Ambiguity*. London and New York: Routledge, 1991.

Foster, Hal, ed. *Postmodern Culture*. London and Sydney: Pluto Press, 1985.

Gatens, Moira. 'Corporeal Representation In/And The Body Politic'. Diprose and Ferrell. 79–87.

Goldberg, Jonathan. *'James I and the Politics of Literature: Jonson, Shakespeare, Donne, and Their Contemporaries*. Stanford: Stanford University Press, 1983.

Haraway, Donna J. 'A Cyborg Manifesto: Science, Technology, and Socialist Feminism in the Late Twentieth Century'. *Simians, Cyborgs and Women: The Reinvention of Nature*. London: Free Association Books, 1991. 149–81.

Heath, Stephen. 'Barthes on Love'. *Sub-Stance* 37/38 (1983): 100–6.

Hillis Miller, J. *Illustration*. Cambridge, Mass.: Harvard University Press, 1992.

Hodge, Bob. 'Monstrous Knowledge: Doing PhDs in the New Humanities'. *Australian Universities' Review* 2 (1995): 35–39.

Hodge, Bob and Alec McHoul. 'The Politics of Text and Commentary'. *Textual Practice* 6.2 (1992): 189–209.

Irigaray, Luce. 'The "Mechanics" of Fluids'. *This Sex Which Is Not One*. Trans. Catherine Porter. Ithaca: Cornell University Press, 1985. 106-18.

Jones, Ann Rosalind and Peter Stallybrass. 'Fetishizing Gender: Constructing the Hermaphrodite in Renaissance Europe'. Epstein and Straub. 80–111.

Jones, Gail. 'Skulls, Fontanelles and the Spaces Between'. *UTS Review* 1.2 (1995): 170–80.

Kantorowicz, Ernst. *The King's Two Bodies: A Study in Medieval Political Theology*. Princeton: Princeton University Press, 1957.

Kauffman, R. Lane. 'The Skewed Path: Essaying as Unmethodical Method'. Butrym 221–40.

Kerr, Heather and Amanda Nettelbeck, eds. *The Space Between: Australian Women Writing Fictocriticism*. Nedlands: University of Western Australia Press, 1998.

King, Noel, Toby Miller, and Stephen Muecke. 'Off the Planet: On Fictocriticism'. Afterword. 'The Morning After the 80s'. Unpublished MS, 1994.

Kristeva, Julia.*'Powers of Horror: An Essay in Abjection*. Trans. Leon S. Roudiez. New York: Columbia University Press, 1982.

—— 'Stabat Mater'. Moi 160–86.

—— 'Psychoanalysis and the Polis'. Moi 300–20.

Landow, George P. ed. *Hyper/Text/Theory*. Baltimore and London: Johns Hopkins University Press, 1994.

Lennon, Kathleen, and Margaret Whitford, eds. *Knowing the Difference: Feminist Perspectives in Epistemology*. London and New York: Routledge, 1994.

Maitland, F. W. 'The Crown as Corporation'. *Maitland: Selected Essays*. Ed. H. D. Hazeltine, G. Lapsley, and P. H. Winfield. Cambridge: Cambridge University Press, 1936. 104–27.

Marlowe, Christopher. *Edward the Second*. Ed. W. Moelwyn Merchant. London: Benn, 1967.

Milton, John. 'Eikonoklastes'. *The Works of John Milton*. Ed. Frank Allen Patterson. Vol 5. New York: Columbia University Press, 1932. 62–309.

Moi, Toril, ed. *The Kristeva Reader*. Oxford: Basil Blackwell, 1986.

Muecke, Stephen. 'Body, Inscription, Epistemology: Knowing Aboriginal Texts'. *Textual Spaces: Aboriginality and Cultural Studies*. Kensington, NSW: New South Wales University Press, 1992. 36–59.

Owens, Craig. 'The Allegorical Impulse: Towards a Theory of Postmodernism'. Wallis 203–35.
Patton, Paul. 'Nietzsche and the Body of the Philosopher'. Diprose and Ferrell. 43–54.
Probyn, Elspeth. 'True Voices and Real People: The Problem of the Autobiographical in Cultural Studies'. Blundell 105–22.
—— 'Queer Belongings: The Politics of Departure'. *Sexy Bodies: The Strange Carnalities of Feminism*. Ed. Elizabeth Grosz and Elspeth Probyn. New York and London: Routledge, 1995. 1–18.
—— *Outside Belongings*. New York and London: Routledge, 1996.
Roof, Judith, and Robyn Wiegman, eds. *Who Can Speak? Authority and Critical Identity*. Ubana and Chicago: University of Illinois Press, 1995.
Rosaldo, Renato. 'After Objectivism'. During. 104–17.
Russo, Mary. *The Female Grotesque: Risk, Excess and Modernity*. New York and London: Routledge, 1995.
Shakespeare, William. *King Richard II*. Ed. Peter Ure. London and New York: Methuen, 1961.
Stallybrass, Peter, and Allon White. *The Politics and Poetics of Transgression*. London and New York: Methuen, 1986.
Stanley, Liz. 'The Knowing Because Experiencing Subject: Narratives, Lives and Autobiography'. Lennon and Whitford. 132–48.
Ulmer, Gregory. 'The Object of Post-Criticism'. Foster. 83–110.
—— 'The Miranda Warnings: An Experiment in Hyperrhetoric'. Landow. 345–77.
Waldman, Diane. *Collage, Assemblage, and the Found Object*. New York: Abrams, 1992.
Wallis, Brian, ed. *Art After Modernism: Rethinking Representation*. New York and Boston: New Museum of Contemporary Art; D. R. Godine, 1984.
Wark, McKenzie. 'Mystery Traces'. *World Art* 12 (1997): 40–45.
Welldon, Estela V. *Mother, Madonna, Whore: The Idealization and Denigration of Motherhood*. New York and London: The Guilford Press, 1992.
Wittig, Monique. *The Lesbian Body*. Trans. Peter Owen. Boston: Beacon Press, 1986.
Young, Iris Marion. 'Pregnant Embodiment: Subjectivity and Alienation'. *Throwing Like a Girl and Other Essays in Feminist Philosophy and Social Theory*. Bloomington and Indianapolis: Indiana University Press, 1990. 160–74.
Žižek, Slavoj. *For They Know Not What They Do: Enjoyment as a Political Factor*. London and New York: Verso, 1991.

Chapter 10

White Trash Lesbianism: Dorothy Allison's Queer Politics

Kelly L. Thomas

The photo on *Bastard Out of Carolina*'s cover features a young, white girl with her head lowered, pressing her body against a barbed wire fence – the sharply focused flora of the print on her dress a shock against the blurred earth and patchy wasteland vegetation. In the background, a gaunt woman (perhaps her mother) with a raised hand shielding her eyes from the sun squints at the child. Although a number of scenarios could be read into this *mise-en-scène*, the image's political significance derives less from its formal content than from its status as one of Dorothea Lange's striking photos of impoverished rural Americans taken during the Great Depression as part of the New Deal's Farm Securities Administration documentation project.[1] Standing as a synecdoche for Lange's celebrated body of work, the photograph plays into popular associations of Lange's images with sympathetic rural whites devastated by economic hardship and natural disaster. Something of an ethnographic pictorial study of poverty, Lange's photographs supported the New Deal's reorganization of US capitalism, working to establish a dominant set of codes with which to represent the poor and positively identifying the embodied effects of the Depression on the corpus of the noble poor. Reminiscent of Lange's sharecroppers and migrant Okies, the woman and child and their desolate environment symbolize undeserved poverty, raising the expectation that the novel, like Lange's familiar (now nostalgic) images of economic crisis, will aestheticize and humanize poor whites whose ability and desire to labor were undermined and eroded by forces beyond their control. Hence, with the melancholic girl's downcast, shadowy visage gracing its cover, Dorothy Allison's 1992 novel is immediately recognizable yet simultaneously overdetermined in its relationship to popular notions of white poverty.

Severing poverty from moral ambiguity and behavioral excess, Lange's photographs and their attendant stereotypes of the Depression reify the notion of the 'good' or 'noble' poor whose poverty is no fault of their own; however, the 'bastard' of the novel's title hints that the impoverished characters therein are hardly deserving of the same kind of sympathy accorded to Lange's ravaged and forlorn subjects. Allison's poor whites don't subscribe to middle-class notions of progress, and hence, do not conform to societal norms regarding sexuality and citizenship as the epithet 'bastard' indicates. Contrary to the nostalgia and pity that Lange's work evokes, the novel takes as its subject the dark underside of white poverty: white trash, those poor whites who are to blame for their own poverty because they are seen as lazy workers, irresponsible parents and citizens, domestically incompetent, excessive and often perverse in their sexuality, and unsound in consumer practices. Emulating the oppositional relationship between the good poor and white trash, the novel and Lange's photograph work against one another, forming a site of tension where the discursive conflict over the definition of whiteness converges with the varied meanings of poverty. The plot of the novel ironically undermines familiar, and perhaps comfortable or safe, ideas of poverty perpetuated by icons of the Depression, highlighting the social and cultural diversity within white racial identity. In fact, the novel foregrounds the ways in which poverty colors whiteness, creating social hierarchies amongst whites that isolate and stigmatize subcultures outside middle-class experience.

As suggested by the iconographic familiarity of Depression-era photographs by Lange and other photojournalists such as Walker Evans, Ben Shahn, Marion Post-Wolcott, and Arthur Rothstein, middle-class American culture understands white poverty through stereotypical images of a body's appearance and context. In the popular American imagination, these fetishistic images of thin, homeless, derelict bodies become oversimplified symbols of past social crises in American history. In contrast, Allison's narrative depicts the intricate ways in which the body visibly registers degrees of poverty and how such embodied indigence can carry vastly different meanings, ranging from aesthetically and morally uplifting to trashy and repugnant. Gravitating toward female experience and the challenges that poverty presents for women's sexuality, motherhood, and child care, Allison is particularly concerned with representing the poor white female. Her works painstakingly illustrate the ways in which poor white women are doubly vulnerable to the physical and emotional effects of poverty in American culture: they dwell at the bottom of the cultural and social hierarchy internal to whiteness while they habitually suffer sexual mistreatment and political disenfranchisement. Indeed, the poor white female body is a politicized locus where economic forces and discourses about race, sexuality, and class converge to enforce traditional social hierarchies.

Taking up the social and political challenge that the poor white female body presents, Dorothy Allison seeks to expose structures of power that underlie such oppressive hierarchies. A lesbian with self-proclaimed 'white trash' roots, Allison undertakes this task in her attempt to integrate facets of her identity rooted in two of the most stigmatized groups in American culture: the poor and the queer. In this essay, I am interested in examining how Allison negotiates and constructs a politically efficacious identity founded upon two radically different (and often contentious) cultures that are united in their disdain for different aspects of her 'perverse' sexual practices. By theorizing and historicizing marginal white identity and analyzing essays from Allison's collection *Skin: Talking About Sex, Class, and Literature* as well as her novel *Bastard Out of Carolina*, I will explore the problems the white-trash body poses for hegemonic as well as alternative notions of sexuality and social hierarchy and demonstrate how the white-trash body cuts across and confuses often opposing political and cultural lines.

Black Sheep

As marginalized populations distinguished from the white American middle class in terms of economic solvency, social status, cultural capital, and political values, 'white trash' people are often constructed as stereotypes simultaneously ridiculed and despised: they are white folk who aren't 'white' enough by middle-class standards; they are the proverbial black sheep of the white flock. Yet, this derision demonstrates that the construction of white racial identity in the US functions not only through its difference from people of color but also through the fragmentation of whiteness itself. Following the racist conflation of blackness and poverty in the US, skin color has functioned, historically, as a primary signifier of class status in hegemonic discourses. But because all 'white' people do not benefit equally from their investment in whiteness as a race, white poverty necessitates a differentiation within whiteness itself, the signs of which are visible characteristics (most frequently in the guise of malnutrition, obesity, physical deformity, bad posture, rotten teeth, and jaundiced or leathery skin) often understood as physical manifestations of class status, occupation, health, cultural capital, and social values. Among the white underclass, however, further distinctions are often made between good poor folk and poor white trash that depend not so much on how poor white people look but on how they conduct themselves. Bodies become coded as trashy when associated with unregulated reproduction, unrestrained or perverse sexuality, and lax work ethic; situated in poor rural environments, these same bodies become the fundament of long-lasting cultural stereotypes.

The trashy poor are despised and degraded because they are white, but never white enough: they don't have enough money; they don't consume properly; they don't believe in narratives of social progress. In *Dangerous Classes*, Lydia Morris questions the fine line between the good and bad poor in the context of public policy in the US and Britain across the generic boundaries of various disciplines, such as sociology, economics, political philosophy, and government policy. She explains that historically, state and other social apparatuses have been plagued by what is perceived as the 'problem' of classifying and treating the 'worthy and unworthy poor' who fall outside of the social system itself and thus are not bound to the government in a conventional manner (2). Implicitly, the division between the good and bad poor revolves around the relationship to labor. The 'worthy' poor are often seen as having fallen upon bad times because of the economy, natural disasters, or other forces beyond their control. The 'unworthy' poor, however, are faulted for their laziness, personal irresponsibility, and immoral lifestyles. Although in the discipline of policymaking the 'underclass' is defined in terms of its dependence on the state and state programs such as the welfare system, Morris points out that the connotation of the term is both 'pejorative and threatening' (1). These dangerous classes are 'not only a threat to social organisation, but also a challenge to [sociologists' and policymakers'] models for portraying and understanding social structure' (2).

Lending depth to the current debate about public policy concerning the poor, Morris sketches a fascinating history of prevalent attitudes (mostly British) toward the lowest classes of society. Historically, poverty has been understood as the fault of its victim; poverty was as a 'sub-culture based on vice, filth and moral ignorance,' and the only antidote could be found in 'moral education and the enforcement of self-reliance' (12). By the mid-nineteenth century, biology had been added to social and economic explanations as a distinguishing factor in accounts arguing that the vagrant is 'physically distinct' and perhaps even a 'race apart' from the ordinary citizen (17). In the US, this concern with biology and visible traits became manifest in concerns about the propensity for immigrants and African-Americans to become dependents on or threats to the state. Contemporary American usage of the term 'underclass' applies primarily to Blacks; consequently, one of the primary debates in policymaking over the last decade has centered around whether issues of class or of race are more central in the 'explanation' of the underclass (4).

Studies focusing upon the relationship between class and race that attempt to circumscribe the impoverished into a 'race' has had a long and infamous history in the United States. In her introduction to a collection of eugenic family studies compiled between 1877 and 1919 fittingly entitled *White Trash*, Nicole Rafter explains that the studies identified poor white rural families[2] or 'tribes' whose abnormal or 'cacogenic' genes, as they were called, were considered the source of such traits as alcoholism, criminal behavior, mental disability, prostitution, hyperactivity, laziness, and poverty. The researchers concluded that society (e.g. the 'white' race) would be cleansed of social problems if these people could be prevented from reproducing. Perhaps most contemptibly, female sexuality was particularly targeted for regulation at the state and national levels through forced sterilization, sexual segregation of women of child-bearing age, and immigration restrictions. In addition, historian Edward Larson suggests that fervent policing of poor white women's bodies through the eugenics project was linked to other contemporary public health campaigns such as those against venereal disease, tuberculosis, and infant mortality (86).

Certainly more of a literature than a science, the discourse of eugenics suggests that profound anxieties existed regarding class position and security on the part of a newly professionalized segment of the middle class. Referring to eugenicists and field practitioners, many of whom, incidentally, were white middle-class women and first-generation female professionals,[3] Rafter elucidates the incipient class oppression involved in scientific discourse and public policy:

> By portraying the cacogenic as insentient subhumans (as well as dangerous), the literature made more palatable the recommendation that a large segment of the population be denied liberty and the right to reproduce. Furthermore, to authors (and readers as well . . .) the family studies gave the reassurance that they, in particular, ranked high in genetic worth. From this perspective, the family studies constitute a graphic rhetorical gesture, an affirmation of class position and entitlement. (16)

Although eugenics began to lose credibility by the 1920s, a legacy of belief in intrinsic social hierarchy as well as the transmission of social characteristics via genetic material endures today. Social policies of the time which governed crime control, education, liquor consumption, marriage, birth control, mental retardation, relief for the poor, and sterilization were strongly influenced by these studies; consequently, not only did these policies directly affect people, but stereotypes regarding the depravity of poor rural whites were perpetuated (30–31). Essentially, concludes Rafter, the eugenic family studies were 'far more than bad science and self-serving doctrine'; they were 'crafted documents' which 'fabricated a mythology' (30). And it is the legacy of this mythology that gives substance to the white trash stereotype.

The cultural and political struggle to define an undeserving 'race' of poor whites created a stereotype of white trash people who seemed to desire their own oppression by refusing established paths to empowerment such as unions and populist politics. This stereotype produces hierarchical relations between the hard-working poor and trash that evaluate poor whites vis-à-vis the standard of dominant white, middle-class, heterosexual discourse. A product of middle-class regimes of signification that construct poverty as a spectacular object of pity, the good poor often escape the degree of contempt experienced by white trash. As I will show, Dorothy Allison's writings suggest that there is room in standards of normativity for the noble poor, for those who show visible signs of their desperate desire for and commitment toward attaining middle-class status. Referring to her own childhood, Allison explains that the distinction between the good and bad poor in her rural South Carolina community was clear to its members, especially to those on the wrong side of the dichotomy such as her family:

> There was an idea of the good poor – hard-working, ragged but clean, and intrinsically honorable. I understood that we were the bad poor: men who drank and couldn't keep a job; women, invariably pregnant before marriage, who quickly became worn, fat, and old from working too many hours and bearing too many children; and children with runny noses, watery eyes, and the wrong attitudes. My cousins quit school, stole cars, used drugs, and took dead-end jobs pumping gas or waiting tables. We were not noble, not grateful, not even hopeful. We knew ourselves despised. (*Skin* 18)

For Allison, the good poor and bad poor are defined primarily in relation to the body, labor, and commodities. She explains that her family never fit the depictions of heroic workers in proletarian novels or the stereotype of 'noble Southern whites portrayed in the movies, mill workers for generations until driven out by alcoholism and a family propensity for rebellion and union talk' because her family didn't believe in or trust unions (*Skin* 25). Because Allison's family members do not seem to acknowledge an alienated relation to labor, their victimization is complicated; they seem to refuse a clear identification with their own labor, placing their identities beyond being simply proletarian victims of capitalist conspiracies. As people who have exhausted themselves without ever getting ahead, they have problems with a belief in the rewards of labor in the first place. Although Allison frequently refers to her family as 'working-class,' their rejection of a theory of exploitation based on an ontological relation to work seems to identify a point where the line between working class and white trash, between the noble poor and bad poor, becomes clear. In this way, Allison's family falls outside the working class and the 'noble' poor and becomes white trash.

Struggling for significant control of poverty, Allison addresses the stigma and effects of being perceived as 'white trash' and attempts to define the 'trashy' quality of her family's economic status as something other than pitiful. In her attempts to mine the political value of that which has no value, she suggests that 'the inescapable impact of being born in a *condition of poverty that this society finds shameful, contemptible, and somehow deserved*, has had dominion over me to such an extent that I have spent my life trying to overcome or deny it' (*Skin* 15, my emphasis). Allison writes that, as a child, she had learned that 'those who cannot change their own lives have every reason to be ashamed of that fact and to hide it' (*Skin* 32). In short, those people who do not adhere to the 'American' dream of social mobility or narrative of progress must be censored because they disrupt the fragile myth which allows the United States' capitalist democracy to function. It is in this way that Allison sees herself not only as poor or working-class but as trash.[4] Trash poverty, then, comes to be defined, at least in part, by the anti-work ethic of those poor people who neither struggle toward class mobility nor aspire to be middle-class by stretching their meager resources to embody middle-class values.

White Trash Lesbianism

Writing about her own experience as a lesbian from a white working-class background, Allison understands firsthand that white trash and queerness are linked indelibly by their relationship to shame and otherness. Recalling the contempt she felt as a child, Allison makes this connection clear: 'Me and my family, we had always been they . . . We die so easily, disappear so completely – we/they, the poor and the queer' (*Skin* 13). Because she claims both seemingly incongruous identities, Allison finds that she never really belongs to either group; the dominant feminist-lesbian community rejects her 'perverse' sexual preferences that she associates with her class background and her childhood experiences of sexual abuse, and similarly, her family has little respect for her sexual orientation and feminist activism. Allison explains that, early in her lesbian activism, she felt compelled to build a closet around her class background and the sexual preferences she associates with conditions of poverty in an effort to become a member of activist lesbian communities of predominantly non-rural, white, middle-class women. Longing for a sense of security and belonging amongst the lesbian-feminists, Allison felt it necessary to muffle her desires and her social circumstances, 'to collapse my sexual history into what I was willing to share of my class background' (*Skin* 17).

While concerns about sexual orientation and anti-patriarchal sentiment dominated the lesbian-feminist discourse of that era, Allison increasingly found that her personal experience demanded a consideration of her class status as well as her sexuality. In opposition to prevailing lesbian-feminist thought in the late 1970s and early 1980s, Allison jeopardized a harmonious alliance by publicly advocating sexual diversity in articles which appeared in *The Advocate*, *American Voice*, *The Village Voice*, and the *Landmark Pleasure and Danger* anthology edited by Carole Vance. Establishing herself as a vocal champion of butch/femme roles, pornography, and sexual practices considered subversive or male-identified such as leather fetishism and penetration, Allison and her 'perverse' sexual preferences deviated from dominant visions of lesbian self-expression. As subversive voices in the lesbian 'sex wars,' an ideological debate over the definition and political import of lesbian sexuality and its relationship to feminism, Allison, Pat Califia, and other sex radicals were accused by more conservative lesbian feminists such as Ti-Grace Atkinson and Robin Morgan of promoting violence toward and objectification of women.

At the heart of this controversy lay a tension between the perceived need for a unified feminist movement and the reality that feminist identities were not constructed by gender or sexual preference alone. Repudiating the prevalent assumption that lesbians, simply by being part of a social minority, naturally understood and sympathized with the plights of various minority groups, Califia admits that 'it was woefully obvious that simply coming out as a lesbian had not eliminated my sexual prejudices or given me any special insight into the way other marginalized people dealt with their stigmatized status' (19). Herein Califia identifies some of problems which led to the third wave's reassessment of the movement's insensitivity toward and discrimination against the vast differences in individual feminists' sexual preferences and practices, class status, race and ethnicity, (dis)ability, religious beliefs, and other determinants of identity outside concerns about gender. Echoing Califia's observation, Allison argues that within this contested ideological environment conflicts over sexual preference and taste frequently stand in for class prejudice: 'my sexual identity is intimately constructed by my class and regional background, and much of the hatred directed at my sexual preferences is class hatred – however much people, feminists in particular, like to pretend this is not a factor' (*Skin* 23). Because taste was not (and, by and large, still is not) considered significant toward constructing a politicized identity, its function as a marker of economic and social standing situates it as a primary locus where class prejudices and social divisions within politically progressive movements are articulated. Taste, then, serves to encapsulate political and cultural differences that exceed the scope of traditional categories of identity politics.

By claiming that her sexuality is shaped by class, Allison doesn't necessarily posit a causal relationship between poverty, sexual abuse and her homosexuality; rather, she seems more invested in exposing the ways in which the politics of taste in lesbian culture can become an expression of class prejudice.[5] She seeks to legitimate her right to cultivate a 'perverse' lesbian sexuality while espousing feminist ideals – to claim her roots and identify as a feminist and lesbian. Catering to her singular circumstances, Allison attempts to reconcile disparate aspects of her experience, linking two seemingly disjunctive marginalized identities: queerness and white trash status. Because her sexual practices and lower class status fall outside of hegemonic value systems, Allison conflates sexual perversion and white trash. In this way, she places sado-masochism under the sign of trashiness because, in her experience, her deviant sexual preferences signify class difference; sexual perversion, for Allison, seems to be the natural result of poverty which fosters violent physical and emotional relationships. Allison, however, seems oblivious to the multitude of meanings s/m carries and its popularity outside both working-class and gay and lesbian communities; she simplifies perversion, forcing its radicalness to correspond to the specific marginality borne by the underclass. Thus, although it relies upon the precedents of the new social movements of the 1960s and 1970s, Allison's white-trash lesbianism seems to be a necessarily idiosyncratic, local sexual politics rather than a widespread movement that provides a structure of identity under which diverse populations unite.

As a lesbian feminist whose sexual practices were often considered deviant or offensive by members of the lesbian community, Allison turns intolerance into a platform for critiquing the lack of attention given to class issues in gay and lesbian politics. Allison's struggle to reconcile these components of her identity, questions the role and limits of identity politics at the same time that she remains invested in asserting the essence of her identity. Although Allison identifies herself as both lesbian and queer, 'queer' seems to carry a specific connotation for her beyond that of object choice and comes to signify her marginalization within the lesbian community. Calling herself queer, Allison sets herself apart from both heteronormative discourse as well as the already queer lesbian-feminist space which she sees as intolerant of her tastes. Queerer than queer, Allison embraces and recovers the shame attributed to poverty and lesbianism in order to forge a distinct identity that validates personal experience while being politically efficacious. Thus, following Michael Warner's argument that queerness is not just defined in opposition to heterosexuality but is 'in favor of a more thorough resistance to regimes of the normal,' I would propose that claiming white trash identity in contemporary culture can be read as a queer act (xxvi). Allison's work does, in some ways, 'queer' gay and lesbian studies. By utilizing queerness' strategy of recuperating stigmatized identity to recover an identity that queer people themselves often stigmatize, Allison puts a twist on left notions of subversion. In this way, Allison not only claims to be white trash but approaches it as a livable, and perhaps even liberating, subjectivity rather than a state of social marginalization. Choosing white trash identity empowers the subject (much as queerness does in the case of gay and lesbian activism) by 'outing' a secret and seizing some degree of control over the discourses and ideologies that work to construct and dominate the lives of marginalized populations. Therapeutic white trash narratives which work toward overcoming the shame and stigma associated with poverty and past marginalization resemble, in large part, coming-out narratives in the tradition of gay and lesbian literature. To come out as white trash entails constructing the closeted remnants of poverty and social stigma not passively as an open secret but defiantly as integral parts of one's identity. In this way, Allison's trashiness operates as a means of opposing class prejudices, heteronormative notions of sexuality, and naturalized constructions of whiteness.

The point of convergence of these components of identity – of sexuality, family, economics, and social context – lies, for Allison, in the body. As a site of desire, inheritance, and lived experience, the body seems to represent a kind of essential truth for Allison. This sentiment is most apparent in 'Skin: Where She Touches Me,' an essay which draws comparisons between her kinship with her mother and her relationship with her first lover:

> Skin, the surface of skin, the outer layer protecting the vulnerable inside, the boundary between the world and the soul, what is seen from the outside and hides all the secrets. My skin, my mama's skin, my sisters' skin. Our outer layer hides our inner hopes. White girls, tough-skinned and stubborn, born to a family that never valued girls. I am my mama's daughter, one with my tribe, taught to believe myself of not much value,

to take damage and ignore it, to take damage and be proud of it. We were taught to be proud that we were not Black, and ashamed that we were poor, taught to reject everything people believed about us – drunken, no-count, lazy, whorish, stupid – and still some of it was just the way we were. The lies went to the bone, and digging them out has been the work of a lifetime. (*Skin* 225)

A racial and cultural marker, a sexual organ, and a metaphor for thinking about experience, skin functions crucially in the construction of Allison's identity as a lesbian, a writer, a feminist activist, and a woman with white working-class origins. Reflecting upon the deaths of two important women in her life, her mother and her first lover, 'Skin' explores the complex ideological space where various discourses and determinants of identity intersect. Joined through their mutual association with the permeable, epidermal boundary of skin, these women represent two distinct components of Allison's identity, her white, working-class heritage and her lesbian sexuality. Skin with its biological, cultural, and racial significance is the physical and semiotic surface where Allison's mother continues to affect, literally touch, her life. Allison inherits her mother's genetic composition along with the socio-economic environment in which the culture of southern, rural poverty is cultivated. Although visibly and racially accepted as white, Allison's relatives are not simply poor but despicably poor because they do not, it seems, sufficiently uphold appearances or behaviors understood as 'white' by prevailing middle-class standards. In this way, Allison seems more concerned with articulating her resentment over having been constantly disparaged for not being white enough than with addressing her own whiteness per se. The presence of an implicitly racialized discourse refers once again to the subject of skin, skin color, and the ideological function of skin in narratives of class identity.

Allison's lover Cathy lives on in her too, but in the context of their relationship skin signifies the erotically charged topography of a non-phallic sexuality. Indeed, Allison recalls of their affair that '[b]efore Cathy I thought I was the only woman in the world who so desperately wanted sex with another woman. But Cathy's desires were so sudden, so explicit and so powerful, I would flush every time I imagined her skin touching mine' (*Skin* 240). The relationship with Cathy transforms Allison's skin into a surface that enables her to envision alternatives to both heteronormative and middle-class lesbian feminist sexual discourses. Shedding her armor allows for an outpouring of promiscuity and irrational desire that cannot be contained by discursive efforts to produce homogeneity and delimit sexual identity. The flowering of what Allison comes to see as her 'trashy' queerness through her first intense lesbian relationship undercuts any notions of health and emotional stability proffered by either heteronormative or lesbian feminist politics. Acknowledging the physical passion she and her lover shared enables Allison to validate her impoverished background, mixing sexual pleasure with the politics of identity. As a result of this formative lesbian relationship,

Allison thus claims that she could finally see herself as having inherited her mother's unabashed and, at times, irrational sexuality and that the women in her family were kin in their queer desires; 'Cathy proved to me,' Allison writes, 'that I was my mother's daughter, my sisters' equal' (*Skin* 233). While her mother and sisters are by no means lesbians, Allison elides the difference of their specific sexual practices. Uniting their sexual 'equality' under the sign of 'poor white trash,' Allison reveals an acute awareness of the centrality of 'deviant' sexual behavior in popular notions of what constitutes white trash. Considered economically and morally impoverished and threatening to the social order, white trash are denounced as ignorant of and unable to take responsibility for their own sexuality.

Although the essay's focus allows Allison to forge connections between her sexuality and class background, the potential impact of her central metaphor is never fully realized because she refrains from addressing the whiteness of her own skin. This omission is most notable in Allison's account of her tentative, somewhat embarrassed approach toward the ambiguity of Cathy's race. Allison recalls Cathy's attempts to dismiss the issue by remarking that people "wonder if I'm not some Black bitch from the projects getting over on them. So I say it before they can whisper it to each other. I say it so they can't pretend nothing. I make them think about who they are" (*Skin* 235-36). Although Allison constantly interrogates her own identity, she does so primarily in terms of class and sexuality, despite her preoccupation with her lover's skin color and indeterminate racial heritage. Perhaps because of the ways in which whiteness maintains its hegemony by asserting its 'naturalness,' race, for Allison, seems to remain a subject that can only be approached indirectly. By not examining her own whiteness, Allison forgoes an opportunity to examine the dominance of whiteness in gay and lesbian studies at the same time that she interjects a much-needed discussion of class. In promoting herself as a white-trash queer, Allison does succeed in making class struggle more visible in gay and lesbian studies. In doing so, however, she emphasizes the class component of *white trash* at the expense of a thorough analysis of the discursive effects of whiteness.[6] Allison's particular use of white trash, though a valuable tool for class analysis, tends to over-simplify and perhaps even erase issues of whiteness from the slate of queer thinking, an action comparable to that of the queer theorists she berates for neglecting class concerns in the context of gay and lesbian issues.[7]

Whiter Than White

Allison's reluctance to problematize some of the issues she brings up in the expository works collected in Skin finds a much more interesting outlet in her fiction. Ruth Anne 'Bone' Boatwright, the semi-autobiographical protagonist of

Bastard Out of Carolina, is the young, illegitimate child of a teen mother living in the rural South of the 1950s. Bone's environment is pockmarked by stereotypical white-trash tropes: lazy, alcoholic men; women who marry young and age quickly; dead-end jobs; sexual and domestic abuse; illegitimacy; racist sentiment; and extreme poverty. Such a bleak socio-economic environment takes its toll upon Bone's pubescent physicality and sexuality, coercing her into pre-determined cycles of poverty and oppression. As an adolescent coming to terms with her body, Bone sees herself in a culture where all she has is her body, and even this is not hers as she is repeatedly violated by her stepfather Daddy Glen. Bone responds to social ostracism and sexual abuse as well as her own anger and confusion about the violence and pleasure of sexuality by turning to autoeroticism and masochistic fantasies which afford her autonomy but leave her feeling ashamed of her desires and her perceived deviance from the dominant culture. But in the same way that Bone is repulsed by her female relatives' sexual and emotional subservience to men, especially her mother's refusal, finally, to renounce Daddy Glen, she is awed by their frank sexuality and comfortable relationship with their bodies, thinking, 'I wished then that I could be like them, easier in my body and not so angry' (*Bastard* 190).

The narrative's solution to Bone's plight is to place her in the care of her Aunt Raylene. Following years of physical and sexual abuse from her stepfather and her mother's refusal to acknowledge the violence, Bone is abandoned by her mother but finds a safe haven in the home of her lesbian aunt, Raylene, an alternative role model whose self-sufficiency allows her to function outside the cycle of despair and abuse her sisters endure. Raylene is part of the novel's larger feminist reconfiguration of the family as an extended matrilineal and sororal network. This reliance on kinship, particularly on the women of the family, is offered as one of the few available ways of coping with shame and despair in such a culture. Although *Bastard Out of Carolina* concludes without resolving Bone's shame about her sexual desires and social status, there is a sense that following her aunt's example of a non-heterosexual lifestyle will allow her to take pleasure in her proto-lesbian sexuality and, ultimately, escape the cycle of so many poor women.

When *Bastard Out of Carolina* captured a front-page notice in the *New York Times Book Review*, Allison was launched into mainstream literary venues, bringing white trash into a popular consciousness.[8] Allison's critically acclaimed first novel became a finalist for the 1992 National Book Award, the first time, according to her publishers, that a 'gay-themed book by an avowed lesbian had been so honored' (Lyall). Published by a national publishing house, *Bastard* was marketed to a wide audience, reflecting an increasing trend in gay and lesbian writing for crossing over genres and across interest groups such as rape and incest survivors, readers of southern fiction, people with an interest in working-class culture, and feminist readers. Despite the praise and widespread recognition, however, Allison seemed uneasy about the commercial success of a book that foregrounded such stigmatized issues; Allison seemed to find disappointment in what she took to be the co-optation of the book's challenge to established literary tastes. In an interview she says, 'I saw myself as a living affront to a kind of literature that I despise. How could the people who were the pantheon of that literature think I did something right? I thought I must have screwed up bad' (quoted in Jetter). In many ways, her unease has become realized in critical responses to the novel. Although *Bastard* functions, in quite an original manner, as what might be considered a white-trash *bildungsroman*, most critics tend to concentrate on its depiction of the sexual abuse and incestuous rape of protagonist Bone Boatwright.[9] By reducing the novel to its most harrowing scene of physical violence, many commentators suspend Allison's complex interplay of class and social hierarchy as well as the construction of rural whiteness such that the novel appears solely to address familiar, if unfortunate, themes of female victimization. However, it is arguable that Allison's celebrity depends, in large part, upon the recent popularity and proliferation of narratives of sexual abuse, perhaps the very literature she disdained. But by utilizing this familiar and fashionable narrative strategy that depicts the female body enduring and surviving victimization, Allison is able to address sexuality in a mainstream venue while she explores the complex, perhaps productive, relationship between incest and sexual pleasure. Gay and lesbian theorist Ann Cvetkovich has examined the therapeutic potential of traumatic experience for queer sexuality, arguing that Bone's inability to separate 'the beating that she hates from the fantasy about it that she loves' (369) illustrates the 'queer interdependence of that which harms and that which heals' (373). While Cvetkovich's thesis might productively be pressed to argue that queerness potentially disrupts the interest in self-preservation that distinctions between harm, healing, and pleasure seem to imply, like most of her contemporaries Cvetkovich limits her analysis to issues of sexual abuse even as she recognizes the novel's celebration of queer desire.

Extending Cvetkovich's interest in queerness' multi-faceted challenge to normativity, I want to analyze a part of the novel much neglected by critics, including Cvetkovich herself. Allison's particular brand of queer politics is exemplified by Bone's charged relationship with Shannon Pearl, the daughter of a couple who scout talent for the gospel tour circuit and manage the local religious supply store that specializes in embroidering gospel singers' costumes with religious images. Born with 'white skin, white hair, and pale pink eyes of an albino,' Shannon is subject to ostracism from not only her neighbors and schoolmates but members of her extended family as well (*Bastard* 155). Moreover, her freakish lack of pigmentation is only compounded by her plump, swollen body, coke-bottle glasses, frail constitution, and evangelist family. Bone meets

Shannon at a crucial point in the novel. After an emergency room physician confronts Bone and her mother about the stepfather's abuse, Bone turns inward in an attempt to conceal her pain and avoid more conflict and hardship in her immediate family. Harboring a moment of social aspiration, Bone fantasizes about leading an entirely different life, one in which she would be an adored and adorned celebrity: 'More than anything in the world, I wanted to be one of the little girls in white fringed vests with silver and gold embroidered crosses – the ones who sang on the revival circuit and taped shows for early-morning television ... I wanted to be a gospel singer and be loved by the whole wide world' (*Bastard* 141). As members of the gospel circuit subculture, the Pearls offer Bone an opportunity to be a spectator, if not a participant, in this cultural realm. When she wants to escape her class condition and social circumstances, Bone turns to gospel and the Pearls as a means and an example for becoming 'whiter'; ironically, however, the Pearls are far *too* white. Part of a marginal subculture centered around religious zeal and hermetic rural lifestyles, the Pearls perform a bourgeois sensibility that doesn't work; if they possess a weird kind of respectability in Bone's eyes, the Pearls' petty aspirations and earnest intentions of being normal sag under the weight of their lack of business sense and their ostentatious piety such that, from a middle-class perspective, they are innocuous anomalies.

Even so, the Pearls offer an attractive alternative to Bone's environment and to what she sees as her destiny:

> This body, like my aunts' bodies, was born to be worked to death, used up, and thrown away. I had read these things in books and passed right over it. The ones who died like that, worked to death or carried off by senseless accidents, they were almost never the heroines ... I was part of the trash down in the mud-stained cabins, fighting with the darkies and stealing ungratefully from our betters, stupid, coarse, born to shame and death. (*Bastard* 206)

Witnessing the poverty and hardship of her mother and aunts, Bone is always cognizant of her trash status. While the tours that the Pearls attend feature second-string artists (in contrast to the commercial radio gospel Bone listens to), they provide a means for community-building and, for Bone, a means of experiencing redemption firsthand. The genre of gospel music, however, performs the unifying action of reminding its patrons that while all people are sinners and moral transgressors, they are also made in God's image and indebted to Christ's sacrifice. As such, gospel simultaneously requires that Christians admit their limitations and celebrate their redemption; in this way, these gospel tours bring redemption and moral discipline to the countryside dotted by white-trash enclaves. As Bone observes, one of the most seductive qualities of gospel is that it will 'make you love and hate yourself at the same time, make you ashamed and glorified' (*Bastard* 136). Bone's particular form of redemption comes not as a religious epiphany, however, but as an epiphany about race, class, and sexuality that she develops through her association with Shannon and her family. In Bone's eyes, the Pearls redeem white trash.

When, upon seeing Shannon, a touring gospel singer exclaims, 'Child, you are the ugliest thing I have ever seen,' Bone defends her friend and feels empowered by Shannon's rage and shame (*Bastard* 165). Despite this kinship founded upon a mutual understanding of stigma, the girls' friendship ends when, after hearing singers from a black church, Bone suggests that Mr. Pearl should invite those singers to join the tour. Shannon cuts Bone short, saying that her father doesn't deal with 'colored.' Because Bone's enthusiasm for gospel music transcends a racist and racially segregated society, she presses Shannon to have her parents make an exception. The girls squabble and trade insults, culminating in Bone's outburst: 'you monster, you greasy cross-eyed stinking sweaty-faced ugly thing! ... You so ugly your own mama don't even love you' (*Bastard* 171–2). Though she lashes out at Shannon's racist attitudes, however, Bone recognizes that Shannon's skin bears the mark of social injustice. Indeed, Bone feels indebted to Shannon's monstrosity: 'I felt as if I belonged to her in a funny kind of way, as if her 'affliction' put me deeply in her debt. It was a mystery, I guessed, a sign of grace' (*Bastard* 156). In a moment of enlightenment about being white trash, Bone, for the first time is allowed a glimpse of a creature worse off than she. Bone's guilt elucidates Shannon's position as society's scapegoat and symbol for evoking moral contrition.

Utterly fascinated with Shannon's abnormality, Bone compares her obsession to that of needing to 'scratch [the scabs on] my ankles' (*Bastard* 156). For Bone, Shannon's glaring whiteness functions as a blemish or site where the boundaries of skin have broken down, a minor irritation that constantly makes itself known and demands attention. A physical abreaction of a healing body, Bone's perverse desire and disgust for Shannon's hyper-whiteness is subject to and representative of intense rage and shame. Envisioning Shannon as a figure of white-trash trauma, Bone concedes, 'All right, she was a little monster, but she was my friend, and the kind of monster I could understand' (*Bastard* 200). Moreover, Bone thinks, '[Shannon] reminded me of myself, or at least the way I had come to think of myself' (*Bastard* 154). It is no coincidence that Bone first makes Shannon's acquaintance by offering the humiliated child a seat on the school bus, not so much as an act of charity but as a move to defy the same people who regularly sneered at Bone and the extended Boatwright clan. Shannon, then, emblematizes Bone's shame about being trash; this, in turn, enables Bone to transform her feelings of victimhood and degradation into a libidinal attraction that fosters fantasies of escaping what she takes to be her bodily destiny – a lifetime of poverty and social stigma. So, when Shannon takes her meager revenge on the world by reciting stories of gruesome 'decapitations, mutilations, murder, and mayhem,'

Bone listens 'openmouthed and fascinated,' both captivated and aroused by the narrative manipulation of the body into snarls of shock and gore (*Bastard* 157).

Allison portrays Bone's sense of her own sexuality as always askew, as desirous of her own violation and open to perverse and inventive bodily combinations. From fantasizing about her stepfather's incestuous groping to masturbating with a metal hook used to dredge drowned bodies from the river, Bone's sexuality rests upon her willing surrender to forces that overtake any sense of volition and possess her physical being, disturbing normative notions of bodily integrity or the 'ownership' of one's self. And though critics such as Jack Kirby argue that Bone's desires result from Daddy Glen's abuse, what Sandell describes as 'an understandable, if ultimately unhealthy, coping strategy,' I want to suggest that such a protracted view crystallizes sexual violence into the *sine qua non* of the novel's vision of feminine sexuality and forecloses the possibilities of Bone's unpleasant, yet creative queerness, a potential sexual and social future prefigured by her lesbian, cross-dressing, neo-hippie Aunt Raylene (Sandell 221). And lest it be forgotten that the history of feminine sexuality is one of occupation and the lack of self-empowerment, Allison retains the tangled relationship of violence, poverty, sexuality, and social abjection, refusing to allow queerness or perversity to resemble anything that might be cleansed or psychologized away. While she is careful to demonstrate the ways in which poor whites labor, live, and make love under the auspices of patriarchal and capitalist power, Allison safeguards Bone's dangerous pleasures – what might be considered the hallmark of queerness – from simple determinism. Bone answers her good-intentioned critics, clinging tenaciously to her idiosyncratic sexual preferences even as she submits to normalizing conceptions of sex and affection which staunchly sever the erotic and the violent:

> I was ashamed of myself for the things I thought about when I put my hands between my legs, more ashamed for masturbating to the fantasy of being beaten than for being beaten in the first place . . . Yet it was only in my fantasies with people watching me that I was able to defy Daddy Glen. Only there that I had any pride. I loved those fantasies, even though I was sure they were a terrible thing. They had to be; they were self-centered and they made me have shuddering orgasms. In them, I was very special. I was triumphant, important. I was not ashamed. (*Bastard* 113)[10]

But if her eroticization of abuse foregrounds the complexities of desire and the radical openness of queer libidinality, Bone's feeling of attraction/repulsion toward Shannon further convolutes her sexual development by negotiating the tricky proximity of whiteness and queer love, representing the whiteness of white skin as a racial erogenous zone.

As an albino, Shannon Pearl is *too* white, signifying a shocking absence of color and pigment. Bone concurs, 'Shannon was wholly monstrous, a lurching hunched creature shining with sweat and smug satisfaction' (*Bastard* 155). Her albinism becomes 'monstrous' – a whiteness that shows itself as white. Indeed, the choice of 'monstrous' to describe this phenomenon is fitting; it is abject whiteness.[11] In the black imagination, bell hooks explains, whiteness is always linked with terror, hence its representational power; correspondingly, she argues, 'without the capacity to inspire terror, whiteness no longer signifies the right to dominate. It truly becomes a benevolent absence' (hooks 345). Whiteness' power, Richard Dyer explains, 'secures its dominance by seeming not to be anything in particular, but also because, when whiteness qua whiteness does come into focus, it is often revealed as emptiness, absence, denial or even a kind of death' ('White' 44). The albino's horror makes clear this latter, terrorizing side of whiteness; her particular threat to white people is to unearth the racist constructions of skin and skin color supporting white power, exposing the means by which whiteness dominates the concept of the 'normal' or 'natural.' Indeed Dyer elaborates upon this notion of an monstrous whiteness in a later work, explaining that 'the extreme, very white white image is functional in relation to the ordinary, is even perhaps a condition of establishing whiteness as ordinary' (*White* 222). In this way, even Bone's tinged, trashy whiteness appears as normal, ordinary whiteness in the face of Shannon's extraordinary lack of pigmentation. Shannon's congenital albinism ironically decries the constructed quality of race, demonstrating how skin pigmentation is overcoded by cultural prejudices. Rather than making her 'whiter,' Shannon's skin marks her as the embodiment of what Dyer calls 'extreme whiteness':

> Extreme whiteness coexists with ordinary whiteness: it is exceptional, excessive, marked . . . It exists alongside non-extreme, unspectacular, plain whiteness. Non-whiteness, on the other hand, is already peculiar, marked exceptional: it is always, in relation to notions of the human in Western culture, particular and has no ordinariness. (*White* 222)

Thus, a pathetic and threatening symbol, Shannon renders whiteness visible and tangible, inspiring nausea as other white characters are forced to witness that which they fetishize – white skin as the bodily origin of their racial power – spiral horribly out of control. The transparency of her skin confuses insides and outsides, provoking radically different interpretations and reactions. Bone reacts with a fascinated disgust because Shannon performs the invaluable service of making Bone feel more normal, more white; without Shannon, Bone and the trashy Boatwright clan stand as signifiers of extreme, extraordinary whiteness – whiteness that is not ordinary. Mrs. Pearl, on the other hand, attempts to whitewash Shannon's monstrousness, literally to make her more or less white; with a sad blindness, Mrs. Pearl speaks rapturously about 'the fine blue blood vessels [that] shone against the ivory of [Shannon's] scalp. Blue threads under the linen, her mama was always saying' (*Bastard* 155). Ironically, even in her effort to deny her daughter's abnormality, Mrs. Pearl, comparing veins to threads, succeeds only in emphasizing the constructedness of Shannon's racial identity, her capillary nets like the stitching in some sort of Pentecostal Frankenstein creature: Shannon's extreme whiteness will not be denied.

Having endured her final insult at a family barbecue, Shannon takes her wretched whiteness into her own hands and sets herself on fire with lighter fluid. Shannon's self-immolation literally turns her black, coloring herself and erasing whiteness' absence. Scorched and smoking, she embodies the spectacular limit of whiteness – truly the black sheep of the novel. Thus, in sympathizing with Shannon's hatred of anything that had ever hurt her, Bone envies Shannon's freakish skin and its capacity for making her abjection obvious; wanting to be monstrous, Bone desires a transparent boundary of self so that what is hidden inside her body – injury, trauma, perversity – might articulate itself shining through her skin. Read in the context of my earlier discussion of Allison's use of skin as a metaphor for queer identity, Bone's obsessive friendship with Shannon parallels and expands upon Allison's discussion of the capacity of skin to function as a site of mediation and even reconciliation of race, class, and sexuality. In *Bastard*, Allison returns to her core concerns, representing skin as a potential locus of identitarian collapse and the rupture of traditional notions of selfhood and whiteness. Shannon, then, becomes Bone's erotic focus, a metaphor for her own yearning to 'show through' her skin and to turn her body inside out, revealing the skeletal framework of a whiteness that denies itself and its racial authority. Bone and Shannon thereby become secret sharers of the deconstructed white girl's body, subverting the racist and patriarchal fetishization of white femininity by loving superwhiteness.[12] Thus Bone finds her 'self' by queering both her race and sexuality. Loving a white girl who's not really 'white,' Bone introduces the discourse of whiteness into homosocial desire and exposes both the peculiar eroticism of white skin and the political ideologies that underpin its seductiveness. In this way, Shannon functions for Bone the way that Bone's narrative functions for Allison: a conflagration waiting to happen, signifying white trash as a social wound and scar for which everyone must answer.

Conclusion

White trash has functioned as a segment of white identity that reveals the complexities of an oppressed social identity that refuses to be incorporated fully in the categories of whiteness or poverty. Studies of the white underclass often negotiate the proximity of the working poor or the white working class to trash by suggesting that fine lines can be drawn on the basis of a body's appearance and behavior. Unlike those poor whites who are victims of unfortunate or uncontrollable circumstances, white trash people tend to bear the blame of their own oppression. While all underclass populations are defined in opposition to a hegemonic white, middle-class, Protestant morality and social standards, white trash's refusal of a prosperous work ethic and normative standards of behavior and good taste disqualifies them from the pity conferred upon hardworking unfortunates down on their luck.

Borrowing strategies from earlier social movements based upon the politics of identity, Allison recuperates the stigma and shame carried by the racial epithet 'white trash.' At the same time Allison works to undermine its pervasive and injurious stereotypes, she transforms white trash into a political identity that provides a sense of community and pride in its cultural difference. Allison's contention that this difference takes the form of perverse sexual practices that frustrate heteronormative regimes of sexuality as well as prevailing lesbian thought locates the political challenge and any potential for social liberation raised by white trash in the body and specific sex acts. Because the basis of her white trash identity is founded upon singular, and often eccentric, social conditions and lifestyle choices, Allison's politics must be approached as an open and flexible strategy that prizes its ability to tailor its critical force to individual circumstances and particular needs. This extreme form of specialization often clashes, as Allison's early feminist writing evidences, with the more inclusive and encompassing organizational efforts of lesbian feminism and other large-scale political movements. Indeed, always striving to maintain and herald some sort of marginal status, Allison is reluctant to join the group that would have her as a member; similarly, white trash eludes representation by political organizations such as labor unions built upon reductive, limited notions of identity. As an admixture of numerous, and frequently contorted and contradictory, forms of marginalized subjectivity, white trash lesbianism forces traditional modes of social analysis to reconsider accepted notions of what counts as fundamental structures of identity. This, then, is white-trash lesbianism's crucial contribution to current discussions of gay and lesbian discourse and queer theory.

Moreover, capturing the critical force of white trash in Bone's pubescent desire, Allison confronts accepted understandings of sexual abuse and trauma. Taking children's sexuality and white poverty seriously, *Bastard Out of Carolina* renders white otherness as visible and tangible as sexual abuse. And, just as she expands the realm of queer, and specifically lesbian, sexuality, Allison splinters the notion of whiteness as a standard of normativity and naturalness. As the novel's white trash characters illustrate, monstrous whiteness can become the basis of community as well as a reconfiguration of patriarchal ideals practiced by men and women. Allison's white-trash lesbianism, then, lays the groundwork for trash to become a livable, if conflicted, subjectivity capable of challenging the social stigma which subjugates poor white bodies and ultimately reinforces the status quo.

Endnotes

1. Lange's most celebrated work is *An American Exodus: A Record of Human Erosion*. As part of a camera team commissioned by the Historical Section of the FSA, Lange and others undertook a mission to "introduce Americans to America" in their documentation of the plight of rural white poor devastated by the Depression's economic hardship and natural disaster (Shindo 75). In his study of popular images of Dust Bowl migrants, Charles J. Shindo contends that these photos have dominated a popular history of the Depression and 'illustrate the pervasiveness of the paternalistic rendering of the rural poor as victims of the environment and the economy' (75).
2. Rafter suggests a number of reasons why white rural families were targeted: professionalization of the social sciences, agricultural labor, lack of regulatory mechanisms in place (13–18).
3. For an enlightening discussion of women professionals' role in eugenics research and regional women's clubs' advocacy of and interest in eugenics, see Larson, especially 71–9.
4. In referring to herself as white trash, Allison does, at times, seem keenly aware of the distinctions between 'white trash' and other labels used to categorize white poverty. Although terms such as lower class, underclass, hillbilly, cracker, Okie, poor whites, redneck, and white working class have often been used interchangeably, they do exhibit subtle differences often related to behavior, geographic location, historical circumstances, or degree of poverty. Studies specifically focused upon white trash as a category of social classification are remarkably spare. More common are investigations about other subcategories of whiteness such as the aforementioned hillbilly, Okie, and redneck. One of the fundamental differences between such terms and white trash – and perhaps the reason for trash's theoretical obscurity – is that, as markers of (often regional) identity, redneck, hillbilly and Okie are suitable for recuperation as politicized identity. In contrast to such marginal white identities, which are often assumed as a point of pride, white trash has historically been an identity conferred onto others – an identity formulated with the purpose of exclusion, degradation, and stigmatization. Indeed, white trash's resistance to recuperation and an identity politics' model of self-identity is precisely what attracts Allison to the term; she prizes the term's connotations of social ostracism and recalcitrance to normative notions of decorum and propriety. Acutely aware of trash's distinction from other subcategories of whiteness, Allison is careful to maintain and delineate such difference.
5. In the essay collection, Allison refers frequently to conflicts among lesbians over tensions between theory and practice; see in particular 'Public Silence, Private Terror' (*Skin* 101–19). For a related discussion of how debates about s/m serve as a vehicle for negotiating differences among lesbians, see Julia Creet's 'Daughters of the Movement.'
6. It is arguable, however, that Allison is making a step in this direction. Referring to the debate between lesbian feminists and sex-radical lesbians, Kate Davy argues that 'Examining the ways in which white women engage in and use a politics of respectability "outs" whiteness, makes it manifest by revealing its investments, operations, and relations of power' (219). By self-identifying as white trash, it is undeniable that Allison 'outs' whiteness.
7. Allison speaks in general terms, but I am thinking here of recent works by Leo Bersani and David Halperin, for example, that attempt to substitute class consciousness with an assessment of the role of the fetish and taste cultures without really investigating the complex relationship between class and style.

8   In this unusually effusive review for the characteristically stolid *New York Times*, George Garrett gushes, 'When I finished *Bastard Out of Carolina* I wanted to blow a bugle to alert the reading public that a wonderful work of fiction by a major new talent has arrived on the scene. It is one of those one-in-a-blue-moon occasions when the jacket copy seems inadequate and all the blurbs are examples of rhetorical understatement. Please reserve a seat of honor at the high table of the art of fiction for Dorothy Allison' (5).
9   Similarly, the movie version of the novel also focuses on the rape scenes. Protesting that the violence and sexuality were too explicit for basic cable, media-mogul Ted Turner refused to air *Bastard Out of Carolina* on his flagship network TNT. Provided with the kind of publicity money can't buy, the film was broadcast on Showtime and garnered mixed reviews for straying far from the novel's central themes of whiteness, poverty, and queer sexuality. For representative reviews of the movie, see Shales, 'Holiday' and Leonard.
10 As one of these good-intentioned critics, Jillian Sandell argues that the trope of storytelling empowers Bone, and in particular, her 'fantasies become a safe space within which she can confront and overcome' her abuse (220).
11 Although the etymological derivation of 'monster' and 'monstrous' is disputed, it is linked to the Latin root words *monere*, meaning to warn, and *monstrare*, meaning to show. Drawing on both of these meanings, 'monstrous' whiteness can be seen as whiteness that shows itself, portending the hidden deformity and hideousness at the core of whiteness.
12 As horrific narratives of miscegenation and mob lynchings make clear, the 'purity' of white womanhood is directly related to masculine guidance and protection in the American imagination. In her contemporary study of white females' attitudes about race, Ruth Frankenberg explains that 'the discourse against interracial relationships entails specifically racialized constructions of white femininity in relation to racialized masculinities ... white women and men were placed, respectively, as victim and rescuer in the discourse against interracial sexuality vis-à-vis the supposed sexual threat posed by men of color toward white women' (*White* 237). By desiring an aberrant whiteness that is homosocial, Bone subverts the patriarchal stipulations of heterosexual, racially homogenous relationships, forgoing the 'threat' of men of color for the less visible threat of an albino girl.

Bibliography

Allison, Dorothy. *Bastard Out of Carolina*. New York: Dutton, 1992.
—— *Skin: Talking About Sex, Class & Literature*. Ithaca: Firebrand Books, 1994.
Bersani, Leo. *Homos*. Cambridge: Harvard UP, 1995.
Califia, Pat. *Public Sex: The Culture of Radical Sex*. San Francisco: Cleis Press, 1994.
Creet, Julia. 'Daughter of the Movement: The Psychodynamics of Lesbian S/M Fantasy.' *differences* 3.2 (1991): 135–59.
Cvetkovich, Ann. 'Sexual Trauma/Queer Memory: Incest, Lesbianism, and Therapeutic Culture.' *GLQ* 2 (1995): 351–77.
Davy, Kate. 'Outing Whiteness.' *Whiteness: A Critical Reader*. Ed. Mike Hill. New York: New York UP, 1997. 204–25.
Dyer, Richard. 'White.' *Screen* 29 (Fall 1988): 44–64.
Frankenberg, Ruth. *White Women, Race Matters: The Social Construction of Whiteness*. Minneapolis: U of Minnesota P, 1993.
Garrett, George. 'No Wonder People Got Crazy as They Grew Up.' *New York Times Book Review* 5 July 1992: 4–5.

Halperin, David. *Saint Foucault: Towards a Gay Hagiography.* New York: Oxford UP, 1995.
hooks, bell. 'Representing Whiteness in the Black Imagination.' *Cultural Studies.* Eds. Lawrence Grossberg, Cary Nelson, and Paula A. Treichler. New York: Routledge, 1992. 338–46.
Kirby, Jack Temple. *The Countercultural South.* Athens: U of Georgia P, 1995.
Lange, Dorothea and Paul Schuster Taylor. *An American Exodus: A Record of Human Erosion.* 1939. New Haven: Yale UP, 1969.
Larson, Edward. *Sex, Race, and Science: Eugenics in the Deep South.* Baltimore: Johns Hopkins UP, 1995.
Leonard, John. "Grief and Blood." *New York* 16 December 1996: 66–7.
Lyall, Sarah. 'The Media Business: A Surge in Gay Book Publishing.' *The New York Times* 26 July 1993: D6.
Morris, Lydia. *Dangerous Classes: The Underclass and Social Citizenship.* New York: Routledge, 1994.
Rafter, Nicole Hahn. Introduction. *White Trash: The Eugenic Family Studies 1877–1919.* Ed. Rafter. Boston: Northeastern UP, 1988. 1–31.
Sandell, Jillian. "Telling Stories of 'Queer White Trash': Race, Class, and Sexuality in the Work of Dorothy Allison." *White Trash: Race and Class in America.* Eds. Annalee Newitz and Matt Wray. New York: Routledge, 1997. 211–30.
Shales, Tom. '*Bastard*: Holiday Chills.' *Washington Post* 14 December 1996: C1.
Shindo, Charles J. *Dust Bowl Migrants in the American Imagination.* Lawrence, KS: UP of Kansas, 1997.
Warner, Michael. Introduction. *Fear of a Queer Planet: Queer Politics and Social Theory.* Ed. Warner. Minneapolis: U Minnesota P, 1993. vii–xxxi.

Chapter 11

The Efficacy of Shock for Feminist Politics: Kathy Acker's *Blood and Guts in High School* and Donald Barthelme's *Snow White*

Ann Bomberger

> In her chamber Snow White removed her coat and then her shirt, and then her bra. The bare breasts remained. – *Snow White* (Barthelme 144)

> That night, for the first time in months, [ten-year-old] Janey and her father slept together because Janey can't get to sleep otherwise. Her father's touch is cold, he doesn't want to touch her mostly 'cause he's confused. Janey fucks him even though it hurts her like hell 'cause of her Pelvic Inflammatory Disease. – *Blood and Guts in High School* (Acker 9–10)

Known for its mixing of genres and styles and its tendency to try to shock through overt sexuality and politicism, postmodern fiction on the surface seems to be an easy match with feminism because it engages issues fundamental to feminism: sexuality, political voice, and language's relationship to authority. Yet, many theorists of postmodernism doubt whether politicism of any kind can mix with postmodernism, because of capitalism's ability to co-opt and render useless any political attack. In his influential essay, 'Postmodernism, or the Cultural Logic of Late Capitalism,' Fredric Jameson suggests that in postmodern society pastiche has replaced parody and with it ineffective shock tactics and apoliticized relativism have overshadowed any potential for radical cultural politics:

> parody finds itself without a vocation; it has lived, and that strange new thing pastiche slowly comes to take its place. Pastiche is, like parody, the imitation of a peculiar mask, speech in a dead language: but it is a neutral practice of such mimicry, without any of parody's ulterior motives, amputated of the satiric impulse, devoid of the laughter and of any conviction that alongside the abnormal tongue you have momentarily borrowed, some healthy linguistic normality still exists. (65)

He further argues that just because a postmodern text has a political edge does not mean that political edge is being employed effectively. Instead, 'aesthetic production today has become integrated into commodity production generally' (Jameson 56).

Many feminists disagree, embracing postmodernism as a political, feminist tool. Ellen G. Friedman and Miriam Fuchs, for instance, view the critiquing of language and meaning-systems as an integral part of feminism:

> In exploding dominant forms, women experimental writers not only assail the social structure, but also produce an alternate fictional space, a space in which the feminine, marginalized in traditional fiction and patriarchal culture, can be expressed. Thus, the rupturing of traditional forms becomes a political act, and the feminine narrative resulting from such rupture is allied with the feminist project. (144)

Other feminists like Magali Cornier Michael, Judith Butler and Joan W. Scott, Linda Nicholson, and Susan Hekman have edited or written book-length studies theorizing even more fully the intersections and disjunctions of feminism and postmodernism.

In the introduction to their book on women's experimental fiction, Friedman and Fuchs rightfully place Kathy Acker's work at the forefront of contemporary feminist experimental writing. Stylistically, Acker suddenly shifts from topic to topic, plagiarizing at will, radically altering format and content, switching genres back and forth, and adding childish pornographic sketches. She admits she at times writes poorly purposefully: 'yes, sure – 'piss, fuck, shit' scrawled over a page – sure, of course. This appalls the literary establishment' ('Conversation' 22). By challenging the structure of writing, Acker attempts to challenge the politics behind writing.

Jameson would disagree with Acker that she 'appalls the literary establishment,' and would probably maintain that she has been co-opted by it. Postmodernism's 'offensive features,' he argues, '– from obscurity and sexually explicit material to psychological squalor and overt expressions of social and political defiance . . . – no longer scandalize anyone and are not only received with the greatest complacency but have themselves become institutionalized and are at one with the official culture of Western society' (56). Peter Bürger in his study of the avant-garde likewise has suggested that shock tactics can actually reinforce long-held beliefs instead of causing political change (80).

This essay explores the political efficacy of shock for feminism by looking at Kathy Acker's postmodernist work *Blood and Guts in High School* (1978). Acker regularly deploys expressions of the perverse in her work in order to shock readers into questioning their understandings of sexuality, gender, capitalism, and language and, in the postmodern vein, elucidates the interconnectedness of all four. I then turn to Donald Barthelme's *Snow White* (1965) to demonstrate some of the limitations of Acker's use of shock. By eroticizing and perverting a cultural icon of innocence, Snow White, then creating an environment where the prevailing sentiment is boredom, Barthelme parodies our shock-addicted society and accents the pitfalls of shock as a political tool. I ultimately turn to a discussion of audience and the effects of shock in the creation and alienation of some audiences, and the political repercussions of audience selection.

Coming out of the punk tradition, Kathy Acker attempts to shock deeply middle America in her novel *Blood and Guts in High School*. Ripe with STDs, Janey, the ten-year-old protagonist, sleeps with a long line of men, most notably her father. As a ten-year old, Janey Smith's sexual involvement with her father becomes a metaphor for the power dynamics involved in contemporary heterosexual relationships and in gender relationships in general. The sexually perverse serves to describe the fundamental structures of the norm: 'Sex in America is S & M' (Acker 99). The names of the parent/child lovers, Jane and John Smith, further signal that they represent societal attitudes rather than individuals and are supposed to be caricatures rather than characters with depth. The law of the Father is here literally rendered as the law of the father.

The film *Spank the Monkey* may have had some success in independent theaters and incest has found a comfortable home on talk shows, but over twenty years after the publication of *Blood and Guts* incest remains one of the strongest cultural taboos and thus offers one of the few remaining resources for those who want to shock. Yet so deep is the cultural revulsion with child molestation that willful naïveté still often protects pedophiles from detection. The child molester is viewed as being so outside of the cultural norm that he could not possibly be the local priest or the concerned father, as he so often is. Acker attempts to shock audiences into connecting the perverse – in this case, child molestation – with the dominant norm, that is, heterosexual adult relationships. Our revulsion with the former, she hopes, will help us see the power dynamics of the latter.

The novel opens with a stereotypical lovers' quarrel, echoing countless clichéd television and movie scripts, where the child, Janey, is placed in the position of the jealous, overly emotional girlfriend and her father acts as the straying male. The associations of the quarrel with the tired dialogue of television spotlights the connection between cultural texts and social discipline. Television serves as a kind of cultural self-hypnosis that enforces certain expectations and understandings of gender. Acker intersperses adult dialogue of infidelity with quick references to childishness in order to disrupt readerly expectations and to link child molestation and adult heterosexual relationships:

> **Janey:** You're going to leave me. (*She doesn't know why she's saying this.*)
> **Father:** (*dumbfounded, but not denying it*): Sally and I just slept together for the first time. How can I know anything?

> **Janey** (*in amazement. She didn't believe what she had been saying was true. It was only out of petulance*): You ARE going to leave me. Oh no. No. That can't be.
> . . .
> **Father** (*ignorant of this huge mess*): We just slept together for the first time tonight.
> **Janey**: You told me you were just friends like me and Peter (*Janey's stuffed lamb*) and you weren't going to sleep together. It's not like my sleeping around with all those art studs: when you sleep with your best friend, it's really, really heavy. (Acker 7–9)

The entrance of Janey's stuffed lamb into the jealous lover dialogue disrupts the overall tone of the scene, using humor and shock to call attention to the gender inequities of heterosexuality. It is our familiarity with the scene – in its allusions to popular culture – that helps produce the jolt with the entrance of the unexpected, a stuffed animal. Like the typical soap opera heroine, Janey cannot control the actions of her lover. She passively voices her worst fears and discovers to her horror that they are true. This is typical of all of Janey's responses. Conditioned completely by the world around her, she can only respond in the way 'she's been programmed to say it' (Acker 27). Clichés control her responses and force her into a position of helplessness.

In an interview, Acker claims that when she wrote *Blood and Guts* she 'thought it was kind of sweet at the time, but of course it's not.' She continues, 'it's about kids and kids are sweet' ('Conversation' 13). Throughout the novel, childhood is demystified as a 'pure' time; even children, represented by the street-wise Janey, have internalized societal concepts of gender and sexuality. Acker signifies on fairy tales throughout the work to deconstruct the rigid gender roles they perpetuate and to disrupt the patriarchal teleological premises of most fairy tales. Using a rather childish, irreverent style similar to the visual style of both her pornographic and non-pornographic sketches, the narrator of *Blood and Guts* creates her own 'fairy tale' of the sexual revolution in order to undercut the sacchariny endings perpetuated by Disney: 'once upon a time there was a materialistic society one of the results of this materialism was a "sexual revolution". Since the materialistic society had succeeded in separating sex from every possible feeling, all you girls can now go spread your legs as much as you want 'cause it's sooo easy to fuck it's sooo easy to be a robot it's sooo easy not to feel' (Acker 99). Out of the mouths of babes comes a story of sexual exploitation and degradation.

In order to extend the discussion of the hierarchical nature of contemporary heterosexuality, Acker introduces the power of the state into the narrative in the form of President Carter. Long after Janey's father has left her for another woman, Janey, now approximately thirteen, first disparages President Carter quite explicitly for pages and then becomes sexually involved with him: 'I didn't want to fall in love with him because I didn't want to put something in my life, but he was screwing me so GOOD and beating me up that I knew I was going to fall in love with him' (Acker 122–3). Just as Janey's masochism draws her to all of her other lovers (one who is her attacker, another her captor) it is precisely the President's abuse which attracts her.[1] As a representative of the power of the state, patriarchy, and capitalism, President Carter can potentially abuse her as no other can. Their relationship highlights the fact that sex is not only not separated from politics, it can become an instrument of governmental oppression (as for instance, rape was a war tactic in Bosnia or, closer to home, allegations of sexual harassment rallied supporters behind a Supreme Court nominee). Although the Monica Lewinsky and Paula Jones scandals have done much to diminish our abilities to be scandalized by questions of 'distinguishing features' on the genitals of the President, certainly at the time of *Blood and Guts'* publication Janey's liaison with the President of the United States would at least verge on the perverse (particularly since she still is a child).

Sexual intercourse is represented in *Blood and Guts* as a diseased, painful, power manipulation of the strong upon the weak, the male upon the female, the father upon the child, and the state upon the citizen. Such a list of dichotomies might seem to suggest that heterosexuality is inevitably evil and yet Acker sees it as a possible liberator. In an interview Acker criticizes Andrea Dworkin for employing the same kind of dichotomy Acker uses in *Blood and Guts*: 'There is an attack on Andrea Dworkin in *Don Quixote* [one of Acker's novels], not her personally (in fact I saw her on a TV show and quite admired how she stood up for feminism), but on her dualistic argument that men are responsible for all of the evil in the world. Her views go beyond sexism. She blames the act of penetration in sexual intercourse' ('Conversation' 13). Sexuality, in *Blood and Guts*, even, or perhaps especially, in its most degraded and perverse forms can be a potentially rebellious political act. In those situations of consensual sex where power dynamics seem most exploitative, there may be positive political consequences; 'EVERY POSITION OF DESIRE, NO MATTER HOW SMALL, IS CAPABLE OF PUTTING TO QUESTION THE ESTABLISHED ORDER OF A SOCIETY; NOT THAT DESIRE IS ASOCIAL; ON THE CONTRARY, BUT IT IS EXPLOSIVE; THERE IS NO DESIRING-MACHINE CAPABLE OF BEING ASSEMBLED WITHOUT DEMOLISHING ENTIRE SOCIAL SECTIONS' (Acker 125). Despite the huge power inequities that Acker highlights by creating father/daughter and President/citizen relationships, there may still be the possibility of political rebellion. Janey tells President Carter, 'everything I do, every way I've seemed to feel, however I've seemed to grasp at you, are war tactics' (Acker 127).

A large portion of Acker's war tactics in the novel arises through the disruption of traditional narrative forms. Sudden, overt political statements, like the section on the explosive nature of sexuality just cited, interrupt what little narrative flow in the novel there is. At other times a paragraph is repeated for seemingly no reason (Acker 21–5). Sketches, pornographic and otherwise, appear without explanation in the text. In the spirit of postmodernist novels like William Burroughs's *Naked Lunch*, Acker continually undermines rhetorical conventions in order to disrupt readerly expectations for narrative, closure, developed characters and the like.

Through these postmodernist techniques the novel shows its connection to poststructural theory as it analyzes the role language plays in social control and exploitation. Janey explains how the power to write definitions and create rules aids the ruling elite in the subjugation of women and people of color: 'for 2,000 years you've had the nerve to tell women who we are. We use your words; we eat your food. Every way we get money has to be a crime. We are plagiarists, liars, and criminals' (Acker 132). By controlling both language and money, Acker maintains, white men can control everyone around them. In a dialogue between two wealthy landowners, Acker lays out her position on language and power in her characteristically blunt way:

> **Mr. Fuckface:** You see, we own the language. Language must be used clearly and precisely to reveal our universe.
> **Mr. Blowjob:** Those rebels are never clear. What they say doesn't make sense.
> **Mr. Fuckface:** It even goes against all the religions to tamper with the sacred languages.
> **Mr. Blowjob:** Without language the only people the rebels can kill are themselves.
> (136)

The importance of this section lies not only in what it says, but also in how it says it. Her use of language demonstrates the principle she is explaining through Mr. Blowjob and Mr. Fuckface. By attempting to break both novelistic and academic conventions – through lack of subtlety, crassness, and overt politicism – the text attempts to launch a guerilla assault against language, patriarchy, and capitalism using the weapon it has stolen, language.

Searching for some type of agency and/or voice, Janey writes at various times in the novel, questioning and analyzing her surroundings. Janey attempts to reverse the traditional role of (active) male author and (passive) female object when in her parody of *The Scarlet Letter* she/Hester says to her lover Reverend Dimwit: 'I want to write myself between your lips and between your thighs' (Acker 95). Fusing writing with sexuality, Acker's metaphor is an exaggerated gender reversal of an idea expressed by Susan Gubar in '"The Blank Page" and Female Creativity'. Gubar comments: 'This model of the pen-penis writing on the virgin page participates in a long tradition identifying the author as a male who is primary and the female as his passive creation – a secondary object lacking autonomy, endowed with often contradictory meaning but denied intentionality' (295). The ability to write rather than be written upon becomes a political, physical struggle for personal agency. Janey says, 'I'm too bruised and I'm scared. At this point in *The Scarlet Letter* and in my life politics don't disappear but take place inside my body' (Acker 97). It is significant in Acker's choice of texts that she selects *The Scarlet Letter*, for it has been taught in nearly every high school in the United States and then taught again in countless universities for decades. Academia's establishment of a literary canon, Acker maintains, has numerous political ramifications and serves as an enforcer of patriarchy, capitalism and colonialism through its shaping of culture.

The canon comes under fire in *Blood and Guts* primarily for its traditionally male perspective and its refusal to acknowledge its political stances. Acker, for instance, attacks another frequently taught writer, John Keats, by including a drawing of a bound, headless, naked woman whose body forms the shape of an urn and labeling it 'Ode to a Grecian Urn,' in a savage send-up of the poem known for its famous lines, 'Beauty is truth, truth beauty' (Acker 63). She compounds the assault further by misnaming the Keats poem. The picture is the only mention of Keats in the novel and refuses to conform to the generic conventions of measured, reasoned academic criticism.[2] Such academic conventions, Acker maintains, only stifle creativity and protect entrenched hierarchies. The narrator of *Blood and Guts* charges academia with policing society in the service of capitalism: 'A scholar is a top cop 'cause he defines the roads by which people live so they won't get in trouble and so society will survive. A scholar is a teacher. Teachers replace living dangerous creatings with dead ideas and teach these ideas as history and meaning of the world. Teachers torture kids. Teachers teach you intricate ways of saying one thing and doing something else' (Acker 68). Acker insists that despite what academia claims, it is not there to get people to think; rather, it helps sustain the current power structure and schools children well in the art of hypocrisy. She elaborates in an interview: 'the culture [of academia] is there to uphold the postcapitalist society, and the idea that art has nothing to do with politics is a wonderful construction in order to mask the deep political significance that art has – to uphold the empire in terms of its representation as well as its actual structure' ('Conversation' 21).

With clear allusions to Michel Foucault, Janey links the controlling functions of prisons, schools, and societal conventions by writing what she calls 'a book report' while in prison (The opening lines of this section read, 'we all live in prison. Most of us don't know we live in prison' [Acker 65]). This book report, however, is anything but a book report; it is a witty, insightful, volatile reading of *The Scarlet Letter* and an application of some of Hawthorne's ideas to current society. Yet, near the conclusion of her analysis Janey tacks on a parody of high school book reports, replete with fawning praise and vague generalizations: '*The Scarlet Letter* is the best book I've read locked up in the Persian slave trader's room and I think everyone should read it. I'm not going to tell you the ending of the book and spoil it for you. I think the author Nathaniel Hawthorne felt that his readers should have fun reading his stories. He didn't think anybody'd learn anything' (100). The petulant, anti-intellectual tone of the resentful student in this passage clashes with the earlier, thought-provoking section that defies the book report genre. Janey has learned well from her teachers 'intricate ways of saying one thing and doing something else.' High school demands anti-intellectualism through its over-reliance on teaching forms and formulas. These formulas become internalized through incessant repetition so that schools can curtail subversive thought and action.

The visual image in the United States, which holds such strong cultural currency, obviously does not lie outside of language. Rather, the primacy of the image helps perpetuate dominant ideologies and is a fundamental part of the controlling nature of representation, thus the image becomes an object of commentary in *Blood and Guts*. Acker positions several pornographic sketches into the opening section of the novel. Unlike most mainstream pornography, most of Acker's drawings are of male nudes, though some are of women. This time the male body is the one on display, the one to be ogled and studied. The sketches also are childishly drawn and cartoonish at times in their exaggeration. For instance, the male figures often have very large penises (one penis is thicker than the woman's arm it is next to [Acker 22]), lampooning pop culture pornography and the cultural discourse which insists 'bigger is better.' The sexual image is taken out of the realm of the fetishized, slickly produced pages of *Playboy* and *Hustler* and mocked through quickly drawn pencil sketches.

The World Wide Web and even magazines combine both the printed word and the visual image, but most books, particularly 'serious' books, still remain wedded to the printed word. Acker breaks these traditional barriers with the inclusion of pornographic sketches.[3] The expectations associated with the printed word are suddenly called into question with the turn of the page. The anonymous person reading privately in public is thus transformed into someone labeled as reading pornography. The sketches are included largely to shock, as their location in the novel suggests. All eight of the explicitly pornographic sketches are found in the first seventy pages, five of which are in the first twenty-five pages. Once their shock value is diminished through repetition the novel moves on to other areas.

It is repetition that both causes Donald Barthelme the most concern with writing and provides him with the most hope for writing. Like Acker, he sees the bridges that connect sexuality and textuality and similarly uses humor to help expose that linkage to others, but he shares Bürger and Jameson's skepticism on the effectiveness of shock as a tool for change. The contemporary reader, bombarded with messages from television, radio, advertising, magazines, and low and high culture books has heard it all, seen it all, and done it all (at least vicariously through popular culture). The perverse, he maintains, can't remain perverse for long because of capitalism's ability to co-opt and render meaningless the controversial. The culture both feeds on shock and is in some sense immune to it.

However, just because Barthelme is skeptical of shock's political effectiveness does not mean he doesn't use it in a revised form. He employs many of the same shock tactics which Acker does – sexualizing icons of innocence, including sudden outbursts of violence, and disrupting expectations of some kind of narrative – but he whitewashes those shocking scenes by making characters react in bored, unimpressed ways.

The abundance of words in contemporary America becomes Barthelme's inroad into a critique of language. *Snow White* suggests that the devaluing of language through its overuse[4] helps create passive citizens unwilling or unable to act outside of the norms. In a lengthy passage on the meaninglessness of most language, Dan, one of the dwarves, muses,

> That part, the 'filling' you might say, of which the expression 'You might say' is a good example, is to me the most interesting part, and of course it might also be called the 'stuffing' I suppose, and there is probably also, in addition, some other word that would do as well, to describe it, or maybe a number of them. But the quality this 'stuffing' has, that the other parts of verbality do not have, is two parted, perhaps: (1) an 'endless' quality and (2) a 'sludge' quality. (Barthelme 96)

Eventually, he maintains, the stuffing will become 100 percent of the writing: 'Now at such a point, you will agree, the question turns from a question of disposing of this 'trash' to a question of appreciating its qualities, because, after all, it's 100 percent, right?' (97). Surrounded by the mundane, Barthelme tries to revitalize a dried up language. So he creates a collage in his book of clichés and tired dialogue, compiling a collection of 'trash' with the hopes that when put together they will create something valuable and new.

His multiple parodies of women's magazines (Barthelme 37, 82–3, 99, 124), menus (18), how-to-manuals (116), academic discourse (24, 54, 59, 61, 66, 124, 143), and pop psychology books (17, 70) clearly illustrate his efforts to break from pop culture by exploiting it. All of these sources, with the exception of the Chinese menu, claim to offer a guide to living to one degree or another. Moral guides from the likes of multibillion dollar publishing conglomerates and self-absorbed academics are not likely to challenge the status quo in any meaningful manner. It is implied that the trash that he finds himself surrounded by is not just an excess of words, but also an excess of texts.

Political discourse has been one of the casualties of the explosion of texts, reduced to a series of clichés pushed into five-second sound bites on television or a much greater number of clichés packed into the pages of *Time* magazine. Any emotions associated with strongly held political beliefs are stripped away. Barthelme, like Acker, calls on the President for a cameo appearance in his novel, replete with the same associations of power, patriarchy, and capitalism that Acker's President has; yet, rather than being an energetic manipulator of power, he is a passive, uninvolved observer just like the other characters in the book. The President muses, 'looking out over this green lawn, and these fine rosebushes, and into the night and the yellow buildings, and the falling Dow-Jones index and the screams of the poor, I am concerned. I have many important things to worry about, but I worry about Bill [one of the dwarves] and the boys too' (Barthelme 81). A falling Dow-Jones index and the screams of the poor are put on a parallel with the green lawn and fine rosebushes, the syntax suggesting that no one thing in the series is more important than the others. The coupling of these dramatically differing items provides a minor shock and a brief laugh and points to elected officials' inability to do much of anything other than express platitudes about concern for the common citizen.

Paul Maltby, when critiquing Jameson's statements that postmodernism is apolitical, uses Barthelme as one of his key examples of what he calls a 'dissident postmodernist' – that is, a political postmodernist – based on sections of the novel like the one just cited. The proliferation of texts and the devaluing of language are directly tied to late capitalism according to Maltby: 'Much of [Barthelme's] best fiction illustrates a thinning out of language in late-capitalist society, a process shown to lead to a loss of critical distance and hence increased susceptibility to social integration (or as Barthelme might have it, "embourgeoisment")' (56). Yet Maltby does not point to the troubling gender politics in the text. Gender and female sexuality become the loci from which Barthelme makes his critique of late capitalism and of language: male characters use voyeurism and sexual fantasy in order to attempt to overcome the humdrum nature of existence, the novel alludes to high culture's treatment of woman as text, and sexual punning abounds in the novel. Like Acker, he parodies the objectification of women, but he is less successful at keeping his parody from reinscribing the stereotypes than Acker is.

Instead of trying to shock his readers into political understanding, as Acker does, Barthelme, realizing the cynicism and near inability of most readers to be shocked, repeatedly creates traditionally 'shocking' scenes and then has his characters react in a disinterested manner. His entire novel is structured around perverting one of the sacred films of American popular culture: Disney's *Snow White*. Barthelme turns the rose colored glasses of the Disney version of *Snow White* into a red light district. His Snow White makes no pretensions about having sex with all of the seven dwarves and is gawked at by every male character. Even the structure of the novel itself is cast in a rather leering frame, focusing on Snow White's obvious sexuality. The novel opens with a description of Snow White's body, down the front and up the back, reminiscent of the cinematic gaze which feminist film critic Laura Mulvey so influentially described:

> **SHE** is a tall dark beauty containing a great many beauty spots: one above the breast, one above the belly, one above the knee, one above the ankle, one above the buttock,

one on the back of the neck. All of these are on the left side, more or less in a row, as you go up and down:

o
o
o
o
o
o

The hair is black as ebony, the skin white as snow. (Barthelme 3)

Barthelme's lascivious inventory of Snow White's various body parts, in John Pizer's mind, 'parodies the beauty of the Grimms' Sneewittchen and severs their linkage of clear skin to a clear soul' (332). Sexuality becomes a way to flaunt cultural conventions of propriety and mock cultural icons of innocence.

High culture originally linked purity of the face with purity of the soul, although popular culture has rushed to co-opt this concept (the Ivory girl is a case in point). By seeing woman as a text to be written upon and philosophized about, high culture envisions woman as the created, not the creator, the image, not the image-maker. Barthelme toys with high culture's assumption of woman-as-text in a parody that changes a historical figure of female strength, Joan of Arc, into an aesthetic object, Joan of Art, as has been so frequently done in artistic renditions of Joan in both literature and painting (Barthelme 109). Being burned at the stake becomes an aesthetic moment rather than an event in history. Later in the novel, Paul takes on the role of the voyeur/literary critic, watching Snow White take off her clothes, thinking, '"It's a good thing I had my reading glasses in my upper robe pocket," Paul read the message written on Snow White's unwrapped breasts' (148). Here the virgin page is the not-so-virginal Snow White. Barthelme employs the metaphor for a third time when woman as text becomes woman as instrument with Hogo watching Jane and thinking of her as a 'cello-shaped girl,' and then thinking of 'the viola da gamba-shaped Snow White' (152). In all these examples a man (or men) compares a woman to art, a beautiful thing to philosophize about, read, or play, rather than someone who philosophizes, reads, or plays. Yet his critique is not really a feminist one.[5] The parody makes fun of the ceaseless repetition of the same tropes in high culture and academic criticism rather than tying those tropes to patriarchy.

Although taking one of the most innocent, over-idealized icons in contemporary society and changing her into a promiscuous twenty-two year old causes some obvious devilish glee, it does not produce the profound shock one might expect. This is because Barthelme creates a world where no one can be shocked by anything, no matter how extreme the situation, and one where the predominating emotion is boredom. Jameson's visions of a shock-proof society are realized in the fictional world of *Snow White*. As Clem tells Snow White, 'most life is unextraordinary' (Barthelme 21). Bill has this exuberant reaction to sex: 'Well it is a pleasure to please her, when human ingenuity can manage it, but the whole thing is just trembling on the edge of monotony, after several years. And yet . . . I am fond of her. Yes, I am. For when sexual pleasure is had, it makes you fond, in a strange way, of the other one, the one with whom you are having it' (35–6).[6] The multiple clauses and interrupters accent his lack of involvement with what he's saying. Most of the characters speak in afterthoughts, suggesting that they could just as easily fall asleep as complete the next sentence. When we consider that Snow White represents the epitome of childhood innocence in contemporary US mass culture, and that Barthelme takes this innocent icon and turns her on her head, and that we are *still* bored with the result, we realize what a serious critique Barthelme is making of the ability to write about anything at all with passion.

As the princess of ennui in this rather absurd kingdom, Snow White similarly must voice her boredom. While having sex in the shower with one of the dwarves, she wonders why they don't show movies in the showers (Barthelme 34). She then contemplates the water on her back, thinking, 'But the water on my back is interesting. It is more than interesting. Marvelous is the word for it' (34). When all words are equally meaningless, words as different as 'marvelous' and 'interesting' can easily be interchanged. Snow White mumbles a lot of pointless, often large words, in a half-hearted attempt to make meaning of life. Perhaps the most frequently used adjective in the novel is 'interesting.' It is a rather nondescript, generic word to explain their nondescript, generic lives. The proliferation of the word 'interesting' is a part of the larger problem of the proliferation of words in general which accompanies the mass marketing of popular culture.

Barthelme's delight with double entendre becomes another way to try to revitalize a dead language, while paradoxically showing the impossibility of reviving that language. Repeatedly the text edges toward a bawdy witticism and then the joke is diffused with an innocent clause. For instance, in a section where the dwarves have been explaining how they were having a marvelous time typing on a typewriter underneath a woman's skirt, the narrator says, 'We all had our hands on the typewriter when it emerged because it had been in that pure grotto, Paul's place' (50). Given the context of the conversation, 'pure grotto' at first appears to refer to the woman's vagina. The clause 'Paul's place' incapacitates the joke (and thus makes it funnier in a rather droll way). Barthelme repeatedly uses this technique in order to amuse his weary readers and to show the predictability of sexual punning (for example, Barthelme 8, 29, 59). Henry comments, 'this language thinking and stinking everlastingly of sex, screw, breech, 'part,' shaft, nut, male, it is no wonder we are all going round the bend with this language dinning forever into our eyes and ears' (30).

When sexuality has been mined as a topic so thoroughly that it has lost even the most remote ability to incite or excite, the novel adds a flash or two of sudden violence. In one scene the dwarves have a dream of a violent, sexual, group fantasy. Snow White is slowly cooked on a rotating spit over an open flame. The rotating motion of the spit parallels the ceaseless repetition of the characters' lives. While some passion and excitement is hinted at (we are told Snow White is screaming and 'making a lot of noise'), the language is still dull and uninviting. The narrator nonchalantly relates the events that occur while they are cooking Snow White in the most detached language possible: 'We regarded Snow White rotating there, in her pain and beauty, in the dream' (Barthelme 109–10). The verb 'to regard' appears repeatedly in the novel as an awkward substitute for 'to see' or another more common term. It gives a certain sense of distance, even intellectual curiosity, to a scene that might otherwise shock. Sexualized murder would normally be considered an extreme expression of the perverse since it crosses the boundaries of most culturally accepted sexual activity, yet in Snow White it is just another unsuccessful attempt to break the monotony of late twentieth-century life.

Robert Siegle opens his section on Kathy Acker in *Suburban Ambush* with a series of student reactions to *Blood and Guts*: 'Reading Kathy Acker is like reading the subway walls.' 'If my mother saw what I was reading, *she'd die*.' 'I never thought I was a prude until I opened this book.' 'I was reading it outside between classes and I found myself holding the book half-closed so the people sitting around me wouldn't see the illustrations.' 'My roommates couldn't believe I was reading this book for a course!' (47). While he is quick to label these students his 'more conservative' students and to dismiss their reactions with only a passing concern, I think it is important to remember those voices because sometimes academics, who have often read widely among all kinds of experimental fiction, forget that most of the country does not read anything more challenging than a John Grisham novel (and many more do not read at all). So that when we talk about shock, it is important really to think about who we are trying to shock.

In order to be effective, political voice needs to have an audience, an audience that will listen and take seriously the ideas expressed. Shock, while an effective form of attention getting for some, will alienate far more. That's not necessarily problematic, but it does put severe limitations on the number of people who will consider the message. Clearly, Donald Barthelme has made it into the mainstream more than Kathy Acker has. His work often appeared in *The New Yorker* (which has a limited audience itself in that it reaches primarily professionals) and his books are more widely published than Acker's. But at what cost? *Snow White* fits into dominant ideologies far more easily than *Blood and Guts* does. As I've mentioned, its gender politics certainly don't challenge prevailing norms. It generally fits within normative standards of taste. For instance, the scene that has the most potential for controversy – the cooking of *Snow White* – is couched in terms of a dream fantasy and thus diffused significantly. Barthelme suggests that shock is close to impossible in the deadened atmosphere of the late twentieth century, but how much has he really tried to shock? The Grimms' Snow White is just seven-years old when she arrives at the dwarves' home and in the Disney version she is a teenager, yet Barthelme increases her years to the very safe age of twenty-two (145). This change suggests Barthelme is not prepared to go to the extremes of taste in order to shock as Acker does.

In a speech delivered to an *Artists and Society* conference a few years before her death, Acker challenged the audience to work to change the assumption that 'experimental writing' equals 'marginal writing.' She outlined the publishing industry's role in marginalizing experimental literature:

> The equation 'experimental writing' equals 'marginal writing' need not be a true equation. Allen Ginsberg's *Howl*, as 'experimental' a text as any when it first appeared, was and is certainly not marginal to certain formations in this society. It is the major publishing houses, the book-chain stores, and the connected media, in search of larger profits, who are maintaining, are reifying the split between commercial and non-commercial or 'experimental' literature. They are telling us, teaching us to read only that fiction and poetry whose structures, the structures of commodity, support the status quo. ('Speech')

Yet, she maintained, it is not solely the publishing industry that contributes to the marginalization of experimental writers. Experimental writers, too, need to break out of the safe, small communities in the margin where they are readily accepted. 'Fortunately or unfortunately,' Acker argues, 'the religious right is putting the margin – that desperate balancing act – out of business. There are no longer any safe places in our world' ('Speech'). She forayed into more hostile territory during a trip to the University of Idaho. She relayed the story of the virulent reaction she received from conservative students when she gave a talk at the University of Idaho during banned book week. Students wrote to the paper in protest, prompting a month long debate in the media about Acker (Olsen). University of Idaho Professor Lance Olsen, who witnessed the event, enthused on the value of the extended debate for the students (he says, 'we should recall a simple, if vital, formula: controversy = education'). Clearly, students were shocked, but that shock prompted greater discussion and reflection, at least for some of the students.

Invariably, Acker's reliance on shocking through representation of the perverse has reinforced traditional opinions in some, caused others to put down the novel within five pages, and not at all affected still others. Politically, *Blood and Guts* is ineffective to change mainstream America because of its insistence on representing the perverse and the political in an extremely confrontational manner. However, I believe *Blood and Guts* has significant potential for political effectiveness, ironically, in the very atmosphere it critiques most thoroughly: the classroom.[7] The classroom provides a unique space in that it brings people to a text who would probably never approach that work otherwise and provides a forum for extended discussion of the intricacies of the ideas presented. As the debate at the University of Idaho and countless similar debates that likely have occurred on a smaller scale in classrooms around the country attest, students are not yet hardened enough not to be shocked by Acker, and perhaps that shock will provoke them to look more closely at the power structures that surround them.

Endnotes

1. Arthur F. Redding views all of Acker's texts as explorations of masochism. See Arthur F. Redding, 'Bruises, Roses: Masochism and the Writing of Kathy Acker.'
2. Larry McCaffery breaks these unwritten rules by trashing an earlier piece on Barthelme he wrote in 1975. In an entertaining and insightful pastiche of abusive marginalia, quotations, autobiography, and biography, McCaffery adopts a toned-down version of the style of both Barthelme and Acker (about both of whom he has written). See Larry McCaffery, 'Towards an Aesthetic of the Aesthetics of Trash: A Collaborative, Deconstructive Reading of: "Barthelme's *Snow White*: The Aesthetics of Trash."'
3. She includes non-pornographic sketches in the novel as well. For an analysis of the dream sketches, see Robert Siegle, *Suburban Ambush: Downtown Writing and the Fiction of Insurgency*.
4. Ironically, the quotation I am about to cite on the 'trash phenomenon' has been so frequently cited in articles on Barthelme that it is beginning to lose its meaning through repetition.
5. See Barthelme's brief, but telling, essay from *The New Yorker* for an elaboration of his romanticized connection between women, the mysterious, and art with brief allusions to what he sees as limitations of the women's liberation movement (*Not-Knowing* 46–7).
6. The obvious reference to 'the other' also allows him to satirize academic jargon again.
7. However, the frequent critiques in the novel of academia's role as an instrument of social discipline will not necessarily protect it from being used as a form of that discipline. For instance, I can see how undergraduate female students might feel silenced and/or intimidated by the masochistic form of sexuality presented in the novel, particularly if the professor were male and/or particularly insensitive to gender politics.

Bibliography

Acker, Kathy. *Blood and Guts in High School*. 1978. New York: Grove Weidenfeld, 1989.
—— Interview with Ellen G. Friedman. 'A Conversation with Kathy Acker.' *The Review of Contemporary Fiction* 9 (Fall 1989): 12–22.
—— 'Speech for the Artist in Society Conference, Chicago, October 1994.' *Fugue: Literature for the Internet*. 28 June 1995. University of Idaho English Department. 15 June 2000. <http://www.uidaho.edu/LS/Eng/Fugue/acker.html>
Barthelme, Donald. *Not-Knowing: The Essays and Interviews of Donald Barthelme*. Ed. Kim Herzinger. New York: Random House, 1997.
—— *Snow White*. 1965. New York: Atheneum, 1972.
Bürger, Peter. *Theory of the Avant-Garde*. Trans. Michael Shaw. Minneapolis: University of Minnesota Press, 1984.
Butler, Judith and Joan Scott. *Feminists Theorize the Political*. New York: Routledge, 1992.

Friedman, Ellen G. and Miriam Fuchs. 'Contexts and Continuities: An Introduction to Women's Experimental Fiction in English.' *Breaking the Sequence: Women's Experimental Fiction.* Eds. Ellen G. Friedman and Miriam Fuchs. Princeton, NJ: Princeton University Press, 1989.

Gubar, Susan. '"The Blank Page" and Issues of Female Creativity.' *The New Feminist Criticism.* Ed. Elaine Showalter. New York: Pantheon Books, 1985.

Hekman, Susan. *Gender and Knowledge.* Boston: Northeastern, 1990.

Jameson, Fredric. 'Postmodernism, or the Cultural Logic of Late Capitalism.' *The New Left Review* 146 (1984): 53–92.

McCafffery, Larry. 'Towards an Aesthetic of the Aesthetics of Trash: A Collaborative, Deconstructive Reading of "Barthelme's Snow White: The Aesthetics of Trash." *Review of Contemporary Fiction* 11 (1991 Summer): 36–49.

Maltby, Paul. *Dissident Postmodernists: Barthelme, Coover, Pynchon.* Philadelphia: University of Pennsylvania Press, 1991.

Michael, Magali Cornier. *Feminism and the Postmodern Impulse: Post-World War II Fiction.* Albany, NY: State University of New York Press, 1996.

Nicholson, Linda, ed. *Feminism/Postmodernism.* New York: Routledge, 1990.

Olsen, Lance. 'Kathy Acker.' *Fugue: Literature for the Internet.* 28 June 1995. University of Idaho English Department. 15 June 2000. <http://www.uidaho.edu/LS/Eng/Fugue/intro.html>

Pizer, John. 'The Disenchantment of Snow White: Robert Walser, Donald Barthelme and the Modern/Postmodern Anti-Fairy Tale.' *Canadian Review of Comparative Literature* 17 (September-December 1990): 330–47.

Redding, Arthur. 'Bruises, Roses: Masochism and the Writing of Kathy Acker.' *Contemporary Literature* 35.2 (1994): 281–304.

Siegle, Robert. *Suburban Ambush: Downtown Writing and the Fiction of Insurgency.* Baltimore: Johns Hopkins, 1989.

Index

References with prefix *n* are to endnotes

abject 76–87 *passim*, 148–50, 154, 157
abjection *see* Kristeva
Acker, Kathy
   Blood and Guts in High School 189–96, 201–3
albinism 179, 182–4
allegory 156–7, 159, 162
Allison, Dorothy
   Bastard Out of Carolina 167–9, 177–86
   Skin 169, 171–7
analogical substantiation 7, 11, 14
androgyne 100–2
anorexic 163–4
Augustine *see* St Augustine

Babar 159–62
Bacon, Francis 129, 134
Barthelme, Donald
   Snow White 189–91, 197–202
Baudrillard, Jean 42–7 *passim*, 50, 114–20
Bell, Currer 61–2, 65
Ben-Levy, Jack 78, 80–7 *passim*
Bersani, Leo 108
Blau-Duplessis, Rachel 102
blazon 27–31, 38
body 4–19, 28–32, 36–7, 76–80, 84–8, 96–9, 132–3, 148–9, 156–64, 168–72, 175, 178–86, 195–9
   as female principle 96–103
Bordo, Susan 97, 163
Brontë, Charlotte 67
Brownmiller, Susan 127
Burns, Jane 1
Butler, Judith 38, 82, 96, 101, 105*n10*, 139–40, 190

Califia, Pat 173–4
Carlson, Marla 16
Carter, Angela 116, 126–44
cartesianism 96–9
chastity 2–4, 9–12, 16–18, 26, 33–8, 127

Chicago, Judy 76–7
child molestation, representations of 191
Christianity 1, 3–4, 7–18 *passim*, 125, 134, 141, 180
circumvallation 109, 111, 114–20
Clair, Jean 106*n20*
class 167–81, 185
collage 150–3, 157, 159, 197
commodification 120, 133
Cowie, Elizabeth 107*n26*
Cvetkovich, Ann 179
cyborg 150, 153, 163–4

Dante Alighieri 48, 51
daughter 42–50, 108–10, 113, 116, 119–20, 177, 193–4
depression era 167–8
Descartes, René 96
desire 2, 11, 16, 19, 25–8, 32–4, 42–52, 61, 81, 84–7, 94, 97, 99, 109–14, 118, 120, 132, 136–40, 153, 155, 163–4, 175–9, 182–5, 193
desiring 27, 34, 153, 155, 159, 163–4, 194
disciplinarity 152, 154, 163–4
Dollimore, Jonathan 2, 148, 150, 153
   Sexual Dissidence 3, 8–10, 14–17
Duchamp, Marcel
   Anémic Cinéma 96
   Étant donnés 92–104
   Fresh Widow 96
   The Large Glass 95, 105*nn4–5*
   L.H.O.O.Q. 100–1, 105*n5*
   The Nude Descending the Staircase 105*n5*
   Readymades 94, 101–2, 105*n5*, 105*n9*
   Rrose Sélavy 96–104
   To Be Looked At 105*n7*
   Trébuchet (Trap) 105*n3*
Dworkin, Andrea 125, 127–8, 193
Dyer, Richard 183

Edward II 157–60
embodiment, virtual 116, 120
enclosure 4, 6, 10, 18, 99

error 10, 152, 163–4
essay 148–57 *passim*, 163–4
essentialism 96–100
ethical 150–5, 163–4
ethics 150
eugenics 170–1
excess 152, 163–4, 167–8, 183
exorbitant 160, 163–4
experimental writing 201–2

fantastic 159–60
fantasy 45–6, 135, 152, 155–7, 163–4, 198, 202
female viewer 103
feminism and postmodernism 70–1, 129, 136–7, 148, 189–91, 194
feminist movement 125–6, 173–4
fetish 94–5, 98–103, 129, 132, 161–4, 168, 171, 173, 184
fetishism and semiotics 92
fictocritical 148, 151–2, 155, 159, 163–4
fictocriticism 150, 153, 163–4
Foucault, Michel 7–8, 14, 108–9, 112, 130, 195
Freud, Sigmund 55–63 *passim*, 76–88, 110, 129, 135, 142; *see also* uncanny
fundamentalism 125, 136–7, 141

gaps 66, 151–60, 163–4
gaze 16, 28–34, 44–5, 53–4, 59, 66–9, 80–4, 92–101 *passim*, 112, 114, 139, 199
gender as artifice 131, 134, 136, 139–43
generic gender categories 94–5, 99, 101
genre 47–51, 111, 126–9, 144, 154, 178, 180, 189–90, 195–6
Gisborne, Maria 51
Gorky, Ashile 78–87
Griffin, Susan 127
grotesque 78, 132, 135–6, 150, 154, 159, 162–4

hermaphroditism 141, 162
Hero 25–6, 30–8
heteroeroticism 25
heteronormative 30, 38, 175–6, 185
Hollywood 125, 130–1, 136, 139, 142
homoeroticism 25, 30, 37–8, 78–85 *passim*, 108, 114
Hrotsvit of Gandersheim 1–3

The Conversion of the Harlot Thais 3–11, 18–19
The Fall and Repentance of Mary 3–11, 18–19
The Martyrdom of the Holy Virgins Agape, Chionia, and Hirena 3–4, 11–19
The Martyrdom of the Holy Virgins Fides, Spes, and Karitas 3–4, 11–19
'Preface to the Dramas' 8–9, 18–19
Hutcheon, Linda 129
hyperreal, hyperreality 116, 120

incest 42–52, 81, 108–12, 116, 119–20, 135, 178–9, 182, 191
Irigaray, Luce 97, 103, 105*n10*, 130, 133, 136–7, 152

Jameson, Fredric 70, 189–90, 197–9
Jay, Martin 97
Jones, Amelia 105*n6*, 106*n22*
Jouve, Nicole Ward 131, 142

Kappeler, Susanne 127–8
king, kingship 113, 148–50, 156–63
Krafft-Ebing, Richard von 129
Krauss, Rosalind 98, 105*nn6–7*, 106*n14*
Kristeva, Julia 69, 76, 78, 87–8, 134, 148–53, 156–7, 163–4

Lacan, Jacques 60, 146*n23*
Lange, Dorothea 167–8
language 2, 46–50, 54–8, 62–8, 72, 87, 114–20, 120, 127–9, 132, 137–8, 155, 163–4, 189–91, 194, 196
Leander 25–38
Leclaire, Serge 121*n4*
Leonardo da Vinci
  Mona Lisa 100, 105*n5*
lesbian-feminist discourse 173, 176, 185
libertine, *libertinage* 110, 113–19 *passim*, 127, 142
Lyotard, Jean-François 106*n23*

MacKinnon, Catherine 125, 127–8
male viewer 54, 98–9, 136
Marlowe, Christopher 25–6, 30–8 *passim*, 157
martyr, martyrs 2–4, 10–17, 86
martyrdom 2, 11, 16, 18

masculinity 78, 80, 126, 140–1, 144
masochism 137–40, 149, 163–4, 178, 191, 193
maternal 26, 45–6, 78, 85–6, 97, 109, 134–8, 142, 148–50, 157, 160–4
maternity 148–9, 157, 159, 163–4
Merck, Mandy 129–30
Middle Ages 1–2, 13–15, 19
mind
　and eye 97, 99
　and fetishism 100
　as male principle 96–100
　as mirror 97, 99
mind-body dualism 96–7
mirror 9, 25, 28, 33, 44, 53–61 *passim*, 65–6, 95–101, 132–3, 136, 160
misrecognition 159–62
monarch 150, 156, 160–3
monarchy 157, 159, 161–2; *see also* king; kingship
monster 134, 150, 154, 159–64, 181
monstrosity 150, 153–5, 163–4, 181–6
mother 42–6, 49, 78–88, 97, 100, 108–19, 130–1, 134–8, 142–4, 149–50, 156–7, 160–4, 167, 175–80, 183
movement 159, 163–4
Mulvey, Laura 92, 95, 102, 105*n8*, 139, 198

naked 26–7, 30–2, 35–8, 93–4, 99, 138, 161; *see also* nude
narcissism 42–4, 48, 50, 59, 102, 136, 140, 149, 160
Nature 26–8, 38, 100, 118, 131, 141
Nead, Lynda 106*n18*
Nelson, Charles 16
Neptune 28–30, 33–8
nude 26, 29–32, 36–7, 98–9, 112, 120, 196; *see also* naked

ocular desire 97, 99
ocularcentrism 97
Œdipus complex 76, 78, 80–8, 125, 135

parody 38, 98, 101, 132, 135–7, 189, 197–9
penance (religious suffering; penitent) 4–10, 50, 113, 117
Perrault, Jean
　Peau d'âne 42–4, 47

perverse 2, 37, 46, 53, 57, 63, 87, 100, 110, 129–31, 135, 140, 148–64 *passim*, 168–9, 173–4, 182, 185, 191–2, 196, 201–2
perverse dynamic 3, 14–17
perversion 2–3, 8–10, 14–19, 46–7, 63, 78, 80, 82, 92–112 *passim*, 128–35, 139–40, 148–53, 174
pornogony 117, 120
pornography 113–19, 125–44, 173, 190–6 *passim*
postcriticism 150–1
postmodernism and feminism 70–1, 129, 136–7, 148, 189–91, 194
poverty 167–86 *passim*, 198
pregnant 149, 163–4
productivity 114–20
'proper' 62–3, 157–64 *passim*
psychoanalysis 125, 131, 134–6, 142, 153

queer 155, 157, 163–4, 168, 173–9 *passim*, 182–5
queerness 173–6, 179, 182

Radcliffe, Ann
　Mysteries of Udolpho 48
Rafter, Nicole 170–1
Ray, Man 100, 106*n24*
Renaissance 28, 38
retrospective narrative 68, 71
Richard II 157–8
Rorty, Richard 97

Sade, Marquis de 126–7, 130–5, 138–41
　'Eugénie de Franval' 108–20
　La Philosophie dans le boudoir 116–19
sadism 139, 191
sadomasochism 133, 137–8, 174
Sartre, Jean-Paul 98
Scarry, Elaine
　The Body in Pain 2–8 *passim*, 11, 14
Schroeder, Peter 10, 19
seduction 19, 28–30, 34–5, 38, 42–52, 111, 114–20
seductiveness 116, 130
sex and violence, representations of 1–3, 18–19, 36, 128, 131–3, 137–9, 179, 182, 193, 197, 201
sexual dissidence as concept 3, 17–18
shadow 154, 162–3

Shelley, Mary
 Fields of Fancy 42
 journal 48
 letters 51
 Mathilda 42–52
Silverman, Kaja 130
simulacrum, simulacra 139
skin 26, 29, 163, 169, 175–7, 181–4, 199
Snitow, Ann 125
Sontag, Susan 119
spaces 5–6, 32, 43, 63, 85, 116–19, 148, 151–60, 163–4, 175–6, 190
specular 54, 92, 95–104, 161
specularity 65, 95, 97, 102–4
Spenser, Edmund
 Faerie Queene 48–9
St Augustine 8, 97
Steefel, Lawrence 106*n14*
Sticca, Sandro 19
Stoller, Robert 129
sublime 159, 162
surface(s) 26–8, 159–60, 163–4

television 160–1, 191, 196–7
Terence (Terentian) 1, 18
theatricality 66, 108–11, 114–15, 118–20, 131–2, 136, 139, 143, 154
tomb 156, 159, 162
tones 153, 155, 163–4
torture 1–16, 19
transgressive knowledge 9–11, 17
transvestism 29, 37–8, 101, 139–40, 182

transvestite 29, 36–7
tyrant 162–3

uncanny 54–72, 100, 110, 154
 and language 55–8, 62–8, 72
 see also Freud
use-value 116
utopian 149, 153–4, 163

Venus 25–7, 33–7, 98, 114
Villette, and present-tense language 68–72
violence and sex, representations of 1–3, 18–19, 36, 128, 131–3, 137–9, 179, 182, 193, 197, 201
virginity, virgin 2–4, 9–19, 31–5, 86, 125–7, 130–1, 136, 138, 142, 200
vision 83, 94–7, 100, 103–4
voyeurism 93–5, 98, 102–3, 112, 114, 198

Walpole, Hugh
 Castle of Utranto 48
Warner, Marina 9, 13, 15
white racial identity 168–9
white trash 168–81, 184–5
whiteness 168–9, 175–86
Williams, Linda 128, 140, 143–4
Wilson, Elizabeth 125–6
Wilson, Katharina 5
women and temporality 63–6, 68–72
women's plots 53–72
writing 19, 50, 67, 138, 148–64, 190, 194, 197, 201–2